INCREASING RETURNS
AND EFFICIENCY

INCREASING RETURNS AND EFFICIENCY

Martine Quinzii

New York   Oxford
OXFORD UNIVERSITY PRESS
1992

Oxford University Press

Oxford   New York   Toronto
Delhi   Bombay   Calcutta   Madras   Karachi
Kuala Lumpur   Singapore   Hong Kong   Tokyo
Nairobi   Dar es Salaam   Cape Town
Melbourne   Auckland   Madrid

and associated companies in

Berlin   Ibadan

Original title of French Edition
"Rendements Croissants et Efficacite Economique"

Copyright ©1992 by Oxford University Press, Inc.

Copyright ©1988 Editions du Centre National de la Recherche Scientifique

Published by Oxford University Press, Inc.,
200 Madison Avenue, New York, New York 10016

Library of Congress Cataloging-in-Publication Data
Quinzii, Martine.
[Rendements croissants et efficacité économique. English]
Increasing returns and efficiency / Martine Quinzii.
p.   cm.
Translation of : Rendements croissants et efficacité économique.
Includes bibliographical references and index.
ISBN 0-19-506553-0
1. Government business enterprises—Costs—Econometric models.
I. Title.   HD3845.6.Q5613   1992   350.009'2—dc20   91-16900

TP

2 4 6 8 9 7 5 3 1

Printed in the United States of America
on acid-free paper

PREFACE

This monograph studies the theory of resource allocation in an economy with increasing returns. Its focus is on the problem of achieving efficient allocations through a mechanism that is as decentralized as possible. Since efficiency cannot be achieved if increasing returns firms are permitted to exploit their monopoly power, such firms must be subject to some measure of regulation. The economy thus consists of two sectors: a private sector with consumers and competitive firms with decreasing returns and a public sector consisting of regulated firms producing with increasing returns. The problem reduces to studying how a price system can coordinate the activities of these two sectors.

The objective of efficiency leads to the concept of a marginal cost pricing equilibrium which is a natural extension of the classical concept of a competitive equilibrium. Even though this concept is motivated by considerations of efficiency, the resulting equilibria are not necessarily efficient. In contrast with a convex economy, conditions of compatibility between the supply and demand for the commodities produced by the public sector are needed to ensure that equilibria are efficient.

Marginal cost pricing introduces a second problem which is not encountered in convex economies, the need to finance the deficit of the public sector. Finding ways of financing the deficit which are acceptable to all agents and more generally to all subgroups of agents leads naturally to the abstract problem of finding allocations which lie in the core of an economy with increasing returns. Once again conditions of compability between the supply and demand sides of the public sector are needed to ensure that core allocations exist.

Here in short is the content of this monograph. While the formal analysis proceeds with the standards of rigor expected of modern theoretical economics, I have attempted to keep the discussion and exposition of the key ideas as intuitive as possible. Simple examples and a geometric approach are used to illustrate basic points and to motivate the reader's intuition. While based on the work of this author, this monograph also draws extensively on the recent literature on increasing returns. Since some of this literature is quite technical the intuitive and geometric approach emphasised in this monograph should provide a more accessible account of recent developments in this field.

While the methods of modern economics provide a more powerful vehicle for understanding the problems posed by the presence of increasing returns, many of the basic issues were clearly understood by the classical authors and were subject to extensive reevaluation during the *marginal cost pricing controversy* of the 1940's. A special effort has been made to connect these earlier discussions with recent developments in this field.

An earlier version of this monograph was presented as a thesis at the University of Paris II in February 1986 and published by the Centre National de la Recherche Scientifique (1988) as *Rendements Croissants et Efficacité Economique*. Material support at various stages was provided by the National Science Foundation and the Sonderforschungsbereich 303 at the University of Bonn. The basic research was undertaken while I was at the Laboratoire d'Econometrie de l'Ecole Polytechnique. I would like to thank Claude Henry as Director for having created the cordial and stimulating intellectual environment at the Laboratoire which was so exceptionally favorable to research. I owe a special debt to Roger Guesnerie for having guided me in my initial research in this area. I am greateful to Bernard Cornet for numerous conversations and for detailed comments on the original thesis. The groundwork for the English version was the diligent work of Sujaya Parthasarathy. Finally I would especially like to thank Michael Magill for much help in bringing the book to its final form.

Los Angeles   M. Q.
June 1991

CONTENTS

INCREASING RETURNS
AND EFFICIENCY

1

INTRODUCTION

1.1 Origin of Ideas

The importance of the phenomenon of increasing returns to scale has been recognized since the origin of modern economic theory. This is natural since the science of economics emerged at the time of the industrial revolution when profound structural changes were occurring in the methods of production and distribution of commodities. The passage to an industrial mode of production which began in the eighteenth century involved exploiting the presence of a zone of increasing returns to scale which exists in most industrial processes. The improved methods of communications (roads, canals, and subsequently railroads) increased the size of the markets to such an extent that large-scale production processes could profitably be employed.

Adam Smith (1776) clearly perceived the benefits of large-scale production which he attributed mainly to the division of labor and the specialization of tasks which are made possible. His well-known example of a pin factory illustrates this point:

> The . . . business of making a pin is, in this manner, divided into about eighteen distinct operations, which, in some manufactories, are all performed by distinct hands, though in others the same man will sometimes perform two or three of them. I have seen a small manufactory of this kind where ten men only were employed, and where some of them consequently performed two or three distinct operations. But though they were poor, and therefore, but indifferently accommodated with the necessary machinery, they could, when they exerted themselves, make among them about twelve pounds of pins in a day. There are in a pound upwards of four thousand pins of a middling size. Those ten persons, therefore, could make among them upwards of forty-eight thousand pins in a day. Each person, therefore, making a tenth part of forty-eight thousand pins, might be considered as making four thousand eight hundred pins in a day. But if they had all wrought separately and independently, and without any of them having been educated to this peculiar business, they certainly could not each of them have made twenty, perhaps not one pin in a day.

At the beginning of the nineteenth century, Charles Babbage (1832) provided an even more detailed analysis of the economies that can be obtained by large-scale production.

If machines be kept working through the twenty four hours (which is evidently the only economical mode of employing them), it is necessary that some person shall attend to admit the workmen at the time they relieve each other, and whether the porter or other person so employed admit one person or twenty, his rest will be equally disturbed. It will also be necessary occasionally to adjust or repair the machine; and this can be done much better by a workman accustomed to machine-making, than by the person who uses it. . . . But in the case of a single lace-frame, or a single loom, this would be too expensive a plan. . . . It ought to consist of such a number of machines as shall occupy the whole time of one workman in keeping them in order: if extended beyond that number, the same principle of economy would point out the necessity of doubling or tripling the number of machines, in order to employ the whole time of two or three skillful workmen. When one portion of the workman's labour consists in the exertion of mere physical force, as in weaving, and in many similar arts, it will soon occur to the manufactories, that if that part were executed by a steam-engine, the same man might, in the case of weaving, attend to two or more looms at once and, since we already suppose that one or more operative engineers have been employed, the number of looms may be so arranged that their time shall be fully occupied in keeping the steam-engine and the looms in order. Pursuing the same principles, the manufactory becomes gradually so enlarged, that the expense of lighting during the night amounts to a considerable sum: and as there are already attached to the establishment persons who are up all night, and can therefore, constantly attend to it, and also engineers to make and keep in repair any machinery, the addition of an apparatus for making gas to light the factory leads to a new extension, at the same time that it contributes, by diminishing the expense of lighting, and the risk of accidents from fire, to reduce the cost of manufacturing.

The early recognition of the importance of increasing returns to scale did not however make it easier to incorporate this phenomenon into the main body of economic theory and in particular into the theory of value. By the end of the nineteenth century the basic elements of the theory of competitive markets had been established and this theory depends in a fundamental way on the assumption of decreasing returns to scale. The partial equilibrium analysis of a market developed by Marshall (1890) is compatible with an initial zone of increasing returns only if the efficient scale of each firm is small relative to the market as a whole. The general equilibrium analysis of a competitive economy introduced by Walras (1874) excludes the possibility of increasing returns to scale.

Marshall was aware that the existence of an equilibrium price which equates consumers' demand to producers' supply is not compatible with a decreasing marginal cost curve. The supply curve of a producer operating under increasing returns to scale is not even defined, since for a given market price of output the production of each additional unit of output, by costing less increases the profit. Marshall introduced an ingenious assumption which allows this difficulty to be overcome: he assumed that the economies of scale were "internal" to an industry but "external" to each firm, so that the supply function of each firm is well defined and an equilibrium price still exists.

This Marshallian hypothesis has recently regained favor in growth theory (see e.g., Romer 1986). In Marshall's time, however, it was strongly criticized as being unrealistic, especially by Sraffa (1920). In the same article, Sraffa developed the basic ideas which led to the theory of monopolistic competition formalized later by Chamberlin (1933) and Joan Robinson (1933): if production takes place under increasing returns, it is the necessity to sell the output that limits the amount produced by a firm and not the increase of its marginal cost. This can be better described by the theory of monopoly than by the theory of competition. Therefore, each firm can be considered as having a monopoly over the good(s) that it produces. The presence of substitutes produced by competing firms is reflected in the price elasticity of demand. Thus, the consideration of increasing returns to scale led naturally to the development of the theory of monopolistic competition. More generally, it underlies the extensive literature on the strategic interactions of a small number of firms on a market since the explanation for the presence of only a small number of firms must ultimately come from the existence of economies of scale.

The classical economists were aware that the productive advantages of increasing returns may well offset the advantages accruing from competition among firms. For example, J.S. Mill (1848) asserts:

> It is obvious, for example, how great an economy of labour would be obtained if London were supplied by a single gas or water company instead of the existing plurality. While there are even as many as two, this implies double establishments of all sorts, when one only, with a small increase, could probably perform the whole operation equally well. Were there only one establishment, it could make lower charges, consistently with obtaining the rate of profit now realized. But would it do so? Even if it did not, the community in the aggregate would still be a gainer.
>
> It is, however, an error to suppose that the prices are ever permanently kept down by the competition of these companies. When competitors are so few, they always end by agreeing not to compete. They may run a race of cheapness to ruin a new candidate, but as soon as he has established his footing they come to terms with him. When, therefore, a business of real public importance can only be carried on advantageously upon so large a scale as to render the liberty of competition almost illusory, it is an unthrifty dispensation of the public resources that several costly sets of arrangements should be kept up for the purpose of rendering to the community this one service. It is much better to treat it at once as a public function.

In the chapter on monopolies in his *Etudes d'Economie Politique Appliquée* (1898), Walras reached the same conclusion for the exploitation of railways.

The conclusion to be drawn from the preceding considerations is clear: the State can and must intervene in the railroad industry for the following two reasons: (1) because the service of railways is a public service as far as concerns the transportation of public goods and services; (2) because the service of railways is a natural and necessary monopoly as far as concerns the transportation of private goods and services. It could not be given legal or economic justification as a private monopoly and must therefore be set up as a state monopoly. A railway monopoly should therefore either be run by the State or as a non-profit private enterprise.

Thus, if increasing returns to scale in the production of some goods and services are present at levels of production relevant for the economy in question—e.g., because of large costs of infrastructure as in the two previous examples—then competition between several firms may lead to wasteful duplication and inefficient use of resources; however, since there is no economic justification for the monopoly rents that a single, profit-maximizing firm can extract from the consumers, the State must consider the provision of these goods and services as one of its functions.

Once this idea is accepted, it is natural to extend the logic of public interest and to consider the best way in which goods and services produced by a natural monopoly should be sold to the public. In his quotation Walras is not specific about the pricing policy that should be adopted beyond the assertion that costs should be covered. A more careful reading of the chapter on monopolies shows that Walras was well aware of the issues involved in the choice of a pricing policy. Although he does not suggest using prices that would not globally cover the cost of investment and operation of the railways, he compares different average cost pricing rules.

> In these conditions, there would be two rather distinct ways in which the State could operate its monopoly. Either it could consider the different railway lines as independent of one another, only beginning the construction and exploitation of a particular line when it is likely to cover its costs, reducing its tariff when it begins to make profits on a regular basis. Or, it could consider all the lines as constituting a global network and instead of reducing the tariffs on those railway lines which earn more than their costs, it could build and operate others which would not completely cover their cost, the profit made by the former covering the losses made by the latter.

To carry the analysis further a criterion needs to be defined for evaluating the social benefit attached to each of these forms of management. Walras does not choose to do this however since he is principally concerned with convincing the reader that the operation of railways should be undertaken by the State.

At the beginning of the twentieth century, interest in the idea of socialism and the theory of planned economies led to the development of welfare economics and to the emergence of the marginal cost principle as a necessary condition for an efficient allocation of resources. The ideas developed by Pigou, Lerner, Lange, and others[1] were crystallized in the classic article of Hotelling (1938):

> In this paper, we shall bring down to date in revised form an argument due essentially to the engineer Jules Dupuit, to the effect that the optimum of the general welfare corresponds to the sale of everything at marginal cost. That means that toll bridges, which have recently been introduced around New York are inefficient reversions, that all taxes on commodities, including sales taxes, are more objectionable than taxes on income, inheritances and site value of land; and that the latter taxes might well be applied to cover the fixed costs of electric power plants, water works, railroads and other industries in which the fixed costs are large, so as to reduce to the level of marginal cost the prices charged for the services and products of these industries.

The Hotelling proposal is unambiguous: marginal cost pricing must be applied in all circumstances, even if it creates a deficit for activities where the marginal cost is low compared to set up costs. The deficit must then be financed from income taxes.

Hotelling's proposal gave rise to a wave of objections and the intense debate that followed came to be known as the *marginal cost controversy*. A useful survey of the arguments exchanged at the time is given by Nancy Ruggles (1950). The controversial issue is the assertion that income taxation is the best way to cover the fixed costs of an industry with low marginal costs. Three types of objections can be raised:

1. More distortions are introduced into the economy by income taxation than Hotelling was ready to recognize.
2. Covering the fixed cost of industries with low marginal cost by income taxes involves a redistribution of income, with high income agents subsidizing the consumers of the goods sold below costs.
3. How is it possible to ensure that a firm which is not exposed to competition and not even required to cover its costs will be run efficiently and will not itself waste resources?

While the third argument was difficult to formalize at a time when no rigorous models were available for exploring the issues of information and incentives,[2] it had a major impact on the way in which public utilities were organized both in the United States and in Europe. In France the industries which were perceived as natural monopolies (electricity, railways, coal mines) were nationalized after the Second World War. The problems of management of these newly nationalized firms led to active research on the theory of resource allocation in the presence of increasing returns. While the theory of marginal cost pricing was actively developed and promoted by the French school of postwar economists (notably by Marcel Boiteux at Electricité De France), the Hotelling proposal (subsidization by the government of a deficit of the nationalized firms created by marginal cost pricing) was opposed by one of the leaders of this school, Maurice Allais, who declared the proposal "psychologically infeasible and economically inadvisable—for lack of appropriate incentives to cost minimization in the absence of a budget restriction."[3] Furthermore, the best-known article of M. Boiteux "On the Management of Public Monopoly Constrained To Budget Balance" (1956) was concerned with optimal second-best pricing and not with marginal cost pricing.

1.2   Recent Developments

The abstract treatment of the theory of value was given a new impetus in the late 1950s when the *Arrow-Debreu theory* of a competitive economy was developed. This theory described precise conditions on the characteristics of an economy (preferences and technology) under which maximizing behavior on the part of individual agents (consumers and firms) can be coordinated via a price system so that the equilibrium of the economy achieves an efficient allocation of resources. The important contribution was to have revealed precise conditions on agents characteristics under which an equilibrium exists and under which such an equilibrium is efficient. The existence and Welfare theorems of the Arrow-Debreu theory thus provided a systematic program for the analysis of a competitive price system.

It was natural to ask how this analysis could be extended to economies with increasing returns. This question was posed by Guesnerie in an important paper (1975) that became the basis for the modern general equilibrium treatment of marginal cost pricing. The extensive literature which has subsequently emerged is summarized in the next four chapters of this book.

Chapter 2 studies the general equilibrium version of the marginal cost principle. The idea is to provide conditions on agents' characteristics under which the Second Welfare Theorem can be extended to non-convex economies. We show that an efficient allocation can be supported by a price vector orthogonal to the agents' indifference curves and to the frontiers of the production sets provided that the appropriate concept of a normal cone is used for the production sets. An assumption of convexity of the input requirement sets of firms is needed to ensure that this property of orthogonality can be interpreted as the equalization of prices to marginal costs.

In the third chapter we show how these first order-conditions for optimality lead naturally to a concept of equilibrium, which has come to be known as a *marginal cost pricing equilibrium*. Two conceptual difficulties emerge. The first concerns the practical issue of how firms with non-convex technology sets should be administered so that the prices of their outputs are set equal to their marginal costs. The second concerns the appropriate specification of a rule by which income is assigned to consumers. Such a rule needs to be defined in order to close the model and any such rule necessarily carries with it an explicit or implicit specification of the way the deficits of firms with increasing returns technologies are covered.

Once the concept of equilibrium has been defined it might seem natural to apply the standard procedure of Arrow-Debreu theory, first analyzing existence and then the optimality of equilibrium. We shall find it convenient, however, to reverse the normal procedure, analyzing first the normative properties of marginal cost pricing equilibria—the subject of chapter 4. It is not surprising that a concept of equilibrium motivated by efficiency conditions can lead to inefficient equilibria; for the first order conditions are necessary conditions which in the absence of convexity are not sufficient. What is perhaps more surprising is that there exist economies (i.e., characteristics and a rule for distributing income) for which *none* of the marginal cost pricing equilibria are efficient. Thus, in a non-convex economy considerations of equity (income distribution) and efficiency cannot be kept separate. In view of this it is important to give conditions under which marginal cost pricing equilibria are known to be efficient. This problem is studied in some detail in chapter 4.

The problem of the existence of a marginal cost pricing equilibrium is the subject of chapter 5. This topic has recently been extensively studied. The main result is that a marginal cost pricing equilibrium exists under relatively weak assumptions. We have chosen to describe in some detail the proof of Bonnisseau and Cornet (1990a) which introduces some interesting techniques to show that the set of feasible production plans, although non-convex, is sufficiently regular to permit the use of the standard Kakutani fixed point theorem.

Chapter 6 is devoted to a more abstract approach to the study of resource allocation in an economy with increasing returns based on the concept of the *core*. While the concept of the core was essentially first introduced by Edgeworth (1881), its application to the study of resource allocation with increasing returns is of much more recent origin. Such an analysis was initiated by Herbert Scarf (1963) soon after the close relationship between the competitive equilibria and the core allocations of an exchange economy were first rigorously established (Scarf 1962; Debreu and Scarf 1963; Aumann 1964). It seemed intuitive that if the possibility of exchange among agents can yield allocations that cannot be improved upon by any subgroup of agents left to its own resources, this property should be all the more true if, in addition to the possibility of exchanging goods, agents have access to a technique of production with increasing returns. On the basis of this intuition Scarf had hoped to find an interesting way of decentralizing core allocations; however, the conjecture that core allocations exist under the general circumstances just described turned out to be false, or at least not true without restrictive conditions.

Scarf obtained essentially the following negative result (1963, published 1986): given a production set Y, the core of all economies for which the production possibilities are described by Y is non-empty if and only if Y is a convex cone. In other words, if Y exhibits true increasing returns, then there exist economies (agents, initial endowments, preferences) for which Y describes the feasible productions and which have an empty core. This result, while apparently disappointing, is not, however, the last word on the subject. For what it really means is that the characteristics on the consumption side of the economy must be compatible with the production possibilities in order for a core allocation to exist. This is most natural. The assumption of increasing returns to scale ensures that production becomes more efficient if all inputs are increased in the same proportions and relative shares of outputs are kept constant. With differences in tastes and endowments, this condition is not sufficient to imply that all agents can agree on a common way of operating a technology with increasing returns. Chapter 6 gives several sets of sufficient conditions—some due to Scarf—under which the core is non-empty.

The problem of the existence of a core allocation is an abstract way of dealing with the problem of the redistribution of income implicit in a pricing rule for a multigood "natural" monopoly. To be more concrete, suppose that a public utility produces two goods—long distance calls and local calls for example—and that the way calls are priced results in the consumers of the first good subsidizing the consumers of the second. Then the core of the economy will be empty since the consumers of the first good will have an incentive to break the monopoly, create their own long distance telephone company and stop subsidizing the others. This problem has been extensively studied in a partial equilibrium, second best context in the literature on contestable markets[4] using cost functions to describe the technologies and the concept of average cost pricing. Even if the structure of the first best problem (existence of a core allocation) and the second best problem (existence of a sustainable price[5]) are not identical, the difficulties involved in proving existence in both approaches gives an idea of the difficulty that is necessarily involved in finding a pricing rule for a multigood monopoly which simultaneously reconciles the interests of all groups of agents in the economy.

Notes

1. For an interesting account of the development of welfare economics and of the emergence of the marginal cost principle prior to Hotelling's paper see Nancy Ruggles (1949).
2. The formal exploration of this issue began with the paper of D. Baron and R. Myerson (1982) "Regulating a Monopoly with Unknown Costs."

A survey of the literature on this subject can be found in Caillaud et al. (1988).

3. The quote is taken from the survey article of J. H. Dreze (1964) "Some Postwar Contributions of French Economists to Theory and Public Policy."

4. Nonexhaustive references are the books of Baumol, Panzar, and Willig (1982) *Contestable Markets and the Theory of Industry Structure* and the book of W. Sharkey (1982) *The Theory of Natural Monopoly.*

5. D. Spulber (1989) has sought to bridge the gap between the two literatures by defining the concept of second best core: however, in the multi-good case its existence is even more problematic than the existence of a core or of a sustainable price.

2

NECESSARY CONDITIONS FOR EFFICIENCY

This chapter introduces the general equilibrium version of the marginal cost pricing principle which asserts that marginal cost pricing is a necessary condition for efficiency. We show that to every Pareto optimal allocation is associated a price system that supports this allocation in a sense which is made precise. Under certain conditions, this price system is such that the price of each good equals its marginal cost.

2.1 The Production Economy

The model that we consider is a natural extension of the standard general equilibrium model of a production economy (Debreu 1959). The differences and subsequent difficulties that emerge arise from the fact that we allow for the possibility of increasing returns or, more generally, of non-convexities in the production sets of some firms.

We consider an economy with H goods. The production sector consists of m firms with production sets $(Y_j)_{j=1,\ldots,m}$. The production set Y_j of firm j is a subset of $\mathbb{R}^H$ which describes the feasible production plans $y_j = (y_{j0},\ldots,y_{jH})$ with the usual sign convention: $y_{jh} < 0$ (> 0) indicates that good h is used as an input (is produced as an output). All production sets Y_j have the following properties:

- $0 \in Y_j$. This simply means that inaction is possible: Using no inputs, firm j produces no output.

- Y_j is closed in $\mathbb{R}^H$. This assumption is mathematically convenient and does not impose a significant restriction from an economic point of view. It means that a limit of feasible production plans is feasible.

- $\forall y_j \in Y_j, \forall z \in \mathbb{R}_-^H, y_j + z \in Y_j$ (or equivalently $\forall y_j \in Y_j, y_j - \mathbb{R}_+^H \subset Y_j$) where $\mathbb{R}_+^H = \{x \in \mathbb{R}^H \mid x_h \geq 0, \forall h = 1,\ldots,H\}$ denotes the positive orthant of $\mathbb{R}^H$ and $\mathbb{R}_-^H = -\mathbb{R}_+^H$ the negative orthant.

This last condition is the assumption of free disposal which is technically convenient but restricts the set of goods that the model can incorporate: it asserts that it is possible to dispose of any quantity of any good without

13

cost. This assumption eliminates consideration of goods which are economic "bads" such as pollution, or more generally of negative externalities associated with industrial production. The H goods to which we restrict consideration are thus assumed to be useful for consumption and production.

The production plans which are of special interests are those which are efficient, that is, those which cannot use less inputs to produce the same outputs or produce more outputs with the same inputs. To give a formal definition, we introduce the following:

NOTATION. *(Vector inequalities) If $x \in \mathbb{R}^H$, $y \in \mathbb{R}^H$,*

$$x \geq y \Longleftrightarrow x_h \geq y_h, \; \forall h = 1, \ldots, H$$

$$x > y \Longleftrightarrow x \geq y, \; x \neq y$$

$$x \gg y \Longleftrightarrow x_h > y_h, \; \forall h = 1, \ldots, H$$

DEFINITION. *Let $Y \subset \mathbb{R}^H$ be a production set. A production plan $y \in Y$ is efficient if there does not exist $y' \in Y$ such that $y' > y$*

An efficient production plan belongs to the boundary (in the sense of real analysis) of the production set Y. Let ∂Y denote the boundary of a set Y. Recall the standard definitions of constant, decreasing, and increasing returns.

DEFINITION. *A production set $Y \subset \mathbb{R}^H$ exhibits constant returns to scale if*

$$\forall y \in Y, \quad \forall \lambda \in \mathbb{R}_+, \quad \lambda y \in Y$$

The scalar λ is to be interpreted as a change in the scale of production. If $\lambda < 1$ ($\lambda > 1$), λy can be calculated from y by decreasing (increasing) all inputs and all outputs by the factor λ. Such a change does not affect the proportions of the different inputs or outputs. $\lambda y \in Y$ implies that it is possible to produce λ times the original outputs by using λ times the original inputs. For a technology with constant returns to scale, this is verified for every $\lambda \geq 0$. But if the original production plan y is efficient, it is not possible to obtain more than λ times the outputs with λ times the inputs. To see this suppose $H = L + K$ with the first L goods being inputs and the last K goods outputs. Let $y = (-z, y^0)$ denote the original production plan where $z \in \mathbb{R}_+^L$ is the vector of inputs, $y^0 \in \mathbb{R}_+^K$ the vector of outputs. Suppose that there exists $\lambda' > \lambda$ such that $(-\lambda z, \lambda' y^0) \in Y$, then by definition of constant returns $y' = (-\frac{\lambda}{\lambda'} z, y^0)$ belongs to Y. Since $y' > y$, this contradicts the efficiency of y. Thus, for a constant returns technology, for fixed proportions of inputs and of outputs no gain and no loss in the output-input ratio is associated with a change in the scale of production.

DEFINITION. *A production set Y exhibits increasing (decreasing) returns to scale if*

$$\forall y \in Y, \ \forall \lambda \geq 1 \ (\forall \lambda \leq 1), \ \lambda y \in Y$$

If a production set exhibits increasing returns to scale, then:

1. If the scale of production is increased in the sense that all inputs are multiplied by a coefficient $\lambda \geq 1$, then the outputs increase at least proportionally. For fixed proportions of inputs and of outputs, there is no loss in the output–input ratio associated with an increase in the scale of production.
2. No gain can be achieved by a decrease in the scale of production. If $y \in Y$ is efficient, $y = (-z, y^0)$, and if $\lambda \leq 1$, then there cannot exist $\lambda' > \lambda$ such that $(-\lambda z, \lambda' y^0) \in Y$. If such a coefficient exists, then $y' = (-\frac{\lambda}{\lambda'} z, y^0)$ belongs to Y. But, $y' > y$ contradicts the efficiency of y.

The definition of increasing returns to scale does not guarantee that there is a gain in the output–input ratio associated with an increase in scale since it covers the case of constant returns to scale. Normally, when we refer to increasing returns to scale, we consider a production set which satisfies the above definition and does not exhibit constant returns to scale. Such a set cannot be convex since a convex production set which contains the origin must exhibit decreasing or constant returns to scale.

It is, however, restrictive to assume that a production set satisfies the global property of increasing returns to scale. A more flexible definition which allows for ranges of production where gains in productivity can be achieved by reasonably increasing the scale of production without requiring it for all possible productions is preferable. In partial equilibrium the concept of local measure of returns to scale has been designed to give this flexibility. In general equilibrium, the assumption that a production set is *non-convex* provides the required flexibility. The source of the non-convexity may be very general and does not need to come from a global property of increasing returns to scale. The analysis of chapters 2 to 5, although motivated by the presence of increasing returns to scale, is made with the general assumption that the production sets of some firms are non-convex.

The consumption sector of the economy consists of n consumers whose preferences orderings over consumption bundles are represented by utility functions $u_i : \mathbb{R}_+^H \to \mathbb{R}, \ i = 1, \ldots, n$.

Each agent i has initial resources $w_i \in \mathbb{R}_+^H$. The total initial resources of the economy are $w = \sum_{i=1}^n w_i$.

DEFINITION. *An allocation for the economy is a vector* $((x_i)_{i=1,...,n},$ $(y_j)_{j=1,...,m}) \in \mathbb{R}_+^{Hn} \times \prod_j Y_j$ *which describes consumption bundles of each agent and production plans of each firm. An allocation* $((x_i)_{i=1,...,n},$ $(y_j)_{j=1,...,m}) \in \mathbb{R}_+^{Hn} \times \prod_j Y_j$ *is feasible if*

$$\sum_{i=1}^{n} x_i \leq \sum_{j=1}^{m} y_j + w$$

An allocation $((x_i^*)_{i=1,...,n}, (y_j^*)_{j=1,...,m})$ is Pareto optimal (efficient) if: (i) it is feasible and (ii) there does not exist another feasible allocation which is preferred by all agents and strictly preferred by at least one agent. More formally,

DEFINITION. $((x_i^*)_{i=1,...,n}, (y_j^*)_{j=1,...,m}) \in \mathbb{R}_+^{Hn} \times \prod_j Y_j$ *is Pareto optimal (efficient) if:*

(i) $\sum_{i=1}^{n} x_i^* \leq \sum_{j=1}^{m} y_j^* + w$

(ii) *there does not exist* $((x_i')_{i=1,...,n}, (y_j')_{j=1,...,m}) \in \mathbb{R}_+^{Hn} \times \prod_j Y_j$ *such that* $\sum_{i=1}^{n} x_i' \leq \sum_{j=1}^{m} y_j' + w$ *and* $(u_i(x_i'))_{i=1,...,n} > (u_i(x_i^*))_{i=1,...,n}$

2.2 Supporting Prices For Efficient Allocations

To give a geometric interpretation to conditions (i) and (ii), let Y denote the aggregate production set, $Y = \sum_j Y_j$. Let $\mathcal{P}_i(x_i^*)$ be the set of consumption vectors preferred to x_i^* by agent i:

$$\mathcal{P}_i(x_i^*) = \{x_i \in \mathbb{R}_+^H \mid u_i(x_i) \geq u_i(x_i^*)\}$$

then $\mathcal{P} = \sum_i \mathcal{P}_i(x_i^*)$ is the set of resource vectors necessary to ensure at least a level of utility $u_i(x_i^*)$ for each agent i. The boundary of $\mathcal{P}$ is known as a social indifference curve or a Scitovski contour.

Condition (i) implies that $\sum_i x_i^* \in w+Y$ and hence that the set $\mathcal{P} \cap w + Y$ contains at least $\sum_i x_i^*$. Condition (ii) implies that $w + Y$ does not intersect the interior of $\mathcal{P}$. Hence, the sets $\mathcal{P}$ and $w+Y$ must be "tangent" at the point $\sum_i x_i^*$.

If the agents' preferences are convex and if the aggregate production set Y is convex (Figure 2.1a), this tangency condition implies the existence of a hyperplane which separates the two sets $w+Y$ and $\mathcal{P}$. The vector normal to this hyperplane is the vector of prices which supports the Pareto optimal allocation. If Y is non-convex (Figure 2.1b where Y is an production set with increasing returns), this separation property will not in general hold but there still exists a hyperplane tangent to $\mathcal{P}$ and $w + Y$ and a vector p orthogonal to the two sets. The boundaries of the production sets in

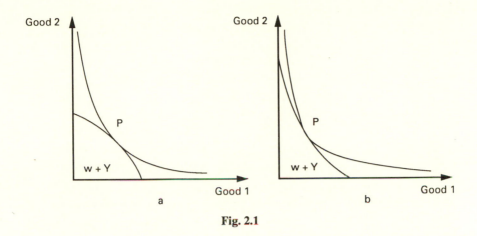

Fig. 2.1

Figure 2.1b are smooth curves having tangents at every point and it is easy to see what is meant by a hyperplane tangent to the sets $\mathcal{P}$ and $w + Y$.

One of the messages of Debreu's *Theorie of Value* (1959) is that for convex economies the assumption of differentiability of $\mathcal{P}$ and ∂Y (as in Figure 2.1) is not needed to obtain the existence of a price which supports an efficient allocation. Existence of a supporting price (hyperplane) follows from Minkovski's separation theorem applied to the convex sets $\mathcal{P}$ and $w + Y$. The same theorem also implies the existence of a cone of normals at each point of the boundary of these sets.

Without the assumption of convexity, one could revert to the differentiable approach to equilibrium theory which was traditional before advent of the Arrow-Debreu theory. This approach has been updated and generalized in recent work (see Mas-Colell 1985 and Balasko 1988) and proves most useful for analyzing the qualitative properties of equilibria. However, beside the fact that differentiability is not really needed to extend the two welfare theorems to non-convex economies, the example that follows shows that it rules out situations that arise quite naturally. Suppose that a firm has two techniques of production at its disposal, one with constant returns to scale which it is efficient to use at low levels of production and another with increasing returns to scale that can be used for higher levels of output. The production set for this firm does not have a smooth boundary because of the "kink" at y (see Figure 2.2).

Production sets with fixed costs do not have smooth boundaries and such production sets cannot be excluded from a systematic study of economies with increasing returns.

Mathematicians have introduced several notions of tangent and normal cones which can be defined for non-convex sets with non-smooth boundaries. R. Guesnerie (1975) and P. Beato (1976, 1982) used the *tangent cone*

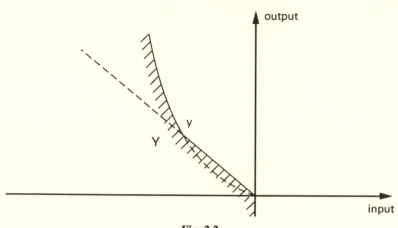

Fig. 2.2

of interior displacements introduced by the mathematicians Dubovickii and Miljutin; however, it is not possible to generalize the second theorem of welfare economics (decentralization of Pareto optimal allocations) in all cases using this notion of a tangent cone: the cone of interior displacements may be non-convex and in such a case the normal cone reduces to {0}.

B. Cornet (1982, published 1990) introduced the use of the Clarke tangent and normal cones in the study of non-convex economies. These concepts, introduced by the mathematician F. Clarke, are well adapted to economic problems of optimization and fixed points and will be used throughout this book. The following section describes the main properties of the Clarke tangent and normal cones. The proofs can be found in Clarke's book (1983) *Optimization and Nonsmooth Analysis*.

2.3   Clarke Normal Cone

DEFINITION. *Let C be a closed set in $\mathbb{R}^n$ and let d denote the euclidean distance in $\mathbb{R}^n$. For $x \in \mathbb{R}^n$ the distance between x and C is given by*

$$d(x, C) = \inf_{x' \in C} d(x, x')$$

DEFINITION. *Let C be a closed set in $\mathbb{R}^n$ and $x \in C$. A vector v is orthogonal to C at x (we write $v \perp C$) if there exists a point $x' \in \mathbb{R}^n$ such that*

$$v = x' - x, \quad d(x', C) = \| v \|$$

It is clear that the null vector is orthogonal to C at every point of C. If x is an interior point of C, then the null vector is the only vector orthogonal to C at x. The points of interest are, therefore, the boundary points of C.

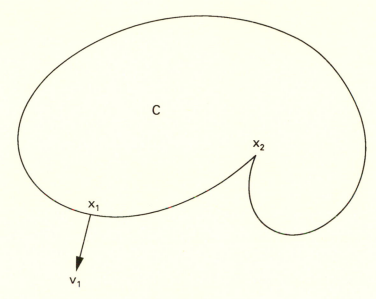

Fig. 2.3

For example, in Figure 2.3, v_1 is orthogonal to C at x_1, but the null vector is the only vector orthogonal to C at x_2.

DEFINITION. *Let C be a closed set in $\mathbb{R}^n$ and $x \in C$. The Clarke normal cone to C at x is the closed convex hull of the set*

$$\{v \in \mathbb{R}^n \mid v = \lambda \lim \frac{v_i}{\| v_i \|}, \lambda \geq 0, \; v_i \perp C \text{ at } x_i, x_i \longrightarrow x \text{ and } v_i \longrightarrow 0\}$$

and is denoted by $N_C(x)$.

By this definition the Clarke normal cone at a point x is the convex cone generated by the vectors orthogonal to C at x and the limits of vectors which are orthogonal to C in the neighborhood of x.

Although the null vector is the only vector orthogonal to C at x_2, the Clarke normal cone at x_2 consists of all vectors of the cone generated by the vectors v_2 and v_2', which are limits of vectors orthogonal to C at points x close to x_2 (Figure 2.4). At x_1, the Clarke cone is the half-line generated by v_1. The normal cone of Clarke is "large." In the case of x_2 in Figure 2.4 it contains vectors which are not really orthogonal to C at x_2. But there is a trade-off between including in the normal cone only vectors which have a real property of orthogonality to the set and "good properties"—like convexity or continuity—of the cone.

The definition of a tangent cone is derived from that of a normal cone by duality.

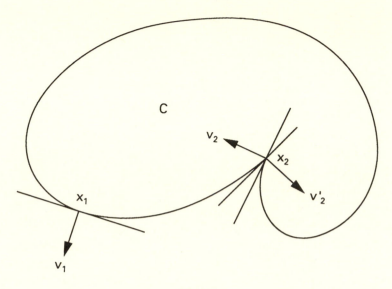

Fig. 2.4

DEFINITION. *Let C be a closed set of $\mathbb{R}^n$ and $x \in C$. The Clarke tangent cone at x denoted by $T_C(x)$, is the polar cone of $N_C(x)$, that is,*

$$T_C(x) = \{u \in \mathbb{R}^n \mid u \cdot v \leq 0, \quad \forall v \in N_C(x)\}$$

By definition $T_C(x)$ is a convex cone. The following theorem gives a direct characterization of the interior of the Clarke tangent cone.

THEOREM 2.1. *Let C be a closed subset of $\mathbb{R}^n$ and $x \in C$. A vector u belongs to the interior of $T_C(x)$ if and only if there exists a number $\epsilon > 0$ such that*

$$x' + t(u + \epsilon B) \in C, \quad \forall x' \in C \cap x + \epsilon B, \quad \forall t \in [0, \epsilon]$$

where B is the unit ball in $\mathbb{R}^n$.

The interpretation of the theorem is as follows: for u to belong to the interior of the tangent cone of C at x, u must be a vector which points into the interior of C not only from x but also from all points x' of C close to x.

The important properties of the Clarke normal cone that will be used in the following chapters are the following:

1. The Clarke normal cone coincides with the standard normal cone when C is convex or when the boundary of C is differentiable.
2. The Clarke normal cone is *convex* and *never reduces to the null vector* for any boundary point of C.

3. If the interior of the tangent cone at x is non-empty, *the correspondence $x \longrightarrow N_C(x)$ has a closed graph.*

These results are formally described in the following theorems.

THEOREM 2.2. *If C is a closed convex set and $x \in C$, $N_C(x)$ coincides with the normal cone of convex analysis*

$$N_C(x) = \{v \in \mathbb{R}^n \mid v \cdot y \le v \cdot x, \ \forall y \in C\}$$

THEOREM 2.3. *Let $C = \{x \in \mathbb{R}^n \mid g_i(x) \le 0, \ i = 1, \ldots, I\}$ where $g_i : \mathbb{R}^n \longrightarrow \mathbb{R}$ is continuously differentiable, $i = 1, \ldots, I$. Let $x \in C$ and $I(x)$ be the set of indices such that $g_i(x) = 0$. If the gradient vectors $(Dg_i(x))_{i \in I(x)}$ are linearly independent, then $N_C(x)$ is the convex hull of the vectors $(\lambda Dg_i(x))_{i \in I(x)}, \lambda \ge 0$.*

THEOREM 2.4. *If C is a closed set and x belongs to the boundary of C, then $N_C(x) \neq \{0\}$.*

THEOREM 2.5. *If the interior of $T_C(x)$ is non-empty, the correspondence $N_C : C \longrightarrow \mathbb{R}^n$, defined by $x \longrightarrow N_C(x)$ is closed at x, that is,*

$$\left.\begin{array}{l} x_i \longrightarrow x \text{ and } x_i \in C, \ \forall i \in \mathbb{N} \\ v_i \longrightarrow v \text{ and } v_i \in N_C(x_i), \ \forall i \in \mathbb{N} \end{array}\right\} \Rightarrow v \in N_C(x)$$

We now have the necessary tools to characterize the properties of the price vector associated with a Pareto optimum when some production sets are non-convex.

2.4 Existence of Supporting Prices

THEOREM 2.6. *Let $\mathcal{E}\big((u_i)_{i=1,\ldots,n}, (Y_j)_{j=1,\ldots,m}, w\big)$ be an economy such that:*

- *the utility functions are continuous, quasi-concave and weakly monotonic, that is,*

$$x_i \gg x_i' \Rightarrow u_i(x_i) > u_i(x_i'), \quad \forall x_i, x_i' \in \mathbb{R}_+^H, \quad i = 1, \ldots, n$$

- *the production sets have the property of free disposal, that is,*

$$y_j - \mathbb{R}_+^H \subset Y_j, \quad \forall y_j \in Y_j, \quad j = 1, \ldots, m$$

Let $\big((x_i^*)_{i=1,\ldots,n}, (y_j^*)_{j=1,\ldots,m}\big)$ be a Pareto optimal allocation. Then there exists a vector of prices $p \in \mathbb{R}_+^H$, $p \neq 0$ such that:

(i) x_i^* minimizes $p \cdot x_i$ over the preferred set
$$\mathcal{P}_i(x_i^*) = \{x_i \in \mathbb{R}_+^H \mid u_i(x_i) \geq u_i(x_i^*)\}, \; \forall i = 1, \ldots, n$$

(ii) $p \in N_{Y_j}(y_j^*), \; \forall j = 1, \ldots, m$.

Proof: Let $\mathcal{P}_i = \mathcal{P}_i(x_i^*)$. The monotonicity of preferences implies that $\mathbb{R}_+^H \subset T_{\mathcal{P}_i}(x_i^*)$ and the assumption of free disposal implies that $\mathbb{R}_-^H \subset T_{Y_j}(y_j^*)$. In particular, the tangent cones $T_{\mathcal{P}_i}(x_i^*)$ and $T_{Y_j}(y_j^*)$ have non-empty interiors. We use the notation "Int" to denote the interior of a set. We show that since $\left((x_i^*)_{i=1,\ldots,n}, (y_j^*)_{j=1,\ldots,m}\right)$ is a Pareto optimal allocation,

$$\sum_i T_{\mathcal{P}_i}(x_i^*) - \sum_j T_{Y_j}(y_j^*) \neq \mathbb{R}^H \tag{1}$$

(This property translates the geometric intuition of the preceding section that the sets $w + Y$ and $\mathcal{P}$ are "tangent.")

Suppose not, then (1) holds with equality. Choose $\xi_i \in \text{Int}(T_{\mathcal{P}_i}(x_i^*))$ for all i and $\eta_j \in \text{Int}(T_{Y_j}(y_j^*))$ for all j and let

$$a = \sum_i \xi_i - \sum_j \eta_j \tag{2}$$

Since the vector $-a$ also belongs to $\sum_i T_{\mathcal{P}_i}(x_i^*) - \sum_j T_{Y_j}(y_j^*)$, there exist vectors $\xi_i' \in T_{\mathcal{P}_i}(x_i^*)$ and $\eta_j' \in T_{Y_j}(y_j^*)$ such that

$$-a = \sum_i \xi_i' - \sum_j \eta_j' \tag{3}$$

Clearly,
$$\xi_i + \xi_i' \in \text{Int}\, T_{\mathcal{P}_i}(x_i^*), \quad \eta_j + \eta_j' \in \text{Int}\, T_{Y_j}(y_j^*)$$

Thus, by Theorem 2.1, $\exists \epsilon > 0$ such that

$$\begin{aligned}
x_i' &= x_i^* + \epsilon(\xi_i + \xi_i') \in \text{Int}\, \mathcal{P}_i, \quad \forall i = 1, \ldots, n \\
y_j' &= y_j^* + \epsilon(\eta_j + \eta_j') \in \text{Int}\, Y_j, \quad \forall j = 1, \ldots, m
\end{aligned} \tag{4}$$

Hence, x_i' is such that $u_i(x_i') > u_i(x_i)$ for all i and y_j' is feasible for all j. (2), (3), (4) imply that

$$\sum_i x_i' - \sum_j y_j' = \sum_i x_i^* - \sum_j y_j^* \leq w$$

The allocation $((x'_i), (y'_j))$ is feasible and preferred by all agents to $((x^*_i), (y^*_j))$, contradicting the Pareto optimality of $((x^*_i), (y^*_j))$. Thus,

$$\sum_i T_{\mathcal{P}_i}(x^*_i) - \sum_j T_{Y_j}(y^*_j)$$

is a convex cone that contains $\mathbf{R}^H_+$ and is strictly included in $\mathbf{R}^H$. Thus, there exists a vector $-p$, $p > 0$, in the dual cone,

$$-p \in \left[\sum_i T_{\mathcal{P}_i}(x^*_i) - \sum_j T_{Y_j}(y^*_j) \right]^{\perp}$$

$$\Longleftrightarrow$$

$$-p \in \cap_i N_{\mathcal{P}_i}(x^*_i) \cap_j (-N_{Y_j}(y^*_j))$$

Thus, $p \in N_{Y_j}(y^*_j)$, $\forall j = 1, \ldots, m$, and the relation (ii) holds.

Since each $\mathcal{P}_i$ is a convex set, by Theorem 2.2, $N_{\mathcal{P}_i}(x^*_i) = \{v \in \mathbf{R}^n \mid v \cdot x_i \leq v \cdot x^*_i, \ \forall x_i \in \mathcal{P}_i\}$. Thus, $-p \in N_{\mathcal{P}_i}(x^*_i)$, implies that $p \cdot x^*_i$ is the minimum of $p \cdot x_i$ for $x_i \in \mathcal{P}_i$ so that (i) holds.

$$\triangledown$$

Remark: It is well known that if $p \cdot x^*_i > 0$, then (i) implies:

(i)′ x^*_i *maximizes* $u_i(x_i)$ *over the budget set* $\{x_i \in \mathbf{R}^H_+ \mid p \cdot x_i \leq p \cdot x^*_i\}$
(for example, Arrow and Hahn 1971).

If the set Y_j is convex then $p \in N_{Y_j}(y^*_j)$ implies that y^*_j maximizes firm j's profit at price p.

Remark: The assumption of monotonicity of the preferences and free disposal of the production sets are stronger than necessary to prove Theorem 1.6. They have been made to keep the proof simple. It is sufficient to assume local non-satiation of the preferences and either that one agent has monotonic preferences or that one production set exhibits free disposal to obtain the existence of a price system satisfying (1) and (2). For further discussion see Bonnisseau and Cornet (1988b).

2.5 Marginal Cost Pricing

Can we deduce from Theorem 2.6 that the vector of prices associated with an efficient allocation has the property that the price of each good equals its marginal cost? More precisely, if the goods are specialized into inputs of a non-convex firm and outputs produced by this firm, does the condition $p \in N_{Y_j}(y^*_j)$ imply that the prices of the outputs are equal to their marginal costs?

Consider a single firm producing good H using $H-1$ inputs. If the technological constraints are described by a continuously differentiable production function $f : \mathbb{R}_+^{H-1} \longrightarrow \mathbb{R}_+$ then the production set is given by

$$Y = \{(-z, y^0) \in \mathbb{R}_-^{H-1} \times \mathbb{R} \mid y^0 \leq f(z_1, \ldots, z_{H-1})\}$$

Let $y^* = (-z^*, y^{0*})$ be an efficient production plan such that $y^{0*} = f(z^*)$ and $z^* \gg 0$.

Does the relationship $p \in N_Y(y^*)$ imply $p_H = C'(y^{0*})$ where C is the cost function derived from the input price vector $(p_1, \ldots, p_{H-1})$?

By Theorem 2.3, $p \in N_Y(y^*)$ is equivalent to the following: $\exists \lambda > 0$ such that

$$\left. \begin{array}{rcc} p_1 & = & \lambda \dfrac{\partial f}{\partial z_1}(z^*) \\[4pt] \vdots & & \vdots \\[4pt] p_{H-1} & = & \lambda \dfrac{\partial f}{\partial z_{H-1}}(z^*) \\[4pt] p_H & = & \lambda \end{array} \right\} \qquad (5)$$

The minimum cost of producing y^{0*} is given by

$$C(y^{0*}) = \inf \{p \cdot z \mid z \geq 0, \ y^{0*} \leq f(z)\}$$

By conditions (5), the point z^* satisfies the first order conditions of this program of minimization. If the domain defined by the constraints is convex, that is, if the set of input combinations for producing a given level of output is convex, these conditions are sufficient: z^* minimizes the cost of producing y^{0*} and (provided C is differentiable)

$$p_H = C'(y^{0*})$$

On the contrary, if the input requirement sets are not convex, it may be that z^* does not minimize the cost of producing y^{0*} (even though the first-order conditions are satisfied). In this case, p_H is no longer related to the marginal cost of production. The following example, due to Arrow and Hurwicz (1960), illustrates this point.

Suppose a firm has two technologies to produce a good y^0. The first technology uses good 1 as an input with the production function $y^0 = (x_1)^2$. The second uses good 2 with the production function $y^0 = (x_2)^2$. The production set Y is shown in Figure 2.5. $y^* = (-z^*, y^{0*})$ is an efficient production plan and p^* is the associated price such that $p^* \in N_Y(y^*)$. The

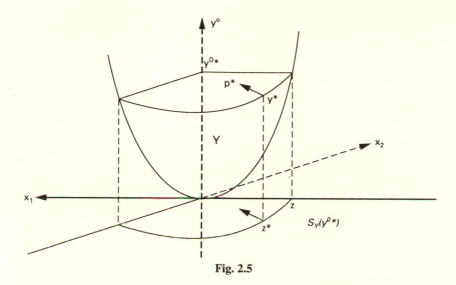

Fig. 2.5

set $S_Y(y^{0*}) = \{z = (x_1, x_2) \in \mathbb{R}^2 \mid (-z, y^{0*}) \in Y\}$ is projected onto the $x_1 0 x_2$ plane. This projection is a non-convex set. The input combination that minimizes the cost of producing y^{0*} at price p^* is the point z and not z^* which is actually a local maximum.

It is easy to associate with this production set an economy which has a Pareto optimum at y^*. The tangency between the social indifference curve and the set $w + Y$ projected onto the $x_1 0 x_2$ plane is shown in Figure 2.6. Thus, we observe the first paradox of non-convex economies: efficiency does not always require cost minimization. The rule of producing at minimum cost which common sense (and the study of convex economies) suggests as the first rule for sound management of the economy does not always lead to an optimal allocation of resources. For this to be the case, the technology must satisfy the following condition: the set of input combinations that produce a given level of output (the input requirement set) must be convex.

The example reveals another difficulty: if the two production techniques that produce the same good are operated by two different firms, if each firm is instructed to produce the appropriate quantity of output and minimizes cost, the the result will be efficient; however, if the two technologies are managed by the same firm, if this firm is instructed to produce the sum of the outputs which would be produced by the two different firms, then cost minimization does not lead to an optimal use of the inputs. This problem of organization of activity does not appear with convex economies in which the rule of profit maximization leads to efficiency whatever the organization of the production technologies between the decision-making units (firms). In non-convex economies, depending on whether production

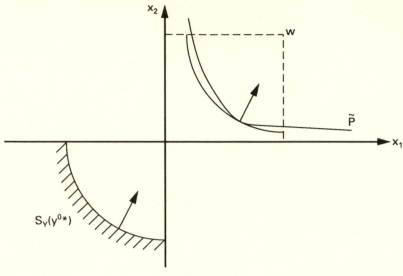

Fig. 2.6

decisions are taken globally or in decentralized units, the same rule (here cost minimization) can give rise to different normative results. We will encounter similar problems with the marginal cost pricing rule in chapter 5.

3

MARGINAL COST PRICING EQUILIBRIUM

In the previous chapter we studied the properties of an efficient allocation given consumers' preferences and production technologies but without assuming any particular organization for the economy. We shall now study how the economy should be organized so as to achieve such an efficient allocation. This will lead us to the basic concept of a marginal cost pricing equilibrium.

3.1 Organization of Decisions

In principle an efficient allocation could be obtained in a totally planned economy if the planning board, perfectly informed of the characteristics of all consumers and firms, decides on the production plans of firms and the consumptions of the agents. The literature on planning has concentrated on the way the planning board can coordinate the actions of the different firms to achieve an efficient production of outputs. The problem is difficult to solve when some production sets are non-convex (see e.g. Heal 1973 for a general presentation of planning procedures; Cremer 1977 and Henry-Zilberberg 1978 for the problem of planning under increasing returns). Furthermore, the way in which produced goods are distributed to the consumers is usually not addressed in this literature.

The experience of the socialist countries has shown that the complexity of the system to be organized coupled with the lack of incentives for firms to reveal the relevant information on their production possibilities to the planning board makes it impossible to achieve efficient allocations through a centrally planned organization of the economy. We are thus led to consider the most decentralized organization by which non-convex firms can be run while still achieving global efficiency. Some control over the non-convex firms is however necessary, in particular to avoid the exploitation of monopoly power by the large firms operating under increasing returns.

Theorem 2.6 of the preceding chapter thus suggests the following organization:

- The decisions of all consumers and the decisions of firms with convex production sets are decentralized and guided by a price system.

27

We assume that consumers and firms operating under decreasing returns are small enough to justify the assumption of perfect competition
(price-taking behavior).

- The non-convex firms are controlled by a planning board which decides
the production plans y_j and sets the tariff policy of the firm to ensure
that

$$p \in N_{Y_j}(y_j) \tag{1}$$

Relation (1) has come to be referred to in the general equilibrium literature as the *marginal cost pricing rule*. The terminology has been adopted
because it is suggestive even though as indicated earlier it is not always correct. Recall that $p \in N_{Y_j}(y_j)$ implies equality between the price of a good
and its marginal cost only if the input requirement sets are convex. With
this qualification in mind we will continue to refer to (1) as the marginal
cost pricing rule.

Condition (1) is usually interpreted as follows: the planning board decides the production plan y_j of each non-convex firm j. Given the market
prices of inputs, the firm is instructed to sell its outputs at prices such
that the resulting combined vector of input and output prices satisfies (1).
In the case where the input requirement sets are smooth and convex, the
procedure can be described as follows: first the planning board must know
the cost functions of the non-convex firms and the aggregate demand functions of the private sector for their outputs. Given this information and the
prices of the inputs in the markets, outputs (y_j^0) must be found such that

- the quantity demanded by the private sector at a price equal to their
marginal cost equals the planned productions,

- the quantities of inputs supplied by the private sector at the market
prices are exactly those necessary to produce (y_j^0) at minimum cost.

Since the non-convex firms must be subject to the detailed monitoring
of the planning board, we will refer to them in the rest of the book as
the *public firms* or more simply as the *public sector*. Does the organization
of the decisions suggested—competitive behavior for the (convex) private
sector, marginal cost pricing for the (non-convex) public sector—lead to a
satisfactory solution of the problem of resource allocation for the economy?
To give an answer to this question we must first define the associated
concept of equilibrium and show that such an equilibrium exists. We shall
then study the normative properties of the resulting equilibria.

3.2   Covering Deficits

To arrive at a concept of equilibrium, we need to show how the incomes
of the consumers are determined. To assume that the planning board com-

pletely controls the incomes of the consumers is not consistent with the idea of a decentralized functioning of the private sector. Even if we assume that a planner can impose taxes on the private sector, it must respect the private nature of the initial resources of agents. The question is then how to share the profits and losses of the firms between the consumers. There is no conceptual difficulty for the distribution of profits of the private, convex firms. We can adopt the traditional solution of the Arrow-Debreu model and assume that agents own shares of these enterprises and receive the corresponding shares of the profits. For non-convex firms, however, the marginal cost pricing rule may result in *losses* rather than profits.

For example, suppose that a firm produces good H using $H - 1$ inputs with a (differentiable) production function $f : \mathbf{R}_+^{H-1} \longrightarrow \mathbf{R}$ exhibiting increasing returns, that is, satisfies the condition

$$f(\lambda z) > \lambda f(z), \ \forall z \in \mathbf{R}_+^{H-1}, \ \forall \lambda > 1$$

The production set of this firm is

$$Y = \{(-z, y^0) \in \mathbf{R}_-^{H-1} \times \mathbf{R} \mid y^0 \leq f(z)\}$$

Let $y = (-\bar{z}, \bar{y}^0)$ be an efficient production plan and p a price vector such that $p \in N_Y(y)$. Since f is differentiable, this is equivalent to

$$p_1 = p_H \frac{\partial f}{\partial z_1}(\bar{z})$$

$$\vdots \qquad \vdots$$

$$p_{H-1} = p_H \frac{\partial f}{\partial z_{H-1}}(\bar{z})$$

The firm's profit at price p is

$$\pi = p_H \bar{y}^0 - \sum_{h=1}^{H-1} p_h \bar{z}_h = p_H \left(f(\bar{z}) - \sum_{h=1}^{H-1} \bar{z}_h \frac{\partial f}{\partial z_h}(\bar{z}) \right)$$

To show that π is negative, consider the function $\psi(\lambda) = f(\lambda \bar{z}) - \lambda f(\bar{z})$. $\psi(1) = 0$ and by assumption $\psi(\lambda) > 0$, $\forall \lambda > 1$. This implies $\psi'(1) \geq 0$. Since $\psi'(1) = \sum_{h=1}^{H-1} \bar{z}_n (\partial f/\partial z_n)(\bar{z}) - f(\bar{z})$, π is non-positive. (If f is homogeneous, $\psi'(1) > 0$ and $\pi < 0$.)

Thus a rule for distributing income among consumers must involve a way of sharing the losses of the public sector. This issue is central and no satisfactory solution has yet been found.

A formal extension of the Arrow-Debreu model where both profits and losses would be distributed with fixed shares $(\theta_{ij})_{\substack{i=1,\ldots,n \\ j=1,\ldots,m}}$ is clearly not satisfactory. First, it is difficult to believe that agents willingly own shares of firms which give them the right to finance the deficit of the firms—firms which may not even try to minimize losses. Second, even if these shares are imposed on the agents, some agents may have insufficient resources to finance the deficit. If the income of the agent is of the form $R_i = p \cdot w_i + \sum_j \theta_{ij} p \cdot y_j$ where some terms $p \cdot y_j$ are negative, then R_i may become negative, which must be excluded from the model.

To avoid this difficulty R. Guesnerie (1975) suggested the following rule: let the *total* income of the economy be divided between the agents according a fixed vector $\alpha = (\alpha_1, \ldots, \alpha_n)$. The ith agent receives the fraction $\alpha_i > 0$ of the total income so that $R_i = \alpha_i (p \cdot w_i + \sum_j p \cdot y_j)$. This ensures that, given a positive total income, each agent has a positive income; however, it is difficult to see how a planner can achieve such a predetermined distribution of the total wealth of the economy while respecting the private ownership of initial resources and of private firms.

Since the problem is essentially a problem of redistribution of income from the private to the public sector, the traditional solution suggested by economic theory is to use lump-sum taxation to cover the losses of the non-convex firms. There is not much loss of generality in assuming that the tax burden is supported directly by the consumers. Then if we denote J_1 the set of convex (or private) firms and J_2 the set of non-convex (public) firms, the income of agent i is given by

$$R_i = p \cdot w_i + \sum_{j \in J_1} \theta_{ij} p \cdot y_j - t_i \qquad (2)$$

where the transfers $(t_i)_{i=1,\ldots,I}$ must be chosen such that

$$\sum_{i=1}^{n} t_i \geq - \sum_{j \in J_2} p \cdot y_j \qquad (3)$$

$$t_i \leq p \cdot w_i + \sum_{j \in J_1} \theta_{ij} p \cdot y_j, \ \forall i = 1, \ldots, n$$

This solution is in the spirit of Hotelling's proposal which suggests covering the deficit of public enterprises by taxes on income and wealth which, according to Hotelling, do not introduce too much distortion in the economy. If tax rates can be personalized, lump-sum taxation is formally equivalent to income taxation since the existence of transfers $(t_i)_{i=1,\ldots,n}$ satisfying (2) and (3) is equivalent to the existence of tax rates $(\tau_i)_{i=1,\ldots,n}$ such that

$$R_i = (1 - \tau_i)(p \cdot w_i + \sum_{j \in J_1} p \cdot y_i) \qquad (4)$$

$$\sum_{i=1}^{n} \tau_i (p \cdot w_i + \sum_{j \in J_1} \theta_{ij} p \cdot y_j) \geq - \sum_{j \in J_2} p \cdot y_j \tag{5}$$

$$(1 - \tau_i) \geq 0, \ \forall i = 1, \dots, n$$

As mentioned in section 1.1, Hotelling's proposal met with many objections. The first concerned the feasibility of covering the losses of the public firms by non-distortive taxation. Lump-sum taxes do not exist in the real world and the equivalent income taxes of formula (4) do not exist either because most of the agents draw a large part of their income from their labor. In the model described in chapter 2 the supply of labor appears as the negative of the consumption of leisure. More precisely, in order to incorporate labor, the model must be interpreted as follows: the first L goods are leisure or "non-work" of quality ℓ, $\ell = 1, \dots, L$. Agent i is endowed with quantities $(w_\ell^i)_{\ell=1,\dots,L}$ of these goods, consumes $(x_\ell^i)_{\ell=1,\dots,L}$ under the form of leisure and thus supplies $w_\ell^i - x_\ell^i$ units of labor ℓ. To be non-distortive, an income tax should bear on $(w_\ell^i)_{\ell=1,\dots,L}$ but not on $(x_\ell^i)_{\ell=1,\dots,L}$. In practice it is impossible to observe or to deduce $(w_\ell^i)_{\ell=1,\dots,L}$ so that income taxes are always levied on the actual quantities of labor supplied $(w_\ell^i - x_\ell^i)_{\ell=1,\dots,L}$ and thus introduce a distortion in the labor–leisure choice. Of course, Hotelling recognized that most forms of income taxation introduce distortions. His point was that some forms of income taxes (on inheritance, on rent, on land) introduce less distortion than excise taxes on the goods produced under increasing returns and can raise enough revenue to cover the deficit created by marginal cost pricing. A serious appraisal of his proposal would involve studying the second best equilibria and comparing the welfare losses implied by either form of distortion. Such a comparison is not likely to be easy.

3.3 Two-Part Tariffs

The second class of objections to Hotelling's proposal concerned income redistribution. If the deficit incurred by public firms pricing at marginal cost is covered by income taxation, the high income agents end up subsidizing the consumers of public firms' goods. Depending on the weight attributed to the welfare of each agent, the resulting allocation, although Pareto optimal, may be less desirable from a social welfare point of view than an allocation resulting from average cost pricing (which is equivalent to the imposition of an excise tax).

There is, however, an alternative to income taxation for collecting the lump-sum taxes necessary to cover the deficit of public firms. Lump-sum taxes are not used because agents would not accept the imposition of arbitrary taxes, but if the taxes are presented as fixed fees that give agents the option to buy (or not to buy) the goods produced by the public sector at their marginal cost, then the taxes become more acceptable since the agents can choose not to pay them. Thus it seems that the use by public firms of personalized two-part tariffs for selling their output should, in many cases, reconcile the requirements of Pareto optimality and of a voluntary financing on the part of the agents. The linear prices of the goods should, of course, be equal to marginal costs while the fixed fees should extract enough of the consumers surplus generated by low linear prices to cover the deficit thus created. Discrimination in the fixed part of the tariff is necessary to prevent some potential consumers of the public firms' goods from being discouraged by too high an entrance fee. This solution is only feasible for goods which are not readily transferred between consumers. If the goods were easy to transfer, only one consumer would pay the required fixed fee and would resell part of what he or she buys from the public firms. The strategic behavior of this agent would again introduce distortion in the prices of the public firms' goods from their marginal cost.

Since the assumption of *nontransferability* is appropriate for many goods produced by public utilities (electricity, telephone, transportation), it is interesting to study more carefully if the use of two-part tariffs leads to a solution of the problem of financing the deficit of public firms producing under increasing returns. The first question is clearly the following: Can an efficient allocation be supported by a two-part tariff? If the answer is negative there is not much hope that an equilibrium concept based on two-part tariff financing for the non-convex firms will lead to efficiency.

It is useful to distinguish three ways of designing two-part tariffs for the public sector:

1. *Good-specific fees*: Each good h produced by the public sector is assigned a (personalized) fixed charge that a consumer must pay to have the right to buying good h at the linear price p_h.
2. *Firm-specific fees*: Each public firm $j \in J_2$ charges a (personalized) fixed fee that a consumer must pay prior to purchasing any good produced by firm j.
3. A *general fee* for the public sector: Each consumer must pay a (personalized) fixed charge prior to purchasing any good produced by the public sector.

Although two-part tariffs of type (i) are more realistic, two-part tariffs of type (iii) are easier to incorporate into our model. With such a system of fees, the income of a consumer is essentially given by (2), the numbers t_i being interpreted as the fixed fee of the two-part tariff.

To formalize the question raised earlier about the possiblity of decentralizing efficient allocation by two-part tariffs, consider the model described in section 2.1.

Let $\left((x_i^*)_{i=1,\ldots,n}, (y_j^*)_{j=1,\ldots,m}\right)$ be an efficient allocation such that $x_i^* \gg 0$, for all $i = 1, \ldots, n$. Suppose J_1 and J_2 denote the sets of convex and non-convex production sets, respectively. By Theorem 2.6, it follows that there exists a price vector p and a distribution of incomes $(R_i)_{i=1,\ldots,n}$ such that:

- x_i^* maximizes $u_i(x_i)$ under the budget constraint $p \cdot x_i \leq R_i$, for $i = 1, \ldots, n$

- y_j^* maximizes $p \cdot y_j$ under the technological constraint $y_j \in Y_j$, for $j \in J_1$

- $p \in N_{Y_j}(y_j^*)$, for $j \in J_2$.

Suppose $H = H_1 \cup H_2$, where H_2 is the set of goods produced by the public sector (by firms $j \in J_2$). To simplify, suppose that the private sector does not produce the goods $h \in H_2$. It is possible to decentralize the allocation $\left((x_i^*), (y_j^*)\right)$ by a two-part tariff (personalized, of type (iii)) if there exist t_i, $i = 1, \ldots, n$, such that:

- $t_i \geq 0$

- x_i^* maximizes $u_i(x_i)$ over the budget set

$$
x_i^* \in \left\{ x_i \geq 0 \left| \begin{array}{ll} p \cdot x_i \leq R_i + t_i, & \text{if } x_{ih} = 0, \ \forall h \in H_2 \\[2mm] p \cdot x_i \leq R_i, & \text{otherwise,} \end{array} \right. \right\}
$$

- $\sum_i t_i + \sum_{j \in J_2} p \cdot y_j^* \geq 0$

Thus, t_i is the fixed charge imposed on agent i if he or she wishes to consume any public sector good. If agent i does not consume any of these goods ($x_{ih} = 0$, $\forall h \in H_2$), his or her income is increased by t_i. The inequality $\sum_i t_i + \sum_{j \in J_2} p \cdot y_j^* \geq 0$ implies that the fixed charges are sufficient to cover the deficit of the public sector.

Although there is a partial equilibrium literature on two-part tariffs, among them the well-known article by Oi (1971), "A Disneyland Dilemma: Two Part Tariff for a Mickey Mouse Monopoly," there is suprisingly little work concerning the compatibility of such a rule with first best optimality. The only published article that deals with the question posed—Is an efficient allocation decentralizable by using two-part tariffs?—is by D. Brown and G. Heal (1980), "Two Part Tariffs, Marginal Cost Pricing and Increasing Returns in a General Equilibrium Model." This article does not really answer the question, but it orients the reader toward a positive answer.

It is clear that in a two good, one firm economy, it is always possible to finance the deficit in production by making consumers pay a fixed charge to buy the produced good. This is shown in Figure 3.1.

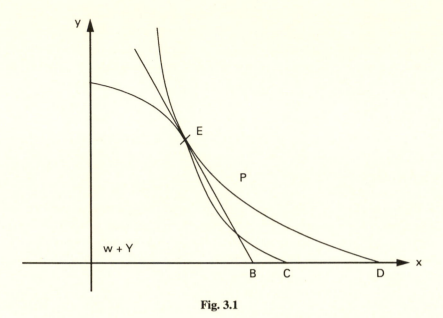

Fig. 3.1

In this figure, the point E where the social indifference curve is tangent to the set of feasible allocations $w + Y$, represents a Pareto optimum. The firm's deficit is given by BC. The social indifference curve must cut the axis $0\,x$ (if it cuts it) to the right of C since E is Pareto superior to the feasible allocation $(w, 0)$ (corresponding to C). Therefore, it is possible to modify the budget constraints so that the agents have access to consumptions whose sum is a point on BC but still prefer the allocation corresponding to E. Brown and Heal established the following result.

THEOREM 3.1. *Consider an economy* $\mathcal{E}\big((u_i)_{i=1,\ldots,n}, (Y_j)_{j=1,\ldots,m}, w\big)$ *satisfying the assumptions of Theorem 2.6. Let* $\big((x_i^*)_{i=1,\ldots,n} (y_j^*)_{j=1,\ldots,m}\big)$ *be an efficient allocation with* $(p, (R_i)_{i=1,\ldots,n})$ *being a vector of prices and a distribution of income which decentralize this allocation.*
If $\bar{z}$ *is a vector satisfying*

$$p \cdot \bar{z} = \max\{p \cdot z \mid z \in w + Y\}$$

and if $(\bar{z})$ *denotes the half-line generated by* $\bar{z}$,

$$(\bar{z}) = \{\lambda \bar{z} \mid \lambda \geq 0\}$$

then there exist $t_i \geq 0$ *such that:*

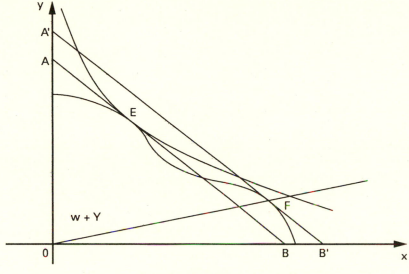

Fig. 3.2

- x_i^* maximizes $u_i(x_i)$ over the budget set

$$\left\{ x_i \geq 0 \;\middle|\; \begin{array}{ll} p \cdot x_i \leq R_i + t_i, & \text{if } x_i \in (\bar{z}) \\[2mm] p \cdot x_i \leq R_i, & \text{otherwise,} \end{array} \right\}$$

- $\sum_i t_i + \sum_j p \cdot y_j^* \geq 0$

This result is similar in spirit to the theorem that we would like to prove; however, the budget constraint modified by the vector $\bar{z}$ does not correspond to a two-part tariff except in special cases. For this property to be satisfied, the vector which maximizes the total value in the economy at prices p must correspond to zero production in the non-convex sector. While this is true in the economy represented in Figure 3.1, even in a two-good model, it is easy to construct a counterexample. The content of Theorem 3.1 is illustrated in Figure 3.2.

E represents the Pareto optimal allocation. For the associated price, F corresponds to the vector $\bar{z}$ which maximizes $p \cdot z$ over the set $w + Y$. It is possible to give agents budget constraints which sum to AB while restricting their consumption on the half line OF if they do not pay the fixed fee in such a way that they still choose the allocation E.

The Brown and Heal theorem does not apply to the usual notion of a two-part tariff since the constraint $x \in (\bar{z})$ which exempts an agent from contributing to the financing of the public sector does not prevent the consumption of public sector goods. Moreover, it does not seem practically

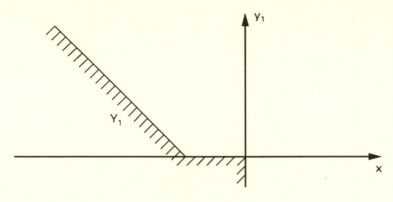

Fig. 3.3

feasible to force agents to consume bundles of goods which have the same compositions as the vector $\bar{z}$ which for them is totally arbitrary.

The following counterexample due to Guesnerie and Quinzii (see Quinzii 1986, 1988a) shows that, in an economy with more than two goods, it is not always possible to decentralize an efficient allocation by a two-part tariff.

Consider an economy with three goods. $[x]$ is the factor of production. A single (representative) consumer owns initially a quantity w of this good. There are two firms: firm 1 produces $[y_1]$ from $[x]$ and firm 2 produces $[y_2]$ from $[x]$. The production of $[y_1]$ requires a fixed cost c and has a constant marginal cost (Figure 3.3). $[y_2]$ is produced under decreasing returns to scale (Figure 3.4). The set of feasible allocations $w + Y$ is shown in Figure 3.5.

$CBAA'B'C$ is the boundary of the set of feasible allocations. AA' represents the feasible allocation with a zero production of $[y_1]$. Allocations

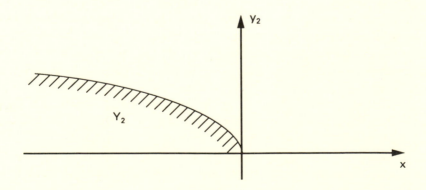

Fig. 3.4

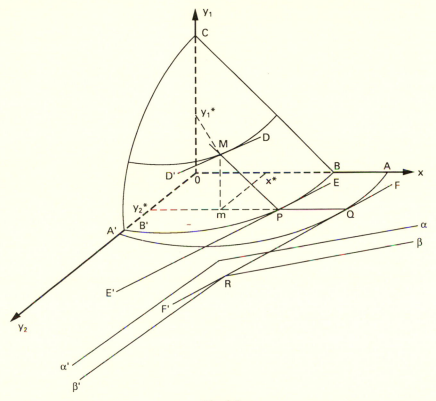

Fig. 3.5

with a positive production of $[y_1]$ where the fixed cost c has to be incurred correspond to CBB'.

At a point like M the consumer consumes the quantity x^* of good $[x]$. The rest, $w - x^*$, is used to cover the fixed cost (PQ) and to produce y_1^* and y_2^* of good $[y_1]$ and $[y_2]$, respectively.

It is easy to assign preferences to the consumer such that the optimal allocation is M, but the losses of firm 1 (the fixed cost) cannot be covered by a two-part tariff for good 1. It is sufficient that the consumer's preferences are such that:

- the indifference surface through M is tangent to the plane generated by PM and DD' and cut the plane $x0y_2$ along a curve outside OAA' (eg., the curve $\alpha\alpha'$ in Figure 3.5),

- there is a consumption on the line FQF' in the plane $x\,0\,y_2$ which is preferred to M (eg. an indifference surface cuts the plane $x\,0\,y_2$ along $\beta'\,R\,\beta$).

It is clear that there are more than enough degrees of freedom to be able to construct convex preferences which satisfy these two conditions.

To verify that a two-part tariff for good $[y_1]$ leads to the budget line FQF', note that the line EPE' is parallel to $D'D$ and belongs to the plane (MP, DD'). If $(1, p_1, p_2)$ is the vector othogonal to the plane (MP, DD'), the equation of EPE' is $x + p_2 y_2 = x^* + p_1 y_1^* + p_2 y_2^* = R^*$. Adding the fixed cost c to the revenue R^* leads to the parallel budget line FQF' whose equation is: $x + p_2 y_2 = R^* + c$. If the preferences of the consumer satisfy the two conditions given earlier, utility maximization under the constraints

$$
\begin{cases}
x + p_2 y_2 \leq R^* + c & \text{if } y_1 = 0 \\[2mm]
x + p_1 y_1 + p_2 y_2 \leq R^* & \text{if } y_1 > 0
\end{cases}
$$

leads to the point R which is not feasible, instead of M which is the Pareto optimal allocation.

The economic intuition behind this example is easy to understand. When an agent considers the two possibilities offered, either to pay a fixed fee and buy some of the two goods or to use all of the budget to buy only good 2, the price vector (p_1, p_2) is not an appropriate guide. To make the correct decision the agent would have to know that good 2 is produced under decreasing returns to scale and that as the demand for it increases so does its price. It is, of course, the essence of competitive behavior that it excludes this kind of information and reasoning.

The nature of the assumption that is needed to ensure that a Pareto optimum can be decentralized by a two-part tariff is clear from this example: the preferences of the consumer must be such that the surplus derived from buying good $[y_1]$ at price p_1 is larger than the fixed cost. Let us formalize this idea. Let u denote the utility function of the consumer, $v^* = u(x^*, y_1^*, y_2^*)$ the utility level at the optimal allocation. Since $((1, p_1, p_2), R^*)$ decentralizes the allocation (x^*, y_1^*, y_2^*),

$$
v^* = \max \left\{ u(x, y_1, y_2) \,\middle|\, \begin{array}{l} x \geq 0, \ y_1 \geq 0, \ y_2 \geq 0 \\[2mm] x + p_1 y_1 + p_2 y_2 = R^* \end{array} \right\} \tag{6}
$$

Let $E : \mathbf{R}_+^3 \longrightarrow \mathbf{R}_+$ denote the expenditure function defined by

$$
E(p_1, p_2, v) = \inf \left\{ x + p_1 y_1 + p_2 y_2 \,\middle|\, \begin{array}{l} x \geq 0, \ y_1 \geq 0, \ y_2 \geq 0 \\[2mm] u(x, y_1, y_2) \geq v \end{array} \right\}
$$

By duality $R^* = E(p_1, p_2, v^*)$.

Let $E_{y_1=0} : \mathbb{R}^2_+ \longrightarrow \mathbb{R}_+$ denote the expenditure function for a consumer constrained to a zero consumption of good $[y_1]$

$$E_{y_1=0}(p_2, v) = \inf \left\{ x + p_2 y_2 \,\middle|\, \begin{array}{l} x \geq 0, \ y_2 \geq 0 \\[6pt] u(x, 0, y_2) \geq v \end{array} \right\}$$

and define

$$\bar{v} = \max \left\{ u(x, y_1, y_2) \,\middle|\, \begin{array}{l} x_1 \geq 0, \ y_1 \geq 0, \ y_2 \geq 0 \\[6pt] x + p_1 y_1 + p_2 y_2 = R^* \quad \text{if } y_1 > 0 \\[6pt] x + p_2 y_2 = R^* + c \quad \text{if } y_1 = 0 \end{array} \right\} \tag{7}$$

Since (x^*, y_1^*, y_2^*) satisfies the constraints in (7), $\bar{v} \geq v^*$. $\bar{v} > v^*$ if and only if the consumer facing a two-part tariff chooses $y_1 = 0$. In this case, $E_{y_1=0}(p_2, \bar{v}) = R^* + c$, so that $E_{y_1=0}(p_2, v^*) < R^* + c$. Conversely, if $E_{y_1=0}(p_2, v^*) < R^* + c$ the consumer can achieve a higher utility level than v^* by not buying good $[y_1]$ and $\bar{v} > v^*$. Thus, a necessary and sufficient condition for (x^*, y_1^*, y_2^*) to be the solution of the utility maximization (7) is

$$E_{y_1=0}(p_2, v^*) > E(p_1, p_2, v^*) + c \tag{8}$$

The additional income needed to compensate the consumer for the absence of the market for good $[y_1]$ must be larger than the fixed cost or, equivalently, the surplus generated by selling good $[y_1]$ at its marginal cost must be larger than the fixed cost.

Condition (8) has recently been introduced by Brown, Heller, and Starr (1990) for a more general model than the example given earlier and called the "Surplus Condition." It is intuitively clear that (8) can be generalized to a multiagent economy and gives a necessary and sufficient condition for an efficient allocation to be decentralizable by a two-part tariff of type (iii). It is also clear that a condition which guarantees decentralization by a two-part tariff of type (i) would be more complicated to express in a multigood economy since the expenditure would have to be evaluated for all possible combinations of positive and zero consumption of the public sector goods. However, we shall not go further into this.

3.4 Marginal Cost Pricing Equilibrium

The problem of balancing the budget of firms producing under increasing returns will be discussed again in chapter 6. In the meanwhile, to circumvent the difficulty of sharing the losses of the public sector, we shall adopt the following abstract procedure for assigning income to the agents.

DEFINITION. *Let $\mathcal{E}\big((u_i, w_i)_{i=1,\ldots,n}, (Y_j)_{j=1,\ldots,m}\big)$ be an economy with H goods. Let Δ_{H-1} denote the simplex in $\mathbb{R}^H$. An income map for the economy $\mathcal{E}$ is a continuous map*

$$r = (r_i)_{i=1,\ldots,n} : \Delta_{H-1} \times \Pi_j Y_j \longrightarrow \mathbb{R}^n$$

such that

(i) $\sum_{i=1}^n r_i(p, (y_j)) = p \cdot \sum_{i=1}^n w_i + p \cdot \sum_{j=1}^m y_j, \; \forall p \in \Delta_{H-1}, \; \forall (y_j) \in \Pi_j Y_j$

(ii) $p \cdot \sum_{i=1}^n w_i + p \cdot \sum_{j=1}^m y_j > 0 \Longrightarrow r_i(p, (y_j)) > 0, \; \forall i = 1, \ldots, n$

This definition is general enough to avoid a precise description of the way in which profits and losses of firms are distributed. The only requirement is that each agent is assured a positive income whenever the total income in the economy is positive. With this definition in hand we define the concept of a marginal cost pricing equilibrium as follows.

DEFINITION. *Let $\mathcal{E}\big((u_i, w_i)_{i=1,\ldots,n}, (Y_j)_{j=1,\ldots,m}\big)$ be a production economy. Let J_1 and J_2 denote the index sets of firms which have convex and non-convex production sets respectively. Let $r : \Delta_{H-1} \times \prod_j Y_j \longrightarrow \mathbb{R}$ be an income map for this economy. A marginal cost pricing equilibrium associated with r is a pair consisting of an allocation and price vector $\big(((x_i^*)_{i=1,\ldots,n}, (y_j^*)_{j=1,\ldots,m}), p^*\big)$ such that:*

- *x_i^* maximizes $u_i(x_i)$ in the budget set $\{x_i \in \mathbb{R}_+^H \mid p^* \cdot x_i \le r_i(p^*, (y_j^*))\}$, $\forall i = 1, \ldots, n$*

- *y_j^* maximizes the profit $p^* \cdot y_j$ over the productions $y_j \in Y_j, \; \forall j \in J_1$*

- *$p^* \in N_{Y_j}(y_j^*), \; \forall j \epsilon J_2$*

- *$\sum_{i=1}^n x_i^* \le \sum_{i=1}^n w_i + \sum_{j=1}^m y_j^*$*

This concept of a marginal cost pricing equilibrium is a natural extension of the concept of a competitive equilibrium for economies in which some firms have non-convex production sets.

Let $\big((x_i^*)_{i=1,\ldots,n}, (y_j^*)_{j=1,\ldots,m}\big)$ be an efficient allocation of a production economy satisfying the assumptions of Theorem 2.6. If p^* is a supporting price for this allocation and if $p^* \cdot x_i^* > 0$ for all agents $i = 1, \ldots, n$, then $\big((x_i^*)_{i=1,\ldots,n}, (y_j^*)_{j=1,\ldots,m}, p^*\big)$ is a marginal cost pricing equilibrium for any income map r satisfying $r_i(p^*, (y_j^*)) = p^* \cdot x_i^*, \; i = 1, \ldots, n$.

For the concept of a marginal cost pricing equilibrium to be of practical relevance, we must establish two properties. First, for a broad class of income rules such an equilibrium should exist. Second, we need to check that the resulting equilibria in fact have the efficiency property that originally motivated the use of the marginal cost pricing rule.

4

EFFICIENCY

In general terms, there are two reasons why a marginal cost pricing equilibrium can be inefficient. The first is linked to the failure of prices to coordinate firms' production decisions; the second arise from a lack of coordination between the consumption and the production sector and has its origin in the way income is distributed among the agents at an equilibrium. The first type of inefficiency, which we call productive inefficiency, will be discussed in chapter 5 in connexion with the problem that it poses for proving existence of an equilibrium. This chapter concentrates on the second type of inefficiency under assumptions which ensure that equilibrium allocations are productively efficient.

The simplest way of avoiding productive inefficiency is to assume that the production sector is aggregated and represented by a production set Y. This is the framework of the following example of an economy in which, for a given income map, all marginal cost pricing equilibria are inefficient. Since there are income maps for which at least one equilibrium is efficient (Theorem 2.6), this example shows that in non-convex economies, efficiency of equilibria and choice of income distribution are not separate questions as they are in convex economies.

These ideas were introduced by Guesnerie (1975) who first presented an example of an economy in which all marginal cost pricing equilibria are inefficient. The analysis which follows is based on the paper of Brown and Heal (1979) which modifies Guesnerie's example so that the analysis of the equilibria can be obtained by simple geometric arguments.

4.1. Inefficiency of All Equilibria

Consider a two-good, two-agent economy with a single firm whose production set exhibits the extreme case of indivisibility (see Figure 4.1).

The production set is

$$Y = \left\{ (x,y) \in \mathbb{R}^2 \left| \begin{array}{ll} x > -7, & y \leq 0 \\ x \leq -7, & y \leq 7 \end{array} \right. \right\}$$

No output can be produced with less than seven units of input and seven units of output can be produced with seven or more units of input. This

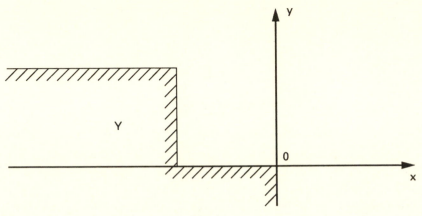

Fig. 4.1

example is not very realistic, but it serves to illustrate the point and leads
to simple calculations. Smoothing the production set and the indifference
curves given later gives the same qualitative results but involves more te-
dious computation.

The only two efficient production plans are the zero production $(0,0)$
and the production plan $(-7,7)$. At all other points on the frontier of Y,
the condition $p \in N_Y(y)$ implies that one of the prices is zero. If consumers
desire both goods, such points cannot be equilibrium points. At the points
$(0,0)$ and $(-7,7)$, the Clarke normal cone is the positive orthant. Hence, all
price vectors $p = (p_x, p_y)$ satisfy $p \in N_Y(y)$ for $y = (0,0)$ and $y = (-7,7)$.

Suppose the utility functions of the two consumers are given by:

$$u_1(x,y) = \begin{cases} y + \frac{4}{3}x & \text{if } y \geq x \\ \frac{700}{312}(y + \frac{4}{100}x) & \text{if } y \leq x \end{cases}$$

$$u_2(x,y) = \begin{cases} \frac{3y+5x}{18} & \text{if } y \geq \frac{x}{3} \\ y & \text{if } y \leq \frac{x}{3} \end{cases}$$

The indifference curves are shown in Figure 4.2.

The income map is defined as follows: the initial resources held by consumers 1 and 2 are $w_1 = (0,5)$ and $w_2 = (15,0)$ respectively, and the loss
or gain of the firm is borne by agent 1. The set of feasible allocations $w + Y$
for the economy is given in Figure 4.3.

As mentioned earlier, the only possible equilibrium points are A and B
corresponding to the production plans $(0,0)$ and $(-7,7)$. Since the condition $p \in N_Y(y)$ does not impose any restriction on the equilibrium prices,
the analysis of a production equilibrium is equivalent to the analysis of
an exchange equilibrium. Every equilibrium with zero production is an

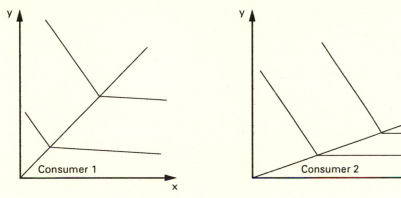

Fig. 4.2

equilibrium of the exchange economy (u_1, u_2, w_1, w_2). Every equilibrium with a production plan $(-7, 7)$ is an equilibrium of the exchange economy $(u_1, u_2, \tilde{w}_1, w_2)$ where $\tilde{w}_1 = (-7, 12)$ are the resources of agent 1, since agent 1 owns the firm which produces $(-7, 7)$. The equilibrium price (p_x, p_y) must guarantee a positive revenue for agent 1, that is, it must be such that $-7p_x + 12p_y > 0$.

These equilibria can be studied in an Edgeworth box since there are two goods and two agents. The first type of equilibrium is represented in the Edgeworth box OEBC and the second type in the box OFAD (Figure 4.3).

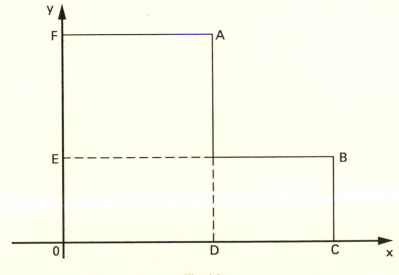

Fig. 4.3

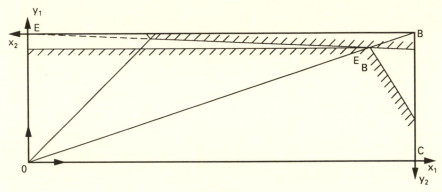

Fig. 4.4

Equilibrium with zero production (Figure 4.4)

The indifference curves of agents are tangent along the line OB which represents the optimal distribution of total resources (15, 5). The equation of the line that separates the two indifference curves at a point on OB is

$$y + \frac{4}{100}x = \text{constant}$$

E represents the initial endowments of the two agents. This point lies on the line $y + \frac{4}{100}x = 5$ which cuts the line OB at the point $x_1 = \frac{1500}{112}, y_1 = \frac{500}{112}$. Thus there exists an equilibrium with zero production characterized by the prices $p_x = 4$, $p_y = 100$ and the consumptions

$$(x_1, y_1) = (13.393, 4.644) \text{ and } (x_2, y_2) = (1.607, 0.536)$$

Equilibrium with production (Figure 4.5)

The Pareto optima in the box OFAD are the allocations of the broken line OHA. For an allocation on OH, the preferred sets are separated by a line of equation $(3y_2 + 5x_2)/18 = \text{constant}$. For an allocation on AH, the preferred sets are separated by a line of equation $y_1 + \frac{4}{100}x_1 = \text{constant}$. The budget line $p_y x_1 + p_y y_1 = R_1$ must pass through the point G (outside the Edgeworth box) of coordinates (15, 0) in the axes $x_2 A y_2$ which represents the initial resources. Thus, there is a unique equilibrium E_A at the intersection of the lines $(3y_2 + 5x_2)/18 = (5 \times 15)/18$ and $x_1 = 0$ (or $x_2 = 8$). This equilibrium corresponds to the prices $p_x = 5, p_y = 3$ and to the consumptions $(x_1, y_1) = (0, \frac{1}{3})$ and $(x_2, y_2) = (8, \frac{35}{3})$.

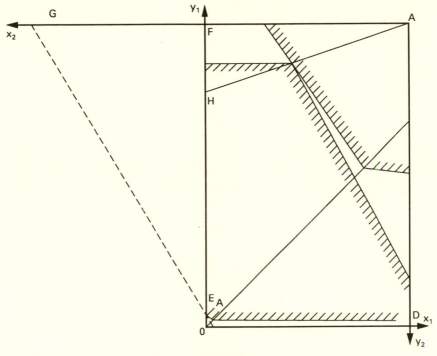

Fig. 4.5

Efficient allocations (Figure 4.6)

We shall now show that neither of the two equilibrium allocations is efficient. First, we determine the set of Pareto optima for the economy. Since at least one agent desires each good, the Pareto optimal allocations can only be obtained by using one of the efficient productions $(0,0)$ or $(-7,7)$. A Pareto optimum with zero production must be an efficient distribution of the vector of goods $(15,5)$ between the two agents. These distributions correspond to the points on the line OB of Figure 4.4, that is, to the allocations of the form

$$0 \le x_2 \le 15, \quad y_2 = \frac{x_2}{3}, \quad x_1 = 15 - x_2, \quad y_1 = 5 - \frac{x_2}{3}$$

The utility levels corresponding to these allocations are

$$\left\{ (U_1, U_2) \mid U_2 + \frac{39}{98} U_1 = 5, \quad 0 \le U_2 \le 5 \right\}$$

A Pareto optimum with production plan $(-7,7)$ must be an efficient distribution of the vector of resources $(8,12)$. These distributions are given

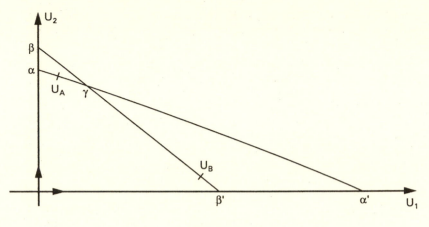

Fig. 4.6

by the broken line 0HA of Figure 4.5. The allocations along OH are of the form:

$$x_1 = 0, \quad 0 \le y_1 \le \frac{28}{3}, \quad x_2 = 8, \quad y_2 = 12 - y_1$$

and the associated utility levels are

$$\left\{ (U_1, U_2) \mid 0 \le U_1 \le \frac{28}{3}, \; U_2 = \frac{76 - 3U_1}{18} \right\}$$

The allocations along HA are of the form

$$0 \le x_1 \le 8, \quad y_1 = \frac{28}{3} + \frac{x_1}{3}, \quad x_2 = 8 - x_1, \quad y_2 = \frac{8}{3} - \frac{x_1}{3}.$$

and the associated utility levels are:

$$\left\{ (U_1, U_2) \mid \frac{28}{3} \le U_1 \le \frac{68}{3}, \; U_2 = \frac{68 - 3U_1}{15} \right\}$$

The feasible utility levels in the economy are described in Figure 4.6. $\beta\beta'$ represents the levels of utility attainable with zero production, $\alpha\alpha'$ corresponds to the levels of utility attainable using the production plan $(-7, 7)$. The set of Pareto optima are the allocations corresponding to the levels of utility $\beta\gamma\alpha'$. The equilibrium allocations E_A and E_B give utility levels $U_B = (11.216, 0.536)$ on $\beta\beta'$ and $U_A = (\frac{1}{3}, \frac{25}{6})$ on $\alpha\alpha'$, both of which are dominated by feasible utility levels.

By modifying the income map one can reestablish efficiency of at least one equilibrium. The modification can either consist of a transfer of initial resources from one agent to another or of a change in the method of financing the losses of firms. Either of these modifications can restore the efficiency of at least one of the equilibrium allocations as shown in the following cases:

(i) Agent 1's initial resources are (8, 5) and agent 2's initial resources are (7, 0). The losses from production are entirely borne by agent 1.

(ii) The initial resources of agents are the same as before, i.e., (0, 5) and (15, 0), but the losses of the firm are borne by agent 2.

The geometric analysis of these two cases are given in Figures 4.7 and 4.8. The utilities associated with the equilibrium are given in Figure 4.9. In these figures, $E_{A'}, E_{B'}, U_{A'}, U_{B'}$ refer to case (i) while $E_{A''}, E_{B''}, U_{A''}, U_{B''}$ refer to case (ii).

4.2. Abstract Condition for Efficiency

The problem of inefficiency of equilibrium allocations exhibited in the given example is specific to non-convex economies. In a convex Arrow-Debreu economy, every distribution of income gives rise to at least one equilibrium and every equilibrium allocation is efficient. The only relevant criterion for comparing two income maps is equity since both give rise to efficient allocations. Thus, in the case of convex economies, it is possible to separate the search for equity (which can theoretically be attained by a direct redistribution of revenues without causing any distortions in the price system) and the search for efficiency (which is guaranteed by decentralized competitive markets).

When the production sets exhibiting indivisibilities or increasing returns the situation is quite different. Although production may be efficient and prices correctly reflect marginal costs, the equilibrium associated with a particular distribution of income may not be Pareto optimal.

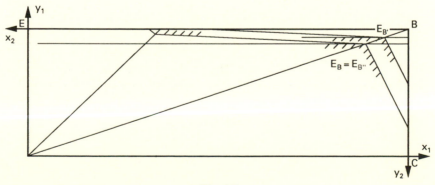

Fig. 4.7

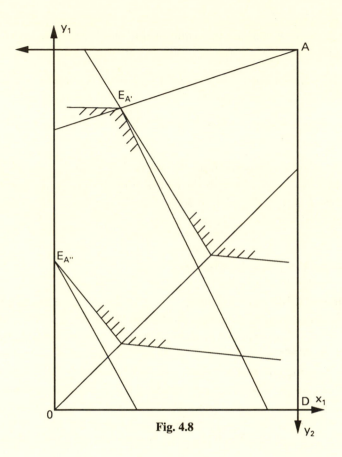

Fig. 4.8

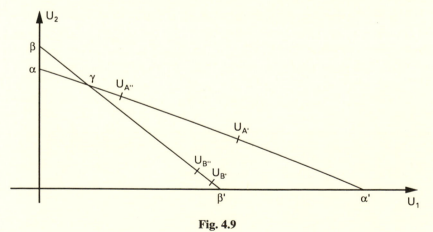

Fig. 4.9

This observation brings us back to the problem of financing deficits of the public sector discussed in section 3.2. To ensure efficiency it is not sufficient that production technologies with increasing returns or large indivisibilities be under the control of a planning board and that prices are set equal to marginal costs. The deficit of these firms must be covered and, even if non-distortive, direct taxation can be used, it is still possible that the induced distribution of income leads to inefficient equilibria.

The economies that we are considering depend on the characteristics $\left((u_i, w_i)_{i=1,\ldots,n}, (Y_j)_{j=1,\ldots,m}\right)$ of consumers and firms and on the income map r. At the current time general conditions on the economies $\mathcal{E}\left((u_i, w_i)_{i=1,\ldots,n}, (Y_j)_{j=1,\ldots,m}; r\right)$ which lead to efficient equilibria are not known. A natural approach is to try to find restrictions on the consumers and firms characteristics so that the economy has efficient equilibria for all income maps r. An obvious case when this property holds is when the economy has only one consumer. In this case, there is only one possible income map since the consumer earns the value of the initial endowment plus the losses or profits of the firms. Any allocation optimal for this consumer in the set of feasible allocations $w + Y$ is an equilibrium allocation for this income map.

It follows readily from this that if the consumption sector can be described by a representative consumer—that is, if the income distribution does not influence the demand of the consumption sector—then there exists at least one efficient equilibrium. As is well known, however, the conditions under which the consumption sector can be described by a representative consumer are extremely restrictive: agents must have identical preferences represented by a utility function homogeneous of degree 1 (identical linear homogeneous utility functions).

We shall now exhibit less restrictive conditions which imply the existence of a Pareto optimal equilibrium. These conditions arise from the following property: non-convex economies are "well behaved" if there is a one to one map between the utility possibility frontier and the feasible allocations which lead to these utilities.

Before establishing this property, recall the preceding example. The set of feasible utilities in the example of section 4.1 is shown in Figure 4.6. The utility frontier is the curve $\beta\gamma\alpha'$. The segment $\beta\gamma$ represents imputations of utility favorable to agent 2 where production is zero. $\gamma\alpha'$ is the segment of utility imputations favorable to agent 1 where production is non-zero. The imputation of utility γ is attainable by two different allocations, one with no production, the other with production. Imagine a planning board which is to achieve an efficient allocation of resources in the economy described in section 4.1. The choice of the level of production will depend on which of the two agents it decides to favor, as shown in Figure 4.10.

The mapping which associates a production decision with every point of the utility frontier is discontinous at γ where two allocations are possi-

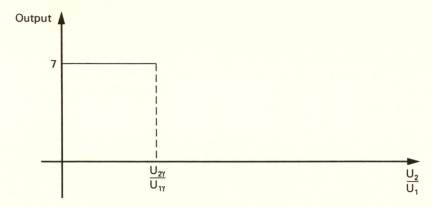

Fig. 4.10

ble (with and without production). In technical terms, this example shows
that in general it is a correspondence and not a function which associates
to a point on the utility frontier the feasible allocations which realize these
utilities. This is true also in convex economies but in this case, the correspondence is convex valued so that discontinuities of the type given in
Figure 4.10 do not occur.

In a non-convex economy, if the occurence of discontinuities is prevented
because there is a *unique* allocation corresponding to every point on the
utility frontier, then it can be shown that for every income map, there exists
a marginal cost pricing equilibrium which is efficient. In economic terms:
if the choice of a production plan is unique once the social objectives have
been fixed then the choice of an income map does not affect the efficiency
of the resulting allocation. However, if the production plan is not uniquely
determined by social objectives, then the choice of financing the public
sector and the distribution of income that results can lead to equilibria
which are all inefficient. The formal result proved by Guesnerie (1980) can
be stated precisely as follows:

THEOREM 4.1. *Let* $\mathcal{E}\big((u_i, w_i)_{i=1,\ldots,n}, (Y_j)_{j=1,\ldots,m}\big)$ *be an economy satisfying the following conditions:*

C. *The utility functions* $u_i : \mathbb{R}_+^H \longrightarrow \mathbb{R}$ *are continuous, quasi-concave and
   strongly monotonic* $(x_i > x_i' \Longrightarrow u_i(x_i) > u_i(x_i'), \ \forall x_i \in \mathbb{R}_+^H, \ \forall x_i' \in
   \mathbb{R}_+^H)$.

P. *The production sets* Y_j *are such that:*

   (i) Y_j *is closed,* $\forall j = 1, \ldots, m$

   (ii) $0 \in Y_j, \ \forall j = 1, \ldots, m$

   (iii) $y_j - \mathbb{R}_+^H \in Y_j, \ \forall y_j \in Y_j, \ \forall j = 1, \ldots, m$

R. Let $w = \sum_{i=1}^{n} w_i$, $Y = \sum_{j=1}^{m} Y_j$. $w + Y \cap \mathbb{R}_+^H$ is compact with a non-empty interior.

Let A denote the set of Pareto optimal allocations of $\mathcal{E}$ and let ρ be the utility map

$$\rho : A \longrightarrow \mathbb{R}^n$$

$$((x_i)(y_j)) \longrightarrow (u_i(x_i))_{i=1,\ldots,n}$$

If ρ is a one-to-one mapping of A onto $\rho(A)$, then for every income map $r = (r_1, \ldots, r_n)$, there exists a marginal cost pricing equilibrium which is Pareto optimal.

Proof:

Step 1. $\rho(A)$ is homeomorphic to Δ_{n-1}, the simplex of $\mathbb{R}^n$.

To prove this property, let us assume without loss of generality that the utilities are normalized so that $u_i(0) = 0$, $\forall i = 1, \ldots, n$. Let V denote the set of feasible imputations (utility levels associated to feasible allocations) in $\mathbb{R}_+^n$. By R and C, V is compact. Consider the map

$$h: \quad \begin{matrix} \Delta_{n-1} & \longrightarrow & V \\ \alpha & \longrightarrow & \lambda(\alpha)\alpha \end{matrix}$$

where $\lambda(\alpha) = \max\{\lambda \mid \lambda\alpha \in V\}$. Let us prove that $h(\Delta_{n-1}) = \rho(A)$. Suppose not. Then would exist α and a point $\lambda(\alpha)\alpha$ on the frontier of V which is not a Pareto imputation. Thus, there exist $v' \in V$ such that

$$v'_i \geq \lambda(\alpha)\alpha_i, \quad \forall i = 1, \ldots, n$$

with strict inequality for some agent i_0. Let $((x'_i), (y'_j)) \in \mathbb{R}^{Hn} \times \Pi_j Y_j$ be a feasible allocation such that $u_i(x'_i) = v'_i$, $i = 1, \ldots, n$. Since $v'_{i_0} > 0$, $x'_{i_0} \neq 0$. Since the utility functions are strongly monotonic, it is possible to redistribute some of the goods of agent i_0 to obtain a feasible allocation $((x''_i), (y''_j))$ such that $u_i(x''_i) > \lambda(\alpha)\alpha_i$, $\forall i = 1, \ldots, n$. But this implies that there exists $\lambda > \lambda(\alpha)$ such that $\lambda\alpha \in V$ which contradicts the definition of $\lambda(\alpha)$. To prove that h is one to one it is enough to prove that $\lambda(\alpha) \neq 0$, $\forall \alpha \in \Delta_{n-1}$. But this follows from assumption R which ensures that there exists $v \in V, v \gg 0$. Since Δ_{n-1} and $\rho(A)$ are compact, to prove that h is an homeomorphism between these sets it is enough to prove that either h or h^{-1} is continuous. It is obvious, however, that $h^{-1} : \rho(A) \longrightarrow \Delta_{n-1}$ is defined by

$$u \longrightarrow \frac{u}{\sum_{i=1}^{n} u_i}$$

which is continuous since, from the preceding remark, $\sum_{i=1}^{n} u_i$ is strictly positive for a Pareto optimal imputation.

Step 2. For all distribution of revenues, there exists a marginal cost pricing equilibrium which is Pareto optimal (i.e., the utility levels achieved in equilibrium are in $\rho(A)$).

For every $v \in \rho(A)$, let $\rho^{-1}(v)$ be the (unique) feasible allocation which gives the utility levels (v_i) to the agents and $S(v)$ be the set of prices which support this allocation, normalized to be in the simplex Δ_{H-1} of $\mathbb{R}^H$. Using the notation of Theorem 2.6,

$$S(v) = \bigcap_i -N_{\mathcal{P}_i}(x_i) \bigcap_j N_{Y_j}(y_j) \bigcap \Delta_{H-1}$$

where $\big((x_i), (y_j)\big) = \rho^{-1}(v)$. By Theorem 2.6, $S(v)$ is non-empty. The correspondence $v \longrightarrow S(v)$ is convex valued (since a Clarke normal cone is convex by definition) and has a closed graph (by Theorem 2.5).

Consider the correspondence $T : A \times \Delta_{H-1} \longrightarrow \Delta_{n-1}$ defined as follows: to a Pareto optimal allocation $\big((x_i), (y_j)\big)$ and a price $p \in \Delta_{H-1}$ we associate:

- the revenues $\big(r_i(p, (y_j))\big)_{i=1,\dots,n}$ generated by the production plans $(y_j)_{j=1,\dots,m}$ at price p,
- the consumption expenditures $(p \cdot x_i)_{i=1,\dots,n}$ of the agents.

We then define

$$T\big((x_i)(y_j), p\big) = \{\beta \in \Delta_{n-1} \mid \beta_i = 0 \text{ if } p \cdot x_i > r_i(p, (y_j))\}$$

If the value of the consumption of agent i at the allocation $\big((x_i), (y_j)\big)$ exceeds the revenue $r_i(p, (y_j))$, the agent is penalized and given the minimum utility.

T is non-empty and convex valued. To show that it has a closed graph, consider a sequence $\big((x_i^\nu), (y_j^\nu), p^\nu\big)$ of $A \times \Delta_{H-1}$ converging toward $\big((x_i), (y_j), p\big)$ and a sequence (β^ν) of Δ_{n-1} converging to β where $\beta^\nu \in T\big((x_i^\nu), (y_j^\nu), p^\nu\big)$. We must show that $\beta \in T\big((x_i), (y_j), p)\big)$. Suppose $p \cdot x_i > r_i(p, (y_j))$ for some i. Since the scalar product and the functions (r_i) are continuous, for ν sufficiently large $p^\nu \cdot x_i^\nu > r_i(p^\nu, (y_j^\nu))$, hence $\beta_i^\nu = 0$ and at the limit $\beta_i = 0$.

The correspondence

$$\Delta_{n-1} \times \Delta_{H-1} \longrightarrow \Delta_{n-1} \times \Delta_{H-1}$$

$$(\alpha, p) \longrightarrow \big(T(\rho^{-1}(h(\alpha)), p), R(h(\alpha))\big)$$

is therefore, a convex valued correspondence with a closed graph. The Kakutani fixed point theorem implies that there exists (α^*, p^*) such that $\alpha^* \in T(\rho^{-1}(v^*), p^*)$ and $p^* \in R(v^*)$ where $v^* = h(\alpha^*)$.

Let $((x_i^*), (y_j^*)) = \rho^{-1}(v^*)$. Since this allocation is Pareto optimal, $\sum_{i=1}^n x_i^* > 0$ (by R) and $p^* \gg 0$ (the utilities are strongly monotonic). Thus, $p^* \cdot (\sum_{i=1}^n w_i + \sum_{j=1}^m y_j^*) > 0$ and by definition of a structure of revenues, $r_i(p^*, (y_j^*)) > 0$. To prove that $((x_i^*, y_j^*), p^*)$ is a marginal cost pricing equilibrium, it is enough to prove that $p^* \cdot x_i^* = r_i(p^*, (y_j^*))$, $\forall i = 1, \dots, n$.

If there exists an agent i for whom $p^* \cdot x_i^* > r_i(p^*, (y_j^*))$, then $\alpha_i^* = 0$ by definition of T. This implies $v_i^* = 0$ and, $p^* \cdot x_i^* = 0$. We just argued, however, that $r_i(p^*, (y_j^*)) > 0$ which contradicts $r_i(p^*, (y_j^*)) < 0$. Therefore, $r_i(p^*, (y_j^*)) \geq p^* \cdot x_i^*$, $\forall i = 1, \dots, n$. Since $\sum_i r_i(p^*, (y_j^*)) = p^* \cdot \sum_i w_i + p^* \cdot \sum_j y_j^*$ (by definition of a structure of revenues) and $\sum_i x_i^* = \sum_i w_i + \sum_j y_j^*$ (since the allocation is Pareto optimal), all the inequalities must be equalities.

$$\triangledown$$

Remark: The assumption of strong monotonicity of preferences is necessary to prove that the set of Pareto optimal imputations is homeomorphic to the simplex Δ_{n-1} of $\mathbb{R}_n$. With the assumption of weak monotonicity, we can only prove that the set of *weak Pareto optimal imputations* is homeomorphic to the simplex. (A feasible allocation is weakly Pareto optimal if there does not exist another feasible allocation which is strictly preferred by all agents.) Thus, if we weaken the assumption of Theorem 4.1 by assuming only that preferences are weakly monotonic, we can prove that for every distribution of revenues, there exists a marginal cost pricing equilibrium which is weakly Pareto optimal.

4.3. Elasticity Condition for Efficiency (One Output)

In Theorem 4.1 the assumption that the map ρ is one to one is not placed directly on the characteristics of the economy (preferences, production sets, endowments). It would be more satisfactory to know what restrictions must be placed on the characteristics to ensure that there is only one allocation associated with a Pareto optimal imputation v. We have seen in chapter 2 that an allocation $((x_i)(y_j))$ is Pareto optimal if the social indifference curve associated with the levels of utility $(v_i)_{i=1,\dots,n}$, where $v_i = u(x_i)$, is tangent to the set of (aggregate) feasible consumptions $w + Y$. Thus, there is a unique feasible allocation which gives the Pareto optimal imputation v if and only if the social indifference curve corresponding to v is tangent to $w + Y$ at only one point. The cases shown in Figure 4.11 must be eliminated.

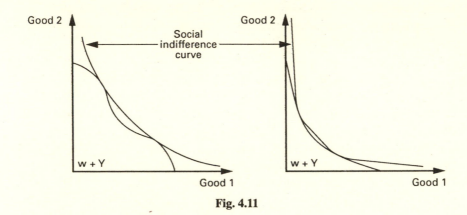

Fig. 4.11

It is clear that this requires restrictions on the curvature of the frontiers of the sets $w + Y$ and $\mathcal{P} = \sum_{i=1}^{n} \mathcal{P}_i$ where

$$\mathcal{P}_i = \{x_i \in \mathbf{R}_+^H \mid u_i(x_i) \geq v_i\}$$

It is difficult to find conditions which hold directly on the utility functions and production sets which can be interpreted and which prevent the cases shown in Figure 4.11. However, natural conditions can be placed on the derived demand and cost functions to prevent the occurence of such cases.

The intuition is as follows: the curvature of a social indifference curve is measured by the size of the substitution effects in the demand of goods when prices vary. The substitution effects in turn are measured by the derivatives of the compensated demand. The curvature of the frontier of a production set is measured by the variation of the vector normal to the frontier when the production plan varies. Under suitable assumptions this variation is directly linked to the change in marginal cost when the level of production varies.

These considerations give the general idea underlying the results which we shall now present. We give conditions on the elasticities of demand and of marginal cost which ensure that the uniqueness property of Theorem 4.1 is satisfied. The analysis that follows is based on the work of the author (Quinzii 1986–1988a, 1988b). Dierker (1986) obtained similar results under slightly stronger assumptions.

To make clear the basic intuition underlying these results, we first study the case of an economy with one non-convex firm producing a single output. The results are then generalized to the case of a non-convex firm producing several outputs and a private sector with many (convex) competitive firms.

Let us first consider an economy with H goods in which the last good H is an output which is produced from the first $H - 1$ goods. Let $L = H - 1$ denote the number of factors of production and let the technology be described by a production function f. We use the following notation: $(-z, y)$ represents a production plan where z is the input vector used for producing the output y. Hence

$$Y = \{(-z, y) \in \mathbf{R}^L_- \times \mathbf{R} \mid y \le f(z)\}$$

ASSUMPTION P'. *The production function* $f : \mathbf{R}^L_+ \longrightarrow \mathbf{R}$ *is continuous, monotonic,* $f(0) = 0$, *and the the sets* $S_y = \{z \in \mathbf{R}_+ \mid f(z) \ge y\}$ *are strictly convex for* $y > 0$. f *is* C^∞ *on* $\cup_{y>0} S_Y(y)$ *with a non-zero gaussian curvature.*

Remark: The assumption of non-zero gaussian curvature is frequently used in the literature on smooth economies and will be used several times in this book. The gaussian curvature of a function can be shown to be the determinant of the bordered hessian

$$\begin{bmatrix} 0 & Df(x)^T \\ Df(x) & D^2 f(x) \end{bmatrix}$$

(see Mas-Colell 1985, pp. 39, 76). The assumption of non-zero gaussian curvature is needed to ensure that the implicit function theorem can be applied to the solution of first-order conditions of the type

$$\begin{cases} Df(x) = \lambda p \\ f(x) = y \end{cases}$$

so that the solution is differentiable.

A price vector for the economy is denoted by (p, θ) where $p \in \mathbf{R}^{H-1}_+$ is the vector of input prices and $\theta \in \mathbf{R}_+$ is the price of the output. We choose the following normalization: p belongs to the simplex Δ_{L-1} of $\mathbf{R}^L$, that is, $\sum_{h=1}^L p_h = 1$. Thus, p indicates the relative prices of factors and θ the level of the price of the output relative to the input prices.

For a given p, the cost of producing y is

$$c(p, y) \stackrel{\text{def}}{=} \inf\{p \cdot z \mid (-z, y) \in Y\}$$

If $p \gg 0$, the lower bound is reached and for $y > 0$, $S_Y(y)$ is strictly convex, so that the cost-minimizing factor combination $z(p, y)$ is unique. The strict convexity of the sets $S_Y(y)$ also implies that the input requirement sets are in the interior of $\mathbf{R}^L_+$ and, hence, $z(p, y) \gg 0$ for $y > 0$:

$$c(p, y) = p \cdot z(p, y)$$

Since f is C^∞ with non-zero gaussian curvature on $\cup_{y>0} S_Y(y)$, $z(p,y)$, the cost function $c(p,y)$, is infinitely differentiable with respect to y for $y > 0$. Assumption P$'$ allows for the presence of a fixed cost which may induce a discontinuity of $c(p,y)$ at $y = 0$. The elasticity of the marginal cost with respect to y, denoted by $e(p,y)$, is defined by

$$e(p,y) = \frac{c''(p,y)}{c'(p,y)} y$$

It is well defined for $y > 0$.

On the consumer side of the economy, we make similar smoothness assumptions in order to obtain differentiable demand functions. The preferences of the agents $i = 1, \ldots, n$ satisfy the following conditions.

ASSUMPTION C$'$. *For each $i = 1, \ldots n$ the utility function $u_i : \mathrm{R}_+^H \longrightarrow \mathrm{R}$ is continuous, monotonic, quasi-concave, $u_i(x,y) = 0, \forall (x,y) \in \partial R_+^H$ (the boundary of R_+^H). On the interior of R_+^H, u^i is C^∞ and strictly quasi-concave with non-zero gaussian curvature.*

We consider the compensated (or Hicksian) demand of each agent i. Let $(\tilde{x}_i(p,\theta,v_i), \tilde{y}_i(p,\theta,v_i))$ denote the consumption of the first L goods (which can also be used as factors of production) and of the output which ensures a utility level v_i at minimum cost for agent i.

From the definition of the compensated demand $(\tilde{x}_i(p,\theta,v_i), \tilde{y}_i(p,\theta,v_i))$ is the unique (by assumption C$'$) consumption bundle that minimizes agent i's expenditure at price (p,θ) while assuring at least a level of utility v_i.

Under the assumptions on u_i, for every $v_i > 0$, the functions $(p,\theta), \longrightarrow \tilde{x}_i$ (p,θ,v_i) and $(p,\theta) \longrightarrow \tilde{y}_i(p,\theta,v_i)$ are differentiable over the domain

$$\{(p,\theta) \in \Delta_{L-1} \times \mathbb{R} \mid p \gg 0, \quad \theta > 0\}$$

The total demand associated with the price vector (p,θ) and utility vector $(v_1, \ldots, v_n)$ is denoted by $\tilde{y}(p,\theta,v)$:

$$\tilde{y}(p,\theta,v) = \sum_{i=1}^{n} \tilde{y}_i(p,\theta,v_i)$$

$\epsilon(p,\theta,v)$ denotes the elasticity of the total compensated demand of output with respect to θ:

$$\epsilon(p,\theta,v) = \frac{\frac{\partial \tilde{y}}{\partial \theta}(p,\theta,v)}{\tilde{y}(p,\theta,v)} \theta$$

The last assumption concerns the initial resources of the agents. It is assumed that there is no initial endowment of the produced good. w denotes the sum of the initial resources:

$$w = \sum_{i=1}^{n} w_i$$

To keep notation simple we let w denote either a vector in $\mathbf{R}_+^L \times \{0\}$ or a vector in $\mathbf{R}_+^L$; the context in each case makes it clear which is appropriate. The assumptions on w may be stated as follows:

ASSUMPTION R′.

$$w \in \mathbf{R}_+^L \times \{0\}$$

$(w + Y) \cap \mathbf{R}_+^{L+1}$ *is compact with a non-empty interior.*

If we denote V the set of feasible imputations of utilities in the economy, the last assumption implies that these exist $v \gg 0$, $v \in V$.

THEOREM 4.2. *Let $\mathcal{E}\big((u_i, w_i)_{i=1,\dots,n}, Y\big)$ be an economy satisfying assumptions C', P' and R'. If in addition one of the two conditions:*

(i) $c''(p, y) \big|_{y=\tilde{y}(p,\theta,v)} \times \dfrac{\partial \tilde{y}}{\partial \theta}(p, \theta, v) < 1 \quad \forall p \gg 0, \quad \forall \theta > 0, \quad \forall v \in \rho(A)$

(ii) $e(p, y) \big|_{y=\tilde{y}(p,\theta,v)} \times \epsilon(p, \theta, v) < 1 \quad \forall p \gg 0, \quad \forall \theta > 0, \quad \forall v \in \rho(A)$

is satisfied, then the utility map $\rho : A \longrightarrow \mathbf{R}^n$ which associates with a Pareto optimal allocation the corresponding vector of utilities is a one-to-one map of A onto $\rho(A)$.

Proof: Let $\{(x_i^*, y_i^*)_{i=1,\dots,n}, (-z^*, y^*)\}$ be a Pareto optimal allocation. Let $v_i^* = u_i(x_i^*, y_i^*)$, $i = 1, \dots, n$. Since all goods are desired

$$\sum_i x_i^* + z^* = w \tag{1}$$

$$y^* = f(z^*) \tag{2}$$

By Theorem 2.6, there exists a vector of prices (p^*, θ^*) such that:

- (x_i^*, y_i^*) minimizes $p^* \cdot x_i + \theta^* y_i$ under the constraint $u_i(x_i, y_i) \geq v_i^*$. This is equivalent to:

$$x_i^* = \tilde{x}_i(p^*, \theta^*, v_i^*) \quad , \quad y_i^* = \tilde{y}_i(p^*, \theta^*, v_i^*) \tag{3}$$

- (p^*, θ^*) is normal to the boundary of Y at $(-z^*, y^*)$, i.e., $(p^*, \theta^*) \in N_Y(-z^*, y^*)$. By Theorem 2.3, this is equivalent to

$$p^* = \theta^* Df(z^*) \qquad (4)$$

Since the set $S_Y(y^*) = \{z \in \mathbb{R}_+^L \mid f(z) \geq y^*\}$ is strictly convex, the unique cost-minimizing combination of inputs for producing y^* at price p^* is given by the first order conditions

$$p^* = \theta Df(z), \quad f(z) = y^*$$

By (2) and (4), z^* is the unique solution and

$$c(p^*, y^*) = p^* \cdot z^* \qquad (5)$$
$$c'(p^*, y^*) = \theta^* \qquad (6)$$

Consider the cost function $\Gamma : \mathbb{R}_+ \longrightarrow \mathbb{R}$ defined by

$$\Gamma(y) = \inf \left\{ p^* \cdot \sum_{i=1}^n x_i + c(p^*, y) \; \middle| \; \begin{array}{l} u_i(x_i, y_i) \geq v_i^*, \; i = 1, \dots, n \\ \sum_{i=1}^n y_i = y \end{array} \right\}$$

$\Gamma(y)$ is the minimum cost of obtaining the utility levels $(v_i^*, i = 1, \dots, n)$ for the agents with a level of production y. If there is no allocation (x_i, y_i) which gives the utility levels $(v_i^*)_{i=1,\dots,n}$ with $\sum_i y_i = y$, then we set $\Gamma(y) = +\infty$.

The objective function is linear and the constraints define a strictly convex domain so that when $\Gamma(y) < +\infty$, the cost-minimizing allocation is the unique solution to the first order conditions. Let λ_i be the multiplier associated with the agent i constraint and let θ be the multiplier associated with the constraint $\sum_i y_i = y$. The first order conditions are

$$p_h^* = \lambda_i \frac{\partial u_i}{\partial x_{ih}}(x_i, y_i), \quad \forall h = 1, \dots, L, \quad \forall i = 1, \dots, n \qquad (7)$$

$$\theta = \lambda_i \frac{\partial u_i}{\partial y_i}(x_i, y_i), \quad \forall i = 1, \dots, n \qquad (8)$$

$$u_i(x_i, y_i) = v_i^*, \quad \forall i = 1, \dots, n \qquad (9)$$

$$\sum_{i=1}^n y_i = y \qquad (10)$$

This sytem of equations can be solved as follows: for a given θ, the solution to equations (7), (8), (9) is: $(\tilde{x}_i(p^*, \theta, v_i^*), \tilde{y}_i(p^*, \theta, v_i^*))_{i=1,\dots,n}$. θ is then determined by the equation

$$\tilde{y}(p^*, \theta, v^*) = y \qquad (11)$$

Since $\tilde{y}$ is a sum of compensated demand, there is no income effect and $\frac{\partial \tilde{y}}{\partial \theta} < 0$. Thus, for y in the range of the function $\tilde{y}(p^*, ., v^*)$, the equation (11) has a unique solution that we denote $\theta(y)$.

By the envelope theorem,

$$\Gamma'(y) = -\theta(y) + c'(p^*, y)$$

and, hence,

$$\Gamma''(y) = -\theta'(y) + c''(p^*, y)$$

Differentiating equation (11) which defines $\theta(y)$, we get

$$\frac{\partial \tilde{y}}{\partial \theta}(p^*, \theta(y), v^*)\theta'(y) = 1$$

which implies

$$\Gamma''(y) = \frac{c''(p^*, y)\frac{\partial \tilde{y}}{\partial \theta}(p^*, \theta(y), v^*) - 1}{\frac{\partial \tilde{y}}{\partial \theta}(p^*, \theta(y), v^*)}$$

If condition (i) holds, then $\Gamma''(y) > 0$, $\forall y > 0$. The function Γ is strictly convex and has a global minimum at the point where $\Gamma'(y) = 0$, that is, where

$$\theta(y) = c'(p^*, y).$$

If condition (ii) holds, then

$$\frac{c''(p^*, y)}{c'(p^*, y)}y\frac{\frac{\partial \tilde{y}}{\partial \theta}(p^*, \theta, v^*)}{\tilde{y}(p^*, \theta, v^*)}\theta < 1 \quad \text{for} \quad y = \tilde{y}(p^*, \theta, v^*), \forall \theta > 0$$

which is equivalent to

$$\frac{c''(p^*, y)}{c'(p^*, y)}\frac{\partial \tilde{y}}{\partial \theta}(p^*, \theta(y), v^*)\theta(y) < 1, \quad \forall y > 0$$

If $\theta(y) = c'(p^*, y)$, then this implies

$$c''(p^*, y)\frac{\partial \tilde{y}}{\partial \theta}(p^*, \theta(y), v^*) < 1$$

Thus, if condition (ii) holds, $\Gamma''(y) > 0$ at every point such that $\Gamma'(y) = 0$. Γ is strictly quasi-convex and has minimum value at the unique point where $\Gamma'(y) = 0$, that is, where $\theta(y) = c'(p^*, y)$.

By (6), $\theta(y^*) = c'(p^*, y^*) = \theta^*$ so that in both cases (i) and (ii), Γ reaches its minimum value at y^*. This minimum value is

$$\Gamma(y^*) = p^* \cdot \sum_i x_i^* + c(p^*, y^*) \quad \text{(since } x_i^* = \tilde{x}_i(p^*, \theta^*, v_i^*))$$

$$= p^* \cdot \sum_i x_i^* + p^* \cdot z^* \quad \text{(by (5))}$$

$$= p^* \cdot w \quad \text{(by (1))}$$

Suppose that there is another allocation $((\bar{x}_i, \bar{y}_i)_{i=1,\dots,n}, (-\bar{z}, \bar{y}))$ which is feasible, that is,

$$\sum_i \bar{y}_i = \bar{y} \tag{12}$$

$$\sum_i \bar{x}_i + \bar{z} \leq w \tag{13}$$

$$(-\bar{z}, \bar{y}) \in Y \tag{14}$$

and which gives each agent i the utility level v_i^*. Then, $\Gamma(\bar{y}) \geq \Gamma(y^*)$. Since $(\bar{x}_i, \bar{y}_i)_{i=1,\dots,n}$ satisfies the constraints of $\Gamma(\bar{y})$,

$$\Gamma(\bar{y}) \leq p^* \cdot \sum_i \bar{x}_i + c(p^*, \bar{y})$$

$$\leq p^* \cdot (w - \bar{z}) + p^* \cdot \bar{z} \quad \text{(by (13) and (14))}$$

$$\leq p^* \cdot w$$

Therefore, $\Gamma(\bar{y}) = \Gamma(y^*) = p^* \cdot w$ and, since the minimum of Γ is unique, $\bar{y} = y^*$. Thus, for $0 \leq t \leq 1$, the allocation $(t\bar{x}_i + (1-t)x_i^*, \bar{y}_i + (1-t)y_i^*)$ is feasible with use of inputs $t\bar{z} + (1-t)z^*$. The strict quasi-concavity of utility functions imply that $(\bar{x}_i, \bar{y}_i) = (x_i^*, y_i^*)$, $\forall i = 1, \dots, n$.

$$\nabla$$

Combining Theorems 4.1 and 4.2, we can conclude that in an economy satisfying the assumptions of Theorem 4.2 there exists, for each income map, at least one marginal cost pricing equilibrium which is Pareto optimal.

Let us explain geometrically why conditions (i) and (ii) prevent a social indifference curve from being tangent at more than one point to the set of feasible allocations (as shown in Figure 4.11). Consider an economy with one input and one output ($L = 1$). Let $((x_i^*, y_i^*)_{i=1,\dots,n}, (z^*, y^*))$ be a Pareto optimum associated with the prices $(1, \theta^*)$ and let $v_i^* = u(x_i^*, y_i^*)$.

If condition (i) holds,

$$c''(1, \tilde{y}(1, \theta, v^*)) \frac{\partial \tilde{y}}{\partial \theta}(1, \theta, v^*) - 1 < 0, \quad \forall \theta > 0$$

which is equivalent to

$$\frac{\partial c'}{\partial \theta}(1, \tilde{y}(1, \theta, v^*)) - 1 < 0$$

which implies that the function

$$\theta \longrightarrow c'(1, \tilde{y}(1, \theta, v^*)) - \theta$$

is decreasing.

If condition (ii) holds,

$$\frac{c''(1, \tilde{y}(1, \theta, v^*))}{c'(1, \tilde{y}(1, \theta, v^*))} \frac{\partial \tilde{y}}{\partial \theta}(1, \theta, v^*)\theta < 1$$

which is equivalent to

$$c''(1, \tilde{y}(1, \theta, v^*))\frac{\partial \tilde{y}}{\partial \theta}(1, \theta, v^*)\theta - c'(1, \tilde{y}(1, \theta, v^*)) < 0$$

which implies that the function

$$\theta \longrightarrow \frac{c'(1, \tilde{y}(1, \theta, v^*))}{\theta}$$

is decreasing.

In both cases, since $\theta^* = c'(1, \tilde{y}(1, \theta^*, v^*))$,

$$\begin{cases} c'(1, \tilde{y}(1, \theta, v^*)) < \theta & \text{if } \theta > \theta^* \\ c'(1, \tilde{y}(1, \theta, v^*)) > \theta & \text{if } \theta < \theta^* \end{cases} \tag{15}$$

As shown in Figure 4.12, $(1, \theta)$ is the normal to the social indifference curve indexed by v^* at the point $(\tilde{x}(1, \theta, v^*), \tilde{y}(1, \theta, v^*))$ and $(1, c'(1, \tilde{y}(1, \theta, v^*)))$ is the normal to the frontier of the feasible set at the point with second coordinate $\tilde{y}(1, \theta, v^*)$. The inequalities (15) imply that the vector $(1, \theta)$ turns more quickly than the vector $(1, c'(1, \theta, v^*))$ which prevents the two curves from having a second tangency point.

From this geometric analysis it is clear that if condition (i) of (ii) holds for any social indifference curve which is tangent in one point to the feasible set $w + Y$, the social indifference curve cannot enter the interior of $w + Y$ and must therefore, correspond to a Pareto optimal imputation of utilities. Since a marginal cost pricing equilibrium is an allocation where a social indifference curve is tangent to $w + Y$ (the first order conditions are satisfied), we readily obtain a sufficient condition ensuring that a given marginal cost pricing equilibrium is Pareto optimal.

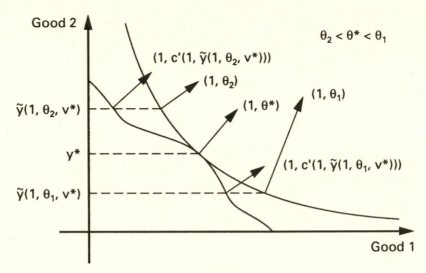

Fig. 4.12

THEOREM 4.3. Let $\mathcal{E}\big((u_i, w_i)_{i=1,\dots,n}, Y\big)$ be an economy satisfying assumptions C', P', R' and let $\big((x_i^*, y_i^*)_{i=1,\dots,n}, (-z^*, y^*), (p^*, \theta^*)\big)$ be a marginal cost pricing equilibrium for some income map r. Let $v_i^* = u_i(x_i^*, y_i^*)$, $i = 1, \dots, n$. If one of the two conditions:

(i) $c''(p^*, y) \big|_{y = \tilde{y}(p^*, \theta, v^*)} \times \dfrac{\partial \tilde{y}}{\partial \theta}(p^*, \theta, v^*) < 1, \ \forall \theta > 0$

(ii) $e(p^*, y) \big|_{y = \tilde{y}(p^*, \theta, v^*)} \times \epsilon(p^*, \theta, v^*) < 1, \ \forall \theta > 0$

is satisfied, then the marginal cost pricing equilibrium is Pareto optimal.

Proof: The proof is an easy adaptation of the proof of Theorem 4.2. Consider a marginal cost pricing equilibrium $((x_i^*, y_i^*)_{i=1,\dots,n}, (-z^*, y^*))(p^*, \theta^*)$ and let $v_i^* = u_i(x_i^*, y_i^*)$, $i = 1, \dots, n$. The relations (1) through (6) are satisfied by this equilibrium. The same arguments as in the proof of Theorem 4.3 show that

$$\min_y \Gamma(y) = \Gamma(y^*) = p^* \cdot w \qquad (16)$$

where

$$\Gamma(y) = \inf \left\{ p^* \cdot \sum_i x_i + c(p^*, y) \ \middle| \ \begin{matrix} u_i(x_i, y_i) \ge v_i^*, i = 1, \dots, n \\ \sum_i y_i = y \end{matrix} \right\}$$

If the equilibrium were not Pareto optimal, there would exist an allocation $((x_i', y_i')_{i=1,\dots,n}, (-z', y')) \in \mathbb{R}_+^{Hn} \times Y$ such that

$$\sum_i x_i' + z' < w \quad , \quad \sum_i y_i' = y'$$

$$u_i(x_i', y_i') \geq v_i^* \quad , \quad i = 1, \ldots, n$$

If it is possible with the resources w to give a higher utility than v_i^* to one agent without hurting the others, then it is possible, by decreasing slightly the consumption of this agent, to give the levels of utility $(v_i^*)_{i=1,\ldots,n}$ with less resources than w. However, $\Gamma(y') < p^* \cdot w$, which contradicts (16).

$\triangledown$

From an applied point of view, Theorem 4.3 is interesting in that it gives sufficient conditions for optimality of a marginal cost pricing equilibrium based on empirically observable functions in the economy. To check if the conditions (i) or (ii) are satisfied, it is sufficient to evaluate:

- the evolution of the (Hicksian) demand for the good produced when its price varies, the prices of the other goods being fixed at their equilibrium value;

- the evolution of the marginal cost of the good produced when the input prices are fixed.

This implies doing a partial analysis of the market of the good produced by the public sector. Condition (i) is familar to partial equilibrium analysis. Since $\tilde{y}(p^*, \theta, v^*)$ is the Hicksian demand, it decreases as the price θ increases. Condition (i) can therefore, be rewritten as

$$c''(p^*, y) > \frac{1}{\dfrac{\partial \tilde{y}}{\partial \theta}}$$

which is an inequality between the slope of the (compensated) demand curve and the slope of the marginal cost curve. It implies that the two curves cut each other at exactly one point and that the demand curve cuts the marginal cost curve from above (Figure 4.13).

Condition (ii) implies the same property of intersection between the demand curve and the marginal cost curve. It is more appealing since it is expressed in terms of elasticities which are easier to evaluate.

From a theoretical point of view, it is easy to derive from Theorem 4.3 a sufficient condition which ensures that *all* marginal cost pricing equilibria are Pareto optimal: it suffices that condition (i) or (ii) hold for all feasible imputations $v \in V$ and all relative prices of the inputs p. Since with assumptions C′, P′, R′ a marginal cost pricing equilibrium must give a positive utility to some agents, it is sufficient to restrict the conditions to the set

$$\tilde{V} = \{v \in V \mid v \neq 0\}$$

THEOREM 4.4. *Let* $\mathcal{E}\big((u_i, w_i)_{i=1,\ldots,n}, Y\big)$ *be an economy satisfying assumptions* C', P', R'. *If one of the two conditions:*

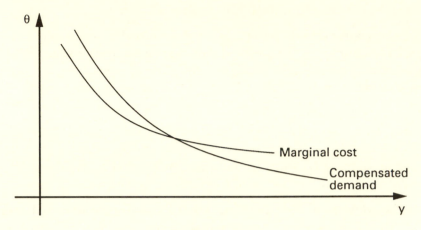

Fig. 4.13

(i) $c''(p,y)\,|_{y=\tilde{y}(p,\theta,v)} \times \dfrac{\partial \tilde{y}}{\partial \theta}(p,\theta,v) < 1,\ \forall p \gg 0,\ \forall \theta > 0,\ \forall v \in \tilde{V}$

(ii) $e(p,y)\,|_{y=\tilde{y}(p,\theta,v)} \times \epsilon(p,\theta,v) < 1,\ \forall p \gg 0,\ \forall \theta > 0,\ \forall v \in \tilde{V}$

is satisfied, then all the marginal cost pricing equilibria are Pareto optimal.

Remark: The hypotheses of Theorem 4.4 identify a class of economies with a non-convex production sector which have the key properties of convex economies: equilibria exist and the two welfare theorems are satisfied. First, for every income map there exists a marginal cost pricing equilibrium (Theorems 4.1 and 4.2). Second, every equilibrium is Pareto optimal (Theorem 4.4). Third, every Pareto optimal allocation can be obtained as an equilibrium allocation with suitable income map (Theorem 2.6).

4.4   Examples

Since conditions (i) and (ii) of Theorem 4.4 do not refer directly to the characteristics of the economy but to the derived demand and cost functions, it is important to verify that the class of economies satisfying the assumptions of this theorem is not empty. We are going to show that the Cobb-Douglas-C.E.S. economies, often used for purpose of computing equilibria, satisfy these assumptions. More precisely, if $\mathcal{E}\big((u_i, w_i)_{i=1,\dots,n}, Y\big)$ is an economy with $L+1$ goods is such that:

- the production function $f : \mathbb{R}_+^L \longrightarrow \mathbb{R}_+$ is strictly quasi-concave and homogeneous of degree α, $\alpha > 1$;

- the functions $u_i : \mathbb{R}_+^{L+1} \longrightarrow \mathbb{R}$ are Cobb-Douglas utility functions or C.E.S. utility functions with less substitution between goods than a Cobb-Douglas function;

• the initial resources satisfy assumption R′;

then the assumptions of Theorem 4.4 are satisfied.

Assumptions C′ and P′ are clearly satisfied. Let us show that the condition (ii) of Theorem 4.4 holds since

$$-1 < e(p, \theta, y) < 0 \quad , \quad -1 < \epsilon(p, \theta, v) < 0$$

for all $p \gg 0, \theta > 0, v > 0$. Both the elasticity of the marginal cost and the elasticity of the compensated demand are, in absolute value, less than 1, which implies that the product is less than one.

Elasticity of the marginal cost of a homogeneous production function

It is well known (e.g., Varian 1978, Ch. 1) that the cost function associated with an homogeneous production function of degree α is of the form

$$c(p, y) = g(p)y^{1/\alpha}$$

Thus, $c'(p, y)$ is of degree $\dfrac{1}{\alpha} - 1$ in y and

$$e(p, y) = \frac{1}{\alpha} - 1$$

If $\alpha > 1$ (increasing returns to scale), then

$$-1 < e(p, y) < 0.$$

Elasticity of the compensated demand if the utility functions are Cobb-Douglas

If $u_i(x, y) = x_1^{\alpha_1^i} \ldots x_l^{\alpha_l^i} y^{\beta^i}$ with $\alpha_1^i + \ldots + \alpha_l^i + \beta^i = 1$, the expenditure function is

$$E(p, \theta, v_i) = \left(\frac{p_1}{\alpha_1^i} \right)^{\alpha_1^i} \ldots \left(\frac{p_L}{\alpha_L^i} \right)^{\alpha_L^i} \left(\frac{\theta}{\beta^i} \right)^{\beta^i} v_i$$

so that the compensated demand of agent i is of the form

$$\tilde{y}^i(p, \theta, v_i) = A_i(p, v_i)\theta^{\beta^i - 1}$$

The elasticity of the aggregate compensated demand is

$$\epsilon(p, \theta, v) = -\frac{\sum_i(1 - \beta_i)A_i(p, v_i)\dfrac{1}{\theta^{1-\beta_i}}}{\sum_i A_i(p, v_i)\dfrac{1}{\theta^{1-\beta_i}}}$$

Since $0 < 1 - \beta_i < 1$, $i = 1, \ldots, n$

$$-1 < \epsilon(p, \theta, v) < 0$$

Since the Cobb-Douglas utility functions are a special case of C.E.S. utility functions, one might think that the same inequality will hold if the utility functions are C.E.S. with less substitution than the Cobb-Douglas function. This is true, but the proof requires some computation.

Elasticity of the compensated demand if the utility functions are C.E.S.

Let

$$u_i(x, y) = (\alpha_1^i x_1^{-\rho_i} + \ldots + \alpha_L^i x_L^{-\rho_i} + \beta^i y^{-\rho_i})^{-\frac{1}{\rho_i}}$$

The Cobb-Douglas function is obtained when $\rho_i \longrightarrow 0$. We shall say that the C.E.S. function exhibits less substitution than the Cobb-Douglas function if $\rho_i > 0$. (In the two-good case, this would imply an elasticity of substitution less than 1.)

The expenditure function is

$$E_i(p, \theta, v_i) = \left(\alpha_1^{i \frac{1}{\rho_i+1}} p_1^{\frac{\rho_i}{\rho_i+1}} + \ldots + \alpha_L^{i \frac{1}{\rho_i+1}} p_L^{\frac{\rho_i}{\rho_i+1}} + \beta^{i \frac{1}{\rho_i+1}} \theta^{\frac{\rho_i}{\rho_i+1}} \right)^{\frac{\rho_i+1}{\rho_i}} v_i$$

$$\overset{\text{def}}{=} \left[A_i(p, \theta) \right]^{\frac{\rho_i+1}{\rho_i}} v_i$$

The compensated demand of agent i is

$$\tilde{y}_i(p, \theta, v_i) = \beta^{i \frac{1}{\rho_i+1}} \theta^{-\frac{1}{\rho_i+1}} \left[A_i(p, \theta) \right]^{\frac{1}{\rho_i}} v_i$$

Thus,

$$\frac{\partial \tilde{y}_i}{\partial \theta} = -\frac{1}{\rho_i+1} \frac{\tilde{y}_i(\theta)}{\theta} + B_i(p, \theta, v_i)$$

where

$$B_i(p, \theta, v_i) = \frac{1}{\rho_i+1} \beta_i^{\frac{2}{\rho_i+1}} \theta^{\frac{-2}{\rho_i+1}} \left[A_i(p, \theta) \right]^{\frac{1}{\rho_i}-1} v_i > 0$$

$$\epsilon(p, \theta, v) = -\frac{\sum_i \frac{1}{\rho_i+1} \tilde{y}_i(\theta)}{\sum_i \tilde{y}_i(\theta)} + \frac{\sum_i B_i(p, \theta, v_i)\theta}{\sum_i \tilde{y}_i(\theta)}$$

If $\rho_i > 0$, $\frac{1}{\rho_i+1} < 1$ and the first term is larger than -1. Adding a positive term cannot change this inequality, therefore,

$$-1 < \epsilon(p, \theta, v) < 0$$

4.5   Elasticity Condition for Efficiency (Many Outputs)

We now generalize the analysis previously discussed to the case of a non-convex production sector producing several goods used for consumption by private agents or as inputs by the private (competitive) production sector. More precisely, let $\mathcal{E}\big((u_i, w_i)_{i=1,\ldots,n}, (Y_j)_{j=1,\ldots,m}, Y\big)$ with:

- H goods

- n consumers with utility functions $u_i : \mathbf{R}_+^H \to \mathbf{R}$ and endowments $w_i \in \mathbf{R}_+^H$, $i = 1, \ldots, n$

- m firms with convex production sets (Y_j), $j = 1, \ldots, m$

- one firm with a non-convex production set Y which produces the last $H - L$ goods using L inputs. Let $K = H - L$.

We write a vector of prices for this economy as $(p, \theta q)$, where p is the vector of relative prices of inputs normalized by $\sum_{\ell=1}^{L} p_\ell = 1$ and q is the vector of relative prices of goods produced by the non-convex firm normalized by $\sum_{k=1}^{K} q_k = 1$. $\theta \geq 0$ indicates the level of prices of the goods produced by the public sector, relative to the input prices. Let Δ_{L-1} denote the simplex of $\mathbf{R}^L$ and Δ_{K-1} the simplex of $\mathbf{R}^K$. $p \in \Delta_{L-1}, q \in \Delta_{K-1}$.

We generalize the method of section 4.3 using the prices p and q to aggregate inputs and outputs, respectively. We compare the change in the cost of inputs (evaluated at prices p) used by the non-convex firm for producing a given level of output (evaluated at the prices q) with the change in the demand for the output as θ varies.

To apply this method, we need assumptions which imply

- the existence of differentiable demand functions for consumers,

- the existence of a differentiable supply function for the competitive production sector.

We also introduce assumptions on the production set Y which are necessary to have a well-defined and differentiable factor demand for each level of production of the public sector.

Assumptions on the private sector

A commodity vector can be written as $(x, y) \in \mathbf{R}^L \times \mathbf{R}^K$.

ASSUMPTION C_1''. *For all $i = 1, \ldots, n$, u_i is continous and quasi-concave on $\mathbf{R}_+^H$, twice continuously differentiable with $Du_i \gg 0$ and a non-zero gaussian curvature on $\mathbf{R}_{++}^H$. If $x_{ih} = 0$ or $y_{ih} = 0$, for $h \in [1, \ldots, H]$, $u_i(x_i, y_i) = 0$.*

Let $(\tilde{x}_i(p, \theta q, v_i),\ \tilde{y}_i(p, \theta q, v_i))$ denote the compensated demand of agent i, that is, the solution to

$$\inf\{p \cdot x_i + \theta q \cdot y_i \mid u_i(x_i, y_i) \geq v_i\}$$

Under Assumption C_1'', this demand function is differentiable for $(p, \theta q) \gg 0$.

ASSUMPTION C_2''. $Y_j \subset \mathbb{R}^L \times \mathbb{R}^K_-$ and is convex, $\forall j = 1, \ldots, m$. The solution to firm j's profit maximizing problem at price $(p, \theta q) \gg 0$ is a twice differentiable supply function $(\tilde{x}_j(p, \theta q), \tilde{y}_j(p, \theta q))$ such that $\tilde{y}_j(p, \theta q) \leq 0$.

We thus assume that the convex production sector uses the goods produced by the non-convex sector as inputs and does not produce the same goods. If $(v_i)_{i=1,\ldots,n}$ denotes agents' utilities and $(p, \theta q)$ is the price vector, the (compensated) demand facing the non-convex firm is

$$\tilde{y}(p, \theta q, v) \stackrel{\text{def}}{=} \sum_{i=1}^{n} \tilde{y}_i(p, \theta q, v_i) - \sum_{j=1}^{m} \tilde{y}_j(p, \theta q)$$

We use the price q to aggregate the demand for the different goods and define the function $\tilde{\eta}$ which we use as the demand function of the private sector:

$$\tilde{\eta}(p, \theta q, v) \stackrel{\text{def}}{=} q \cdot y(p, \theta q, v)$$

The elasticity of demand with respect to the price level θ of public sector goods is denoted by $\epsilon(p, \theta q, v)$:

$$\epsilon(p, \theta q, v) = \frac{\frac{\partial \eta}{\partial \theta}(p, \theta q, v)}{\tilde{\eta}(p, \theta q, v)} \theta$$

Assumptions on the non-convex production sector

ASSUMPTION P_1''.

(i) $Y \subset \mathbb{R}^L_- \times \mathbb{R}^K_+$ is closed, contains $(0,0)$ and satisfies the assumption of free disposal. $\{(z, y) \in \partial Y,\ y \gg 0\}$ is a smooth submanifold of $\mathbb{R}^{H-1}$.

(ii) The set $S_Y(y) = \{z \in \mathbb{R}^H_- \mid (z, y) \in Y\}$ is non-empty, strictly convex. Its frontier has a non-zero gaussian curvature, for all $y \in \mathbb{R}^K_{++}$.

Let $g(p, y)$ denote the cost of production of every vector y of $\mathbb{R}^K_+$ when the prices of inputs is p:

$$g(p, y) \stackrel{\text{def}}{=} \inf\{-p \cdot z \mid z \in S_Y(y)\}$$

Assumption P_1'' implies that for all $p \gg 0$ this function is differentiable to every order. In addition, we assume:

ASSUMPTION P_2''. *For all $p \in \Delta_{L-1}$, the function $y \longrightarrow g(p, y)$ is increasing, strictly quasi-convex on $\mathbf{R}_-^K$.*

Remark: The assumptions P_1'' and P_2'' severely restrict the degree of non-convexity of the set Y. By P_1'', the set of factors which are required to produce at least a vector $y \in \mathbf{R}_+^K$ are convex. By P_2'', the set of vectors of outputs which cost less than a given amount is convex. This property depends on the form of the sections

$$S_Y'(z) = \{y \in \mathbf{R}^K \mid (z, y) \in Y\}$$

Let us show that P_1'' and P_2'' imply that these sections are convex. Let $y_1, y_2 \in S_Y'(z)$. Suppose there exists $\lambda \in (0, 1)$ such that

$$\lambda y_1 + (1 - \lambda)y_2 \notin S_Y'(z)$$

This is equivalent to:

$$z \notin S_Y(\lambda y_1 + (1 - \lambda)y_2)$$

By P_1'', this set is convex and z can be separated from $S_Y(\lambda y_1 + (1 - \lambda)y_2)$. There exists $p \neq 0$ such that:

$$p \cdot z > \sup\{p \cdot z' \mid z' \in S_Y(\lambda y_1 + (1 - \lambda)y_2)\}$$

Since all the components of z' could go to $-\infty$, p is non-negative and

$$g(p, \lambda y_1 + (1 - \lambda)y_2)) > -p \cdot z$$

However, $g(p, y_1) \leq -p \cdot z$ and $g(p, y_2) \leq -p \cdot z$. The quasi-convexity of g implies

$$g(p, \lambda y_1 + (1 - \lambda)y_2) \leq -p \cdot z$$

which contradicts the earlier inequality. Therefore, the production sets Y that we consider have all the "good" properties possible, except for convexity. The sections corresponding to a fixed vector of output or a fixed vector of factors are convex. Moreover, the quasi-convexity of the function g implies that the sections $\{y \in \mathbf{R}^K \mid (z, y) \in Y \mid -p \cdot z \leq c\}$ are convex for all $p > 0$ and all $c \geq 0$.

Finally, note that although the assumptions P_1'' and P_2'' are strong, they are satisfied in the two important cases:

- $K = 1$ (only one good is produced) and the production function is smooth, strictly quasi-concave (assumptions of Theorem 4.2).

- $L = 1$ (a single factor of production). The set Y can be represented by a cost function $Y = \{(z, y) \mid -z \geq c(y)\}$. The cost function then must be differentiable and strictly quasi-convex.

Assumption P_2'' implies that the indirect cost function

$$c(p, q, \eta) \overset{\text{def}}{=} \inf\{g(p, y) \mid q \cdot y \geq \eta\}$$

is, for all $p \gg 0$ and $q \gg 0$, strictly increasing and differentiable at any order. This function gives the minimum cost of inputs required for producing an aggregate output η, when the prices of inputs are $p \in \Delta_{L-1}$ and the relative prices of outputs are $q \in \Delta_{K-1}$. $\frac{\partial c}{\partial \eta}(p, q, \eta)$ represents the marginal cost of the composite good η where the different outputs are weighted by their respective prices. The elasticity of the marginal cost is denoted by $e(p, q, \eta)$:

$$e(p, q, \eta) = \frac{\frac{\partial^2 c}{\partial \eta^2}(p, q, \eta)}{\frac{\partial c}{\partial \eta}(p, q, \eta)}\eta$$

Finally, we shall make a series of assumptions regarding the initial resources which guarantee that there are no initial resources of the goods produced by the public sector, that there are sufficient input resources to guarantee each agent a positive utility and that the set of feasible allocations is compact.

ASSUMPTION R''.

- $w \in \mathbb{R}_+^L \times \{0\}$
- $(w + \sum_{j=1}^m Y_j + Y) \cap \mathbb{R}_+^H$ is compact
- $0 \in \text{Int}(w + \sum_{j=1}^m Y_j + Y)$

THEOREM 4.5. *Let $\mathcal{E}\big((u_i, w_i)_{i=1,\ldots,n}, (Y_j)_{j=1,\ldots,m}, Y\big)$ be an economy satisfying assumptions C_1'', C_2'', P_1'', P_2'', R''. If one of the two conditions:*

(i) $\frac{\partial \tilde{\eta}}{\partial \theta}(p, \theta q, v) \times \frac{\partial^2 c}{\partial \eta^2}(p, q, \eta) \mid_{\eta = \tilde{\eta}(p, \theta q, v)} < 1$

(ii) $\epsilon(p, \theta q, v) \times e(p, q, \eta) \mid_{\eta = \tilde{\eta}(p, \theta q, v)} < 1$

is satisfied for all $\theta > 0$, $p \gg 0$, $q \gg 0$, $v \in \rho(A)$, then the utility map $\rho : A \longrightarrow \mathbb{R}^n$ which associates with a Pareto optimal allocation the corresponding vector of utilities is a one-to-one map of A onto $\rho(A)$.

Proof: Let $((x_i^*, y_i^*)_{i=1,\ldots,n}, (x_j^*, y_j^*)_{j=1,\ldots,m}, (z^*, y^*))$ be a Pareto optimal allocation for the economy $\mathcal{E}$. Let $v_i^* = u_i(x_i^*, y_i^*)$, $\forall i = 1, \ldots, n$. We want to show that there exists no other feasible allocation which gives a utility level v_i^* to every agent i. Without loss of generality, we can assume that $v_i^* \neq 0, i = 1, \ldots, n$, since the only allocation compatible with Pareto optimality which gives $v_i^* = 0$ is $x_i^* = 0$, $y_i^* = 0$. Note that assumption C_1'' implies that $y^* \gg 0$.

By Theorem 2.4, there exists a vector of prices $(p^*, \theta^* q^*)$ which supports this allocation. This price is such that

$$(p^*, \theta^*, q^*) \gg 0$$
$$x_i^* = \tilde{x}_i(p^*, \theta^* q^*, v_i^*)$$
$$y_i^* = \tilde{y}_i(p^*, \theta^* q^*, v_i^*)$$
$$x_j^* = \tilde{x}_j(p^*, \theta^* q^*)$$
$$y_j^* = \tilde{y}_j(p^*, \theta^* q^*)$$
$$(p^*, \theta^* q^*) \in N_Y(z^*, y^*)$$

Let η^* denote the aggregate output $q^* \cdot y^*$.

Step 1. We first prove that $c(p^*, q^*, \eta^*) = -p^* \cdot z^*$, $\frac{\partial c}{\partial \eta}(p^*, q^*, \eta^*) = \theta^*$.

The strict convexity of the set $S_Y(y^*)$ implies that the solution to the problem $\inf\{-p \cdot z \mid z \in S_Y(y^*)\}$ is unique. Since the boundary of Y is differentiable, it can be locally represented by a function of the form $f(z, y) = 0$ around the point (z^*, y^*). Since $(p^*, \theta^* q^*) \in N_Y(z^*, y^*)$, there exists $\lambda > 0$ such that (Theorem 2.3)

$$p^* = \lambda D_z f(z^*, y^*)$$
$$\theta^* q^* = \lambda D_y f(z^*, y^*)$$

The first equality implies that z^* satisfies the first-order conditions for the convex problem $\inf\{-p^*.z \mid f(z, y^*) = 0\}$ and, hence,

$$g(p^*, y^*) = -p^* \cdot z^* \tag{17}$$

The assumption of non-zero gaussian curvature of $S_Y(y^*)$ implies that the equations

$$p^* = \lambda D_z f(z, y), \qquad f(z, y) = 0$$

have a solution $\tilde{z}(y)$ which is differentiable around y^*. Since $g(p^*, y) = -p^* \cdot \tilde{z}(y)$,

$$D_y g(p^*, y^*) = -p^* \cdot D_y \tilde{z}(y^*) = -\lambda D_z f(z^*, y^*) D_y \tilde{z}(y^*) = \lambda D_y f(z^*, y^*).$$

Hence,

$$D_y g(p^*, y^*) = \theta^* q^* \tag{18}$$

We can now show that assumption P_2'' implies that

$$c(p^*, q^*, \eta^*) = -p^* \cdot z^* \tag{19}$$

$$\frac{\partial c}{\partial \eta}(p^*, q^*, \eta^*) = \theta^* \tag{20}$$

By (18), the first-order conditions for the problem

$$c(p^*, q^*, \eta^*) = \inf\{ g(p^*, y) \mid q^* \cdot y \geq \eta^* \}$$

are satisfied by y^*. Since g is strictly quasi-convex, y^* is the only solution so that $c(p^*, q^*, y^*) = g(p^*, y^*) = -p^* \cdot z^*$. The assumption of non-zero gaussian curvature of g implies that c is differentiable with respect to η and since, by (18), θ^* is the multiplier associated to the constraint $q^* \cdot y \geq \eta^*$, (20) holds.

Step 2. *Properties of the function $\Gamma(\eta)$*
  Consider the cost function $\Gamma : \mathbb{R}_+ \longrightarrow \mathbb{R}$ defined by

$$\Gamma(\eta) =$$

$$\inf \left\{ p^* \cdot (\sum_{i=1}^{n} x_i - \sum_{j=1}^{m} x_j) + c(p^*, q^*, \eta) \; \middle| \; \begin{array}{l} u_i(x_i, y_i) \geq v_i^*, i = 1, \dots, n \\ (x_j, y_j) \in Y_j, \; j = 1, \dots, m \\ q^* \cdot (\sum_i y_i - \sum_j y_j) = \eta \end{array} \right\}$$

which is a generalization of the function Γ introduced in the proof of Theorem 4.2. The same method of solution for the first order conditions leads to the solution

$$\begin{array}{llll} x_i = \tilde{x}_i(p^*, \theta q^*, v_i^*), & y_i = \tilde{y}_i(p^*, \theta q^*, v_i^*), & i = 1, \dots, n \\ x_j = \tilde{x}_j(p^*, \theta q^*), & y_j = \tilde{y}_j(p^*, \theta q^*), & j = 1, \dots, m \end{array}$$

where θ is the multiplier associated to the constraint $q^* \cdot (\sum_i y_i - \sum_j y_j) = \eta$ and is determined by the equation

$$q^* \cdot \tilde{y}(p^*, \theta q^*, v^*) = \eta \Leftrightarrow \tilde{\eta}(p^*, \theta q^*, v^*) = \eta \tag{21}$$

We show that $\theta \longrightarrow \tilde{\eta}(p^*, \theta q^*, v^*)$ is decreasing. Let (p, Q) denote the vector of prices for the economy. The matrix of partial derivatives of the total compensated demand as a function of the prices (p, Q):

$$\tilde{M}(p, Q, v^*) = \frac{\partial(\tilde{x}(p, Q, v^*), \tilde{y}(p, Q, v^*))}{\partial(p, Q)}$$

is symmetric, negative semidefinite, and its kernel is generated by the vector (p, Q) (classical properties of the compensated demand of consumers and of the supply function of competitive firms). Then,

$$\frac{\partial \tilde{\eta}}{\partial \theta} = < q^*, \frac{\partial \tilde{\eta}}{\partial Q}(p^*, \theta q^*, v^*)q^* > = < (0, q^*), \tilde{M}(p^*, \theta q^*, v^*)(0, q^*) >$$

The first scalar product is the scalar product on $\mathbf{R}^K$ and the second is the scalar product on $\mathbf{R}^H$. Since $(0, q^*)$ does not belong to the kernel of $\tilde{M}(p^*, \theta q^*, v^*)$, $\frac{\partial \tilde{\eta}}{\partial \theta} < 0$.

On the other hand, it is easy to see that if $\theta \to 0$, the prices of the last K goods tend toward 0 and $\tilde{\eta}(p^*, \theta q^*, v^*) \to +\infty$. If $\theta \to +\infty$, $\tilde{\eta}(p^*, \theta q^*, v^*) \to 0$. Hence, the equation $\tilde{\eta}(p^*, \theta q^*, v^*) = \eta$ has a unique solution for every $\eta > 0$.

Since $\frac{\partial \tilde{\eta}}{\partial \theta} < 0$, the function $\theta(\eta)$ defined by the equation (21) is differentiable on $(0, +\infty)$ and

$$\theta'(\eta) = \frac{1}{\frac{\partial \tilde{\eta}}{\partial \theta}(p^*, \theta(\eta)q^*, v^*)}$$

It follows from the Envelope Theorem that

$$\Gamma'(\eta) = -\theta(\eta) + \frac{\partial c}{\partial \eta}(p^*, q^*, \eta)$$

$$\Gamma''(\eta) = -\frac{1}{\frac{\partial \tilde{\eta}}{\partial \theta}(p^*, \theta(\eta) \cdot q^*, v^*)} + \frac{\partial^2 c}{\partial \eta^2}(p^*, q^*, \eta)$$

Condition (i) implies $\Gamma''(\eta) > 0, \forall \eta \in (0 + \infty)$ and, hence, if there exists a point where $V'(\eta) = 0, V$ attains a minimum at this point. Condition (ii) implies that $\Gamma''(\eta) > 0$ at any point where $\Gamma'(\eta) = 0$, which implies that Γ is strictly quasi-convex and has a minimum at the point where $\Gamma'(\eta) = 0$.

Now, $\Gamma'(\eta^*) = 0$ since:

- the equation $q^* \cdot \tilde{y}(p^*, \theta q^*, v^*) = \eta^*$ is satisfied by θ^* (by definition of η^*)
- $\frac{\partial c}{\partial \eta}(p^*, q^*, \eta^*) = \theta^*$ (by 20).

Therefore,

$$\min \Gamma(\eta) = \Gamma(\eta^*) = p^* \cdot (\sum_i x_i^* - \sum_j x_j^*) + c(p^*, q^*, \eta^*)$$

$$= p^* \cdot (\sum_i x_i^* - \sum_j x_j^* - z^*)$$

$$= p^* \cdot w$$

Step 3. $((x_i^*, y_i^*)_{i=1,\ldots,n}, (x_j^*, y_j^*)_{j=1,\ldots,m}, (z^*, y^*))$ *is the only feasible alloca-tion which gives the utilities* $(v_i^*)_{i=1,\ldots,n}$.

Suppose that there exists another feasible allocation $((x_i, y_i)_{i=1,\ldots,n}, (x_j, y_j)_{j=1,\ldots,m}, (z, y))$ *such that* $u_i(x_i, y_i) = v_i^*$.

If $\eta = q^* \cdot y$, *this allocation satisfies the constraints of the program* $\Gamma(\eta)$.
Therefore,

$$\Gamma(\eta) \le p^* \cdot \left(\sum_i x_i - \sum_j x_j\right) + c(p^*, q^*, \eta)$$

$$\le p^* \cdot \left(\sum_i x_i - \sum_j x_j - z\right) = p^* \cdot w$$

Hence, $\Gamma(\eta) = \Gamma(\eta^*)$, $\eta = \eta^*$ *and by uniqueness of the solution of* $\Gamma(\eta^*)$,
it follows that

$$x_i^* = x_i, \ y_i^* = y_i, \ \forall i = 1, \ldots, n$$

$$x_j^* = x_j, \ y_j^* = y_j, \ \forall j = 1, \ldots, m$$

$\triangledown$

As in section 4.2, the proof can be easily modified to prove the following theorem:

THEOREM 4.6. *Let* $\mathcal{E}\left((u_i, w_i)_{i=1,\ldots,n}, (Y_j)_{j=1,\ldots,m}, Y\right)$ *be an economy which satisfies assumptions* C_1'', C_2'', P_1'', P_2'', R''. *Let*

$$((x_i^*, y_i^*)_{i=1,\ldots,n}, (x_j^*, y_j^*)_{j=1,\ldots,m}, (z^*, y^*), (p^*, \theta^* q^*))$$

be a marginal cost pricing equilibrium for an income map r. *Let* $v_i^* = u_i(x_i^*, y_i^*)$. *If one of the two conditions*

(i) $\dfrac{\partial^2 c}{\partial \eta^2}(p^*, q^*, \eta)\Big|_{\eta = \tilde{\eta}(p^*, \theta q^*, v^*)} \times \dfrac{\partial \tilde{\eta}}{\partial \theta}(p^*, \theta q^*, v^*) < 1, \ \forall \theta > 0$

(ii) $e(p^*, q^*, \eta)\Big|_{\eta = \tilde{\eta}(p^*, \theta q^*, v^*)} \times \epsilon(p^*, \theta q^*, v^*) < 1, \ \forall \theta > 0$

is satisfied, then the equilibrium is Pareto optimal.

Again as in Section 4.2, the following theorem can be obtained as a corollary of Theorems 4.5 and 4.6.

THEOREM 4.7. *Let* $\mathcal{E}\left((u_i, w_i)_{i=1,\ldots,n}, (Y_j)_{j=1,\ldots,m}, Y\right)$ *be an economy satis-fying assumptions* C_1'', C_2'', P_1'', P_2'', R'', *and one of the two conditions:*

(i) $\dfrac{\partial^2 c}{\partial \eta^2}(p, q, \eta)\Big|_{\eta = \tilde{\eta}(p, \theta q, v)} \times \dfrac{\partial \tilde{\eta}}{\partial \theta}(p, \theta q, v) < 1$

(ii) $e(p, q, \eta)\Big|_{\eta = \tilde{\eta}(p, \theta q, v)} \times e(p, \theta q, v) < 1$

for all $\theta > 0$, $p \gg 0$, $q \gg 0$, $v \in \tilde{V}$. *Then every marginal cost pricing equilibrium of* $\mathcal{E}$ *is Pareto optimal.*

Thus, under assumptions C_1'', C_2'', P_1'', P_2'', R'', the many outputs case can be treated as the one output case by using the relative prices q of the goods produced by the public sector to aggregate the production and the demand for these goods. More generally, these assumptions allow us to reduce the general equilibrium problem to the study of the market for the aggregate output of the non-convex sector (Theorem 4.6) or to a series of markets for this output under different aggregating weights and levels of utility for the consumers (Theorems 4.5 and 4.7).

The analysis which has been carried out in this section applies to the case where there are several non-convex firms, each one of which produces specific goods not produced by any other firm in the economy. In this case there is no difficulty in aggregating these firms in a non-convex sector Y; however, the analysis does not apply to the case where the same good is produced by several firms, one of which has a non-convex technology. In the next chapter we will see that this case introduces additional difficulties, in particular other sources of possible inefficiency in a marginal cost pricing equilibrium than the ones analyzed in this section which are related to the distribution of income in the economy.

5

EXISTENCE

5.1 Single Firm Existence Theorem

It may seem surprising that we have discussed the normative properties of a marginal cost pricing equilibrium before establishing conditions under which such an equilibrium exists. In analyzing the normative properties, however, we have already obtained an existence result: under the assumptions of Theorem 4.1 an equilibrium exists for every income map. We shall now show, however, that the assumptions of this theorem are unnecessarily restrictive for the purpose of proving existence.

The methods of proof which have been successful for proving existence of equilibrium for a convex economy do not directly apply to non-convex economies. In particular, Debreu's method of proof (1959) which (essentially) consists in applying the Kakutani fixed point theorem to the excess demand correspondence $p \longrightarrow Z(p) \longrightarrow p'$ (prices which maximize the value of excess demand) cannot be used. Without the assumption of convexity of production sets, the supply correspondence (productions where the vector normal to the boundary of the production set is colinear to the price p), is generally non-convex.

The method of proof used by Negishi (1960) and Arrow and Hahn (1972) which consists in applying a fixed point theorem to the boundary of the feasible utilities can be applied only if the assumptions of Theorem 4.1 hold. This proof requires that the allocations associated with a given vector of utility levels be convex, which is generally not the case (except if it is unique as assumed in Theorem 4.1).

A modification of this approach, which applies in the case where there is a single aggregate production set, has been introduced by P. Beato (1976, 1982) and R. Mantel (1979) and later improved by B. Cornet (1982, published 1990). It consists in applying a fixed point theorem to the boundary of the production set. Let us explain heuristically the idea behind this approach.

Suppose that there is only one firm in the economy. Consider the part of the boundary of the set $(w + Y)$ which is in $\mathbb{R}_+^H$. First, one has to show that this boundary is homeomorphic to the simplex of $\mathbb{R}^H$. Then,

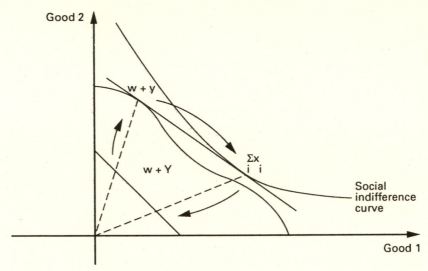

Fig. 5.1

- to every element of the simplex of $\mathbb{R}^H$, one can associate an efficient production y and the price p normal to Y at y (in the simplest case the price is unique),
- knowing y and p, consumers incomes $r_i(p, y)$ can be deduced,
- p and $r_i(p, y)$ determine the demand $x_i(p, r_i)$ of consumer i,
- one returns back to the simplex of $\mathbb{R}^H$ by considering the vector

$$\frac{\sum\limits_{i=1}^{n} x_i(p, r_i)}{\| \sum\limits_{i=1}^{n} x_i(p, r_i) \|}$$

This construction is illustrated in Figure 5.1 in the case of a two-good economy.

This construction leads to a continuous map from the simplex into itself. A fixed point is a marginal cost pricing equilibrium. The formal statement of the theorem is as follows.

THEOREM 5.1. *Let* $\mathcal{E}\left((u_i, w_i)_{i=1,\dots,n}, Y\right)$ *be an economy such that:*

A1. *Agent i's preferences are represented by a utility function u_i strictly quasi-concave, monotonic, and continuous on $\mathbb{R}_+^H, \forall i = 1, \dots, n$.*

A2. *The production set Y is such that:* $0 \in Y, Y$ *is closed,* $y - \mathbb{R}_+^H \subset Y, \forall y \in Y$ *(free disposal).*

A3. $0 \in \text{Int}(w + Y)$ and $w + Y \cap \mathbf{R}_+^H$ is compact, where $w = \sum_{i=1}^n w_i$.

A4. $\forall y \in \partial Y$, $y + w \geq 0 \Longrightarrow p \cdot (w + y) > 0$, $\forall p \in N_Y(y) \backslash \{0\}$
(where ∂Y denotes the boundary of the set Y).

Then for every income map r, $\mathcal{E}$ has a marginal cost pricing equilibrium.

Proof: To apply the method of proof explained above, we must first show that $w + \partial Y \cap \mathbf{R}_+^H$ is homeomorphic to the simplex of $\mathbf{R}^H$. More formally:

LEMMA 5.2. *The set* $\tilde{E} = \{w + y \mid y \in \partial Y, \ w + y \geq 0\}$ *is homeomorphic to the simplex* Δ_{H-1}.

Proof of Lemma 5.2: By assumption A3, $0 \notin \tilde{E}$. Therefore, we can consider the map $\varphi : \tilde{E} \longrightarrow \Delta_{H-1}$ defined by

$$\varphi(w + y) = \frac{w + y}{\displaystyle\sum_{h=1}^H (w_h + y_h)}$$

Step 1. *φ is one to one.*

$\varphi(w + y_1) = \varphi(w + y_2) \Longrightarrow \exists \lambda > 0$ such that $w + y_1 = \lambda(w + y_2)$. Let us show that $\lambda = 1$. If $w + y_1 \gg 0$, this is obviously true. If $w + y_1$ has a zero component, we use assumption A4 to exclude configurations of the type shown in Figure 5.2.

Suppose that $\lambda > 1$. By A4, $p \in N_Y(y_1) \Longrightarrow p \cdot (w + y_1) > 0$. Therefore, $-w - y_1$ belongs to the interior of the tangent cone $T_Y(y_1)$ (since $T_Y(y_1)$ is the dual cone of $N_Y(y_1)$). By Theorem 2.1, there exists $\epsilon > 0$ such that

$$z = y_1 + t(-w - y_1 + \epsilon e) \in Y, \ \forall t \in [0, \epsilon]$$

where e is the vector $(1, 1, \dots, 1) \in \mathbf{R}^H$. Then,

$$-y_2 + z = - \left(w \frac{1 - \lambda}{\lambda} + \frac{y_1}{\lambda} \right) + y_1 + t(-w - y_1 + \epsilon e)$$

$$= (-w - y_1)(\frac{1}{\lambda} + t - 1) + t\epsilon e$$

For t small enough, $1/\lambda + t - 1 < 0$. Then, $-y_2 + z \gg 0 \Longleftrightarrow z \gg y_2$. But, y_2 is strictly less than a vector $z \in Y$, which contradicts the assumption that $y_2 \in \partial Y$. Thus, $\lambda \leq 1$

Reversing the roles of y_1 and y_2 implies $\lambda \geq 1$, so that $\lambda = 1$.

Step 2. *φ is onto.*

Let $\alpha \in \Delta_{H-1}$. Let $\Lambda(\alpha) = \{\lambda \geq 0 \mid \lambda\alpha - w \in Y\}$. Since $-w \in \text{Int } Y$, for λ sufficiently small, $\lambda\alpha - w \in Y$. Therefore, $\Lambda(\alpha)$ is non-empty. It is compact

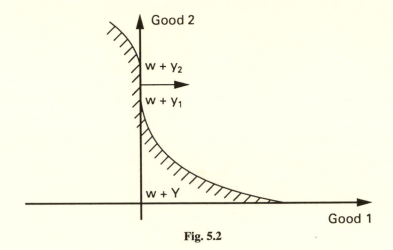

Fig. 5.2

since $w + Y \cap \mathbb{R}_{+}^{H}$ is compact. Thus, there exists $\bar{\lambda} = \max\{\lambda \mid \lambda \in \Lambda(\alpha)\}$. It is easy to check that $\alpha = \varphi(w + \bar{\lambda}\alpha)$.

Hence, φ is a continuous bijection of $\tilde{E}$ onto Δ_{H-1}. It is easy to verify that A3 implies that $\tilde{E}$ is compact. Thus, φ is a homeomorphism.

$$\nabla$$

Proof of Theorem 5.1: Let α, p be two elements of the simplex Δ_{H-1}. Let y be such that $w + y = \varphi^{-1}(\alpha)$ (y exists by the preceding lemma) and define

$$G(\alpha, p) = \{q \in \Delta_{H-1} \mid q \in N_Y(y)\}$$

By the properties of the Clarke cone (Theorems 1.3, 1.4, and 1.5), the correspondence G from $\Delta_{H-1} \times \Delta_{H-1} \longrightarrow \Delta_{H-1}$ has non-empty compact and convex values and has a closed graph.

Consider the demand $d_i(p, r_i)$ of consumer i. By A1, this function is continuous over the domain $\{(p, r_i) \in \Delta_{H-1} \times \mathbb{R} \mid p \gg 0, \ r_i > 0\}$ and if $p \longrightarrow \bar{p} \in \partial\Delta_{H-1}$ and $r_i \longrightarrow \bar{r}_i > 0$, then $\| d_i(p, r_i) \| \longrightarrow +\infty$ (classical properties of demand). These properties imply that the correspondence F from $\Delta_{H-1} \times \Delta_{H-1}$ to Δ_{H-1} defined by

- $\dfrac{\sum_i d_i(p, r_i(p, y))}{\sum_h \sum_i d_{ih}(p, r_i(p, y))}$ if $p \gg 0$ and $r_i(p, y) > 0$

- $\{q \in \Delta_{H-1} \mid q \cdot p = 0\}$ if $p \in \partial\Delta_{H-1}$ and $r_i(p, y) > 0$, $\forall i = 1, \dots, n$

- Δ_{H-1} if $\exists i$ such that $r_i(p, y) \leq 0$

has compact and convex values and a closed graph.

By Kakutani's theorem, the correspondence

$$(F, G): \ \Delta_{H-1} \times \Delta_{H-1} \longrightarrow \Delta_{H-1} \times \Delta_{H-1}$$

$$(\alpha, p) \longrightarrow (F(\alpha, p), G(\alpha, p))$$

has a fixed point $(\bar{\alpha}, \bar{p})$. Let $\bar{y} = \varphi^{-1}(\bar{\alpha}) - w$ be the corresponding production.

Let us show that $\big((d_i(\bar{p}, r_i(\bar{p}, \bar{y}))_{i=1,\ldots,n}, \bar{y}, \bar{p}\big)$ is a marginal cost pricing equilibrium. Since $\bar{p} \in G(\bar{\alpha}, \bar{p})$, $\bar{p} \in N_Y(\bar{y})$ and by A4, $\bar{p} \cdot (w + \bar{y}) > 0$. From the properties of r (definition in section 3.4), $r_i(\bar{p}, \bar{y}) > 0$, $\forall i = 1, \ldots, n$. If $\bar{p}$ were in $\partial \Delta_{H-1}$, we would have, since $\bar{\alpha} \in G(\bar{\alpha}, \bar{p})$, $\bar{p} \cdot \bar{\alpha} = 0$. Since there exists $\lambda > 0$ such that $w + \bar{y} = \lambda \bar{\alpha}$, this would imply $\bar{p} \cdot (w + \bar{y}) = 0$, which contradicts $\bar{p} \cdot (w + \bar{y}) > 0$.

Thus, $\bar{p} \gg 0$ and

$$\bar{\alpha} = \frac{\displaystyle\sum_i d_i(\bar{p}, r_i(\bar{p}, \bar{y}))}{\displaystyle\sum_h \sum_i d_{ih}(\bar{p}, r_i(\bar{p}, \bar{y}))}$$

Thus, there exists $\mu > 0$, such that

$$w + \bar{y} = \mu \left(\sum_i d_i(\bar{p}, r_i(\bar{p}, \bar{y})) \right)$$

By Walras's law, $\mu = 1$, and $\sum_i d_i(p, r_i(p, \bar{y})) = w + \bar{y}$, completing the proof.

$$\triangledown$$

A few remarks are in order concerning the hypotheses of Theorem 5.1. The assumptions on the consumer side have been deliberately strengthened to keep the structure of the proof simple. These assumptions can be weakened to convexity, continuity, and local non-satiation of preferences at the cost of some additional technical constructions.

The chief restriction on production is the existence of a single production set. Given this, the other assumptions on Y are not restrictive since they do not preclude the presence of fixed costs, or of "kinks" in the boundary of Y. The only restriction imposed by A4 is that the vector of marginal costs of production of all goods must be non-zero for a production plan that exhausts all of at least one factor of production available in the initial resources w. This does not seem to be a severe restriction.

The generality of the assumptions on the aggregate production set Y is made possible by the definition of normal cone that we have adopted. The properties of continuity and convexity of a Clarke normal cone lead to a

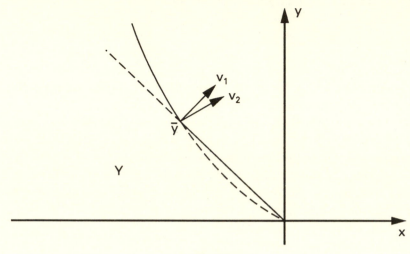

Fig. 5.3

straightforward application of the fixed point theorem. The cost, however, as mentioned earlier, is that the Clarke normal cone is large at kinks of the boundary of Y (see Figure 2.4). This property makes it impossible to use Theorem 5.1 for proving the existence of a marginal cost pricing equilibrium for desaggregated production sets.

To see why, suppose that the economy is such that there are two techniques for producing the same good, one with constant returns, one with increasing returns, so that Y is the sum of Y_1 and Y_2 where

$$Y_1 = \left\{(x,y) \in \mathbf{R}_- \times \mathbf{R} \mid y \leq -x\right\}$$
$$Y_2 = \left\{(x,y) \in \mathbf{R}_- \times \mathbf{R} \mid y \leq x^2\right\}$$

$Y = Y_1 + Y_2$ is shown in Figure 5.3. The boundary ∂Y has a kink at the point $\bar{y} = (-1,1)$. The vector $v_1 = (1,1)$ is normal to the line $y = -x$ at this point and the vector $v_2 = (2,1)$ is normal to the curve $y = x^2$ at this point.

The cone $N_Y(\bar{y})$ is the convex cone generated by v_1 and v_2. $\bar{y}$ can be obtained as the sum of a vector $y_1 \in Y_1$ and a vector $y_2 \in Y_2$ in two different ways:

$$\bar{y} = \bar{y} + 0, \ \bar{y} \in Y_1, \ 0 \in Y_2$$

$$= 0 + \bar{y}, \ 0 \in Y_1, \ \bar{y} \in Y_2$$

and

$$N_{Y_1}(\bar{y}) \cap N_{Y_2}(0) = v_1$$
$$N_{Y_1}(0) \cap N_{Y_2}(\bar{y}) = v_2$$

The only vectors of $N_Y(\bar{y})$ which can be equilibrium prices for a decentralized economy with production sets Y_1 and Y_2 are the vectors v_1 and v_2.

Thus if the two technologies Y_1 and Y_2 are operated by different firms and if the equilibrium given by Theorem 5.1 results in the production $\bar{y}$ and a price $\bar{p}$ in the interior of the cone $N_Y(\bar{y})$, then this equilibrium is not a marginal cost pricing equilibrium of the decentralized economy involving two firms with technologies Y_1 and Y_2, respectively.

It follows that Theorem 5.1 does not prove the existence of a marginal cost pricing equilibrium in the case where there are several firms in the production sector. The following example due to P. Beato and P. Mas-Colell (1983) shows that the existence of a marginal cost pricing equilibrium for a decentralized economy cannot be deduced from a fixed point theorem applied to the boundary of the aggregate production set Y. The reason is that the total production may be inefficient (i.e., in the interior of the aggregate production set) for *all* the marginal cost pricing equilibria of some economies.

5.2 Example of Productive Inefficiency

The economy consists of two goods, a factor of production (denoted by x) and an output y which is produced using this factor.

The consumption sector consists of two agents who consume positive quantities of these two goods. Agent 1's preferences are represented by the utility function $u^1(x^1, y^1) = y^1$. (This agent is not interested in the factor of production.) Agent 1's initial endowment consists of 50 units of good $y : w^1 = (0, 50)$. Agent 2's preferences are represented by the utility function $u^2(x^2, y^2) = \min(6x^2, y^2)$. Agent 2's initial endowment consists of 20 units of the factor of production: $w^2 = (20, 0)$.

The production sector is similar to the one described in the previous section. There are two firms with production possibilities given by:

$$Y_1 = \{(x_1, y_1) \in \mathbb{R}_- \times \mathbb{R} \mid y_1 \leq -x_1\}$$
$$Y_2 = \{(x_2, y_2) \in \mathbb{R}_- \times \mathbb{R} \mid y_2 \leq \frac{1}{16}(x_2)^2\}$$

The profits and losses of the two firms go to consumer 1, while consumer 2 only gets revenue from selling the factor of production. The characteristics of this economy are shown in Figure 5.4.

A marginal cost pricing equilibrium for this economy consists of: a price vector $\bar{p} = (\bar{p}_x, 1)$, consumption bundles $(\bar{x}^1, \bar{y}^1), (\bar{x}^2, \bar{y}^2)$, productions $(\bar{x}_1, \bar{y}_1), (\bar{x}_2, \bar{y}_2)$ such that:

- $(\bar{x}_1, \bar{y}_1)$ maximizes $y_1 + \bar{p}_x x_1$ under the constraints $y_1 \leq -x_1, x_1 \geq 0$

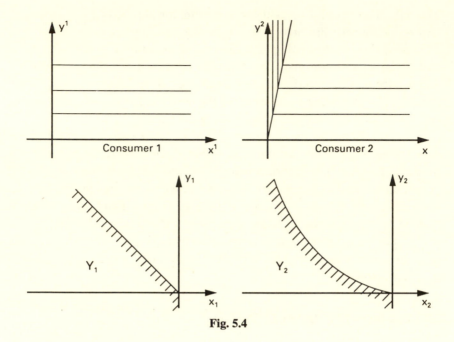

Fig. 5.4

- $(\bar{x}_2, \bar{y}_2)$ satisfies $\bar{y}_2 = 1/16(x_2)^2$ with either $\bar{x}_2 = 0$ or $\bar{x}_2 = -8\bar{p}_x$ (to ensure that $\bar{p} \in N_{Y_2}(\bar{x}_2, \bar{y}_2)$)
- the revenue of agent 1, $50 + (\bar{y}_2 + p_x\bar{x}_2)$ is strictly positive and the consumption $(\bar{x}^1, \bar{y}^1)$ is such that $\bar{x}^1 = 0$, $\bar{y}^1 = 50 + (\bar{y}_2 + p_x\bar{x}_2)$
- $(\bar{x}^2, \bar{y}^2)$ maximizes $\min(6\bar{x}^2, \bar{y}^2)$ under the constraint $\bar{p}_x x^2 + y^2 = 20\bar{p}_x$
- $\bar{x}^1 + \bar{x}^2 = 20 + \bar{x}_1 + \bar{x}_2$
- $\bar{y}^1 + \bar{y}^2 = 50 + \bar{y}_1 + \bar{y}_2$

It is sufficient that $\bar{p}_x$ clears the input market to be an equilibrium price for the economy. Walras's law then guarantees equilibrium in the output market. Consider the input market:

- consumer 1's supply of the factor is 0,
- given the utility function consumer 2's supply is:

$$20 - \frac{20p_x}{p_x + 6} = \frac{120}{p_x + 6}$$

- firm 1's demand is equal to 0 if $p_x > 1$, indeterminate if $p_x = 1$, infinite if $p_x < 1$,
- firm 2's demand is equal to $8p_x$ or 0.

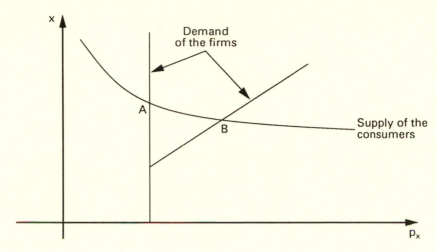

Fig. 5.5

The total supply and demand correspondences are shown in Figure 5.5. There are two points of intersection A and B. The point A corresponds to $\bar{p}_x = 1$ and $x = 120/7$. This quantity can be

- either used entirely by firm 1 to produce $\bar{y}_1 = 120/7$ units of output (equilibrium 1),

- or divided between firm 2 which uses 8 units and produces $\bar{y}_2 = 4$, and firm 1 which uses the remaining 64/7 units to produce $\bar{y}_1 = 64/7$ (equilibrium 2).

The point B corresponds to $p_x = 2\sqrt{6} - 3$ and $x = 8(2\sqrt{6} - 3)$. The input is entirely used by firm 2 to produce $\bar{y}_2 = (33 - 12\sqrt{6}/4)$. The characteristics of the three equilibria are:

Equilibrium 1:

$$\bar{p}_x = 1, \quad \bar{x}_1 = \frac{-120}{7}, \quad \bar{y}_1 = \frac{120}{7}, \quad \bar{x}_2 = 0, \quad \bar{y}_2 = 0$$

$$\bar{x}^1 = 0, \quad \bar{y}^1 = 50, \quad \bar{x}^2 = \frac{20}{7}, \quad \bar{y}^2 = \frac{120}{7}$$

Equilibrium 2:

$$\bar{p}_x = 1, \quad \bar{x}_1 = \frac{-64}{7}, \quad \bar{y}_1 = \frac{64}{7}, \quad \bar{x}_2 = -8, \quad \bar{y}_2 = 4$$

$$\bar{x}^1 = 0, \quad \bar{y}^1 = 46, \quad \bar{x}^2 = \frac{20}{7}, \quad \bar{y}^2 = \frac{120}{7}$$

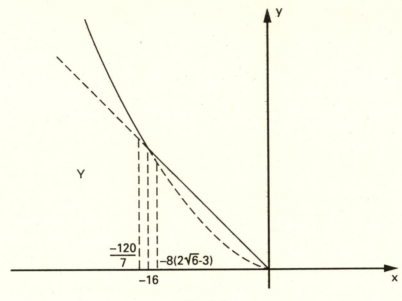

Fig. 5.6

Equilibrium 3:

$$p_x = 2\sqrt{6} - 3, \quad \bar{x}_1 = 0, \quad \bar{y}_1 = 0 \quad \bar{x}_2 = -8(2\sqrt{6} - 3), \quad \bar{y}_2 = \frac{33 - 12\sqrt{6}}{4}$$

The exact consumption of agents 1 and 2 in equilibrium 3 are not calculated since they are unimportant.

The interest of this example is to show that none of the equilibria corresponds to an efficient distribution of the factor of production between the two firms. Consider the global production set $Y = Y_1 + Y_2$ represented in Figure 5.6. To use efficiently the $\frac{120}{7}$ units of input, only firm 2 should produce, which is not the case in either equilibrium 1 or 2. An efficient utilization of $8(2\sqrt{6} - 3)$ units of input, would require that the output is produced entirely by firm 1, which is not the case in equilibrium 3.

The example shows the importance of the organization of the production sector in a non-convex economy. If the two firms were combined into a single firm, the production set of this single firm would be Y. The demand for input by this single firm selling at marginal cost would be:

- $-8p_x$ or 0 if $p_x > 2$
- 16 or 0 if $1 < p_x \leq 2$
- any value in the interval $[0, 16]$ if $p_x = 1$
- indeterminate if $p_x < 1$.

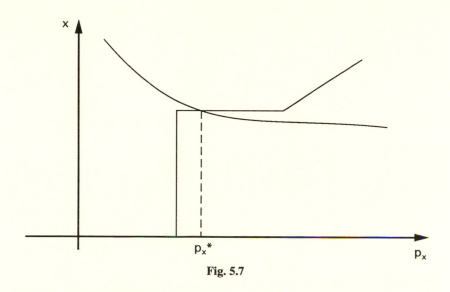

Fig. 5.7

Therefore, the equilibrium in the factor market would be as indicated in Figure 5.7. The equilibrium would be obtained at a price p_x^* between 1 and 2 and the production plan at equilibrium would be $(-16, 16)$. This is the equilibrium guaranteed by Theorem 5.1; however, this equilibrium cannot be decentralized since the price $p^* = (p_x^*, 1)$ does not represent the marginal cost of either firm 1 or firm 2. $p^* \notin N_{Y_1}(-16, 16)$ and $p^* \notin N_{Y_2}(-16, 16)$.

5.3 General Existence Theorem

A number of existence results for the multi-firm case have been obtained (Beato and Mas-Colell 1985; Dierker, Guesnerie, and Neuefeind 1985; Brown et al. 1986; Vohra 1988, 1990a; Kamiya 1988; Bonnisseau and Cornet 1988a, 1990a,b) under a variety of assumptions. Some of these papers consider more general pricing rules than marginal cost pricing. Since the emphasis of this monograph is on first best optimality and marginal cost pricing, we shall give an existence proof which is specific to the marginal cost pricing rule. The theorem that we prove uses slightly stronger assumptions than Bonnisseau and Cornet (1990a), which allows us to simplify the structure of the proof.

THEOREM 5.3. *Let* $\mathcal{E}\left((u_i, w_i)_{i=1,\ldots,n}, (Y_j)_{j=1,\ldots,m} \right)$ *be an economy with H goods, n agents and m firms with the following properties:*

B1. *The utility function u_i defined on $\mathbb{R}_+^H$ is continuous, quasi-concave, and locally non-satiated, $\forall i = 1, \ldots, n$.*

B2. (a) *Y_j is closed, contains 0 and $Y_j - \mathbb{R}_+^H \subset Y_j$, $\forall j = 1, \ldots, m$.*

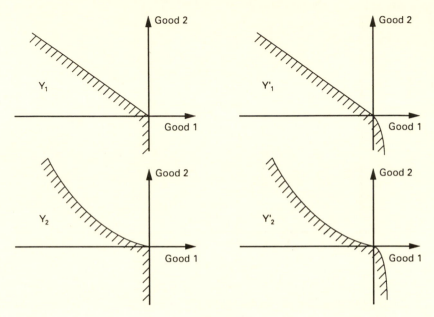

Fig. 5.8

(b) $Y_j = \{y \in \mathbb{R}^H \mid g_j(y) \le 0\}$ where $g_j : \mathbb{R}^H \longrightarrow \mathbb{R}$ is a twice continuously differentiable function with $Dg_j(y) \neq 0$ if $g_j(y) = 0$, $\forall j = 1, \ldots, m$.

B3. The set $\{(y_j) \in \prod_j Y_j \mid \sum_{j=1}^m y_j \ge z\}$ is compact for all $z \in \mathbb{R}^H$.

B4. For $(y_j) \in \prod_j Y_j$ such that $\bigcap_j N_{Y_j}(y_j) \neq \{0\}$, $p \cdot (\sum_{j=1}^m y_j + w) > 0$ for all price vectors $p \neq 0$ belonging to $\bigcap_j N_{Y_j}(y_j)$.

Under assumptions B1 to B4, for every income map r there exists a marginal cost pricing equilibrium of the economy $\mathcal{E}$.

Remark: Typically, a production set does not satisfy assumption B2(b) if the roles of the factors of production and output produced are not reversible. Therefore, Theorem 5.3 must be applied to an approximation of the actual production set and then a limit argument proves existence of an equilibrium in the original economy (Figure 5.8).

Remark: The assumption of differentiability B2(b), although restrictive, is more acceptable for individual production sets than it is for the aggregate production set since, as we have seen, the sum of production sets with smooth boundaries can give an aggregate production set whose frontier exhibits kinks. The proof given here can be extended to the case where individual production sets also exhibit kinks at the cost of an extra effort in technique (see Bonnisseau and Cornet 1990b).

Remark: Assumption B4 is called a "survival" assumption. It ensures that the total income generated by a production plan such that all marginal productivities are equalized is strictly positive. Since by definition of an income map each agent has a positive income when the total income is positive, assumption B4 ensures that, for all such production plans, each agent has a positive income and can "survive." This assumption is strong since it applies to all production plans such that the frontiers of the production sets of the individual firms have a common normal vector, *whether these production plans are feasible or not* with the resources available in the economy. It would be more satisfactory to require the positive income property only for those production plans which are feasible. The natural assumption would be:

B4′. *All production plans* $(y_j) \in \prod_j Y_j$ *which are feasible (i.e.,* $\sum_j y_j + w \geq 0$) *and such that* $\bigcap_j N_{Y_j}(y_j) \neq \{0\}$ *verify:* $p \cdot (\sum_j y_j + w) > 0$ *for all* $p \in \bigcap_j N_{Y_j}(y_j)\backslash\{0\}$.

A counterexample by Kamiya (1988b) shows that this assumption, together with B1 to B3, is not sufficient to imply existence of an equilibrium. Bonnisseau and Cornet (1990a) prove existence under the assumption B4″ which is intermediate between B4 and B4′.

B4″. *For all* $w' \geq w$, *the production plans* $(y_j) \in \prod_j Y_j$ *which are feasible with* w' *(i.e.,* $\sum_j y_j + w' \geq 0$) *and such that* $\bigcap_j N_{Y_j}(y_j) \neq \{0\}$ *verify:* $p \cdot (\sum_j y_j + w') > 0$ *for all* $p \in \bigcap_j N_{Y_j}(y_j)\backslash\{0\}$.

This assumption is satisfied in the example of Beato and Mas-Colell given in the previous section although B4 is not. We will retain assumption B4 since this allows us to keep the mathematics of the proof at a relatively straightforward level and to give a proof with a clear structure. The method that we describe can be refined to give existence with a weaker survival assumption. The interested reader is referred to the article by Bonnisseau and Cornet (1990a) for a proof of existence under the assumptions B1 to B3, B4″ and an additional assumption on the income map.

Idea of the proof

The key idea of the method of proof used in Theorem 5.1 is contained in Lemma 5.2 which asserts that the set

$$E = \{y \in \partial Y \mid w + y \in \mathbb{R}_+^H\}$$

is homeomorphic to the $(H-1)$-dimensional simplex of $\mathbb{R}^H$. (The proof is made for $\tilde{E}$ which is a translation of E.) The natural extension of this property to an economy with m firms involves showing that the set of *individually efficient production plans*

$$E = \{(y_1, \ldots, y_m) \in \partial Y_1 \times \ldots \times \partial Y_m | \sum_{j=1}^{m} y_j + w \in \mathbf{R}_+^H \}$$

is homeomorphic to the simplex or equivalently to a ball of $\mathbf{R}^{(H-1)m}$. The fact that E is homeomorphic to a ball of $\mathbf{R}^{(H-1)m}$ has been proved by Cornet (1988), but involves the use of a considerable amount of technique. It is simpler to prove the weaker property that the set

$$E_\epsilon = \{(y_1 \times \ldots \times y_m) \in \partial Y_1 \times \ldots \times \partial Y_m \mid d(\sum_j y_j + w, \ \mathbf{R}_+^H) \le \epsilon\}$$

is homeomorphic to a retract of a ball in $\mathbf{R}^{(H-1)m}$. E_ϵ is the set of *individually efficient, ε-feasible production plans*, namely, the individually efficient plans which allow for an ϵ violation of the feasibility condition with the existing resources. This property of E_ϵ is sufficient to permit an application of Kakutani's fixed point theorem, albeit at the cost of some complication in the definition of the fixed point map (see Section 5.5).

5.4   Structure of the Set E_ϵ

In this section we prove that the set E_ϵ is homeomorphic to a retract of a ball in $\mathbf{R}^{(H-1)m}$ (Lemma 5.11). To do this we introduce a basic result from the theory of Morse functions (Lemma 5.4) and some techniques from convex analysis (Lemmas 5.5 to 5.8).

Results used in studying the structure of E_ϵ

LEMMA 5.4. *Let X be an euclidean space of finite dimension, $\theta : X \longrightarrow \mathbf{R}$ be a differentiable function with a locally lipschitzian derivative and a and b be two real numbers such that:*

(i) *the set $\{x \in X \mid a \le \theta(x) \le b\}$ is compact*

(ii) *$D\theta(x) \neq 0 \ \forall x \in X$ such that $a \le \theta(x) \le b$.*

There exists a continuous mapping α from the set $\{x \in X \mid \theta(x) \le b\}$ to the set $\{x \in X \mid \theta(x) \le a\}$ such that:

- *if $\theta(x) \le a$, $\alpha(x) = x$;*

- *if $a \le \theta(x) \le b$, $\theta(\alpha(x)) = a$*

The application α is called a retraction of the set $\{x \in X \mid \theta(x) \le b\}$ onto the set $\{x \in X \mid \theta(x) \le a\}$.

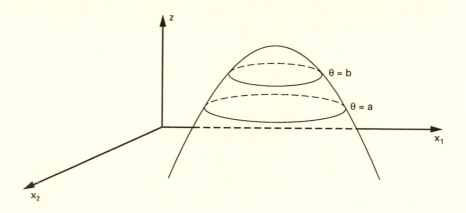

Fig. 5.9

The proof of Lemma 5.4 which is the first lemma in the theory of Morse functions on smooth manifolds is not given here. The proof can be found in Gramain (1971) or Milnor (1969). It is easy to give a geometric intuition of the result (Figure 5.9).

Figure 5.9 represents the graph of a function $\theta : \mathbb{R}^2 \longrightarrow \mathbb{R}$. If θ does not have an extremum between the level curves $\theta = a$ and $\theta = b$, the set $\{x \mid \theta(x) \leq b\}$ can be smoothly retracted into the set $\{x \mid \theta(x) \leq a\}$ following the vector field $-D\theta(x)$. If the function θ admits an extremum between the two level curves, this property is not always true, as suggested by Figure 5.10.

The function θ that will be used in the proof of Theorem 5.3 is derived from the distance function from a point of $\mathbb{R}^H$ to the positive orthant $\mathbb{R}^H_+$. We will use the following classical results of convex analysis. In the

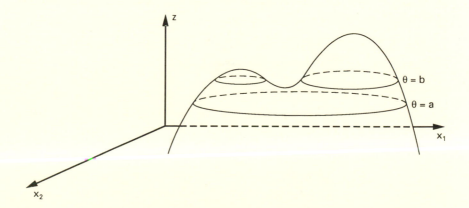

Fig. 5.10

economic literature, they are used and proved in Mas-Colell (1985). Denote the euclidian norm of $\mathbf{R}^H$ by $\|\ \ \|$ and the associated distance by d.

THEOREM AND DEFINITION 5.5. *Let C be a closed convex set of $\mathbf{R}^H$. For every point x of $\mathbf{R}^H$, there exists a unique $y \in C$ such that*

$$d(x, y) = d(x, C) \stackrel{\text{def}}{=} \inf_{x' \in C} \| x - x' \|$$

y is called the projection of x on C and denoted by $y = \text{proj}_C(x)$

THEOREM 5.6. *Let C be a closed convex set of $\mathbf{R}^H$. The map proj_C : $\mathbf{R}^H \longrightarrow C$ is Lipschitzian. More precisely,*

$$\| \text{proj}_C(x_1) - \text{proj}_C(x_2) \| \leq \| x_1 - x_2 \|, \ \forall x_1 \in \mathbf{R}^H, \ \forall x_2 \in \mathbf{R}^H.$$

THEOREM 5.7. *Let C be a closed convex set of $\mathbf{R}^H$. The mapping f : $\mathbf{R}^H \longrightarrow \mathbf{R}$ defined by $f(x) = \frac{1}{2}d^2(x, C)$ is convex and differentiable with a gradient vector $Df(x) = x - \text{proj}_C(x)$.*

THEOREM 5.8. *Let K be a closed convex cone of $\mathbf{R}^H$ and $x \in \mathbf{R}^H$. $y \in K$ is the projection of x on K if and only if,*

$$(x - y) \cdot y = 0$$

$$(x - y) \cdot x' \leq 0, \ \forall x' \in K$$

Properties of E_ϵ

In order to work in an euclidean space, it is convenient to project the boundary of each production set onto the hyperplane orthogonal to the vector $e = (1, \ldots, 1)$ (see Figure 5.11).

Let $\mathbb{H} = e^\perp$ denote this hyperplane. Let $\pi : \mathbf{R}^H \longrightarrow \mathbb{H}$ denotes the orthogonal projection onto $\mathbb{H}$ and let $\pi_j : \partial Y_j \longrightarrow \mathbb{H}$ denote the restriction of π to ∂Y_j.

LEMMA 5.9. *Under assumption B2, the orthogonal projection π_j : $\partial Y_j \longrightarrow E$ is a C^2 diffeomorphism whose inverse is denoted by φ_j.*

Proof:

Step 1. $\pi_j : \partial Y_j \longrightarrow \mathbb{H}$ is injective.

$$\pi_j(y_j^1) = \pi_j(y_j^2) \Longleftrightarrow \exists \lambda \in \mathbf{R} \quad y_j^1 - y_j^2 = \lambda e$$

If $\lambda > 0$, $y_j^1 \gg y_j^2$ which implies, by the assumption of free disposal, that y_j^2 belongs to the interior of Y_j and is not on the boundary.

If $\lambda < 0$, y_j^1 is in the interior of Y_j and not on ∂Y_j. Therefore, $\lambda = 0$ and $y_j^1 = y_j^2$.

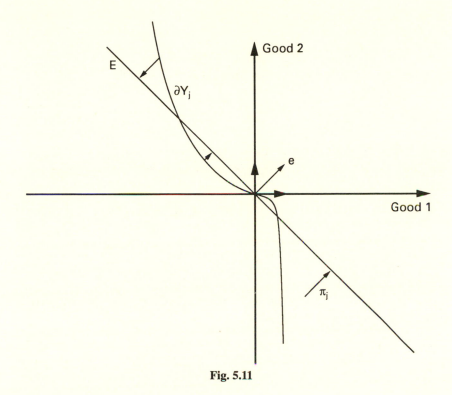

Fig. 5.11

Step 2. π_j *is onto.*

Let t be an element of $\mathbb{H}$. Consider the set $\{t + \lambda e \mid \lambda \in \mathbb{R}\}$. For $\lambda < 0$ and sufficiently large in absolute value, $t + \lambda e \in -\mathbb{R}^H_{++} \subset \text{Int} \, Y_j$. For $\lambda > 0$ and sufficiently large, $T + \lambda e \notin Y_j$ since assumption B3 implies that $Y_j \cap \mathbb{R}^H_+$ is bounded. Therefore, by the intermediate value theorem, there exists $\bar{\lambda} \in \mathbb{R}$ such that $t + \bar{\lambda} e \in \partial Y_j$. Thus, $t = \pi_j(t + \bar{\lambda} e)$.

Step 3. *The inverse of π_j, φ_j is differentiable.*

It is sufficient to show that for every $y_j \in \partial Y_j$, the derivative of π_j : $T_{Y_j}(y_j) \longrightarrow \mathbb{H}$ is bijective. This map is the projection of the tangent plane $T_{Y_j}(y_j)$ at y_j to ∂Y_j on $\mathbb{H}$. Since T_{Y_j} and $\mathbb{H}$ have the same dimension $(H-1)$, the projection is bijective except in the case where $T_{Y_j}(y_j)$ contains vectors parallel to e. $T_{Y_j}(y_j)$ is orthogonal to the vector $Dg_j(y_j)$. It is easy to show that the assumption of free disposal implies that $Dg_j(y_j) \in \mathbb{R}^H_+$. Therefore, $e \cdot Dg_j(y_j) > 0$ and $T_{Y_j}(y_j)$ cannot contain vectors parallel to e.

Step 4. *Computation of the derivative map $D\varphi_j$.*

The map $D\varphi_j : \mathbb{H} \longrightarrow T_{Y_j}(y_j)$ is the inverse mapping of $D\pi_j$: $T_{Y_j}(y_j) \longrightarrow \mathbb{H}$. Let $t_j \in \mathbb{H}$, $y_j = \varphi_j(t_j)$, $h_j \in \mathbb{H}$. Let us compute the value of $u_j \stackrel{\text{def}}{=} D\varphi_j(t_j) \cdot h_j$:

$$u_j = D\varphi_j(t_j) \cdot h_j \Longleftrightarrow h_j = D\pi_j(y_j) \cdot u_j \longleftrightarrow u_j = h_j + \lambda e$$
$$u_j \in T_{Y_j}(y_j) \Longleftrightarrow u_j \cdot Dg_j(y_j) = 0 \Longleftrightarrow (h_j + \lambda e) \cdot Dg_j(y_j) = 0 \Longleftrightarrow \lambda =$$
$$-\frac{h_j \cdot Dg_j(y_j)}{e \cdot Dg_j(y_j)}$$

If we denote the normalized gradient of g_j by $\mu_j(y_j)$ $(\mu_j(y_j) = Dg_j(y_j)/e \cdot Dg_j(y_j))$, we get: $D\varphi_j(t_j) \cdot h_j = h_j - h_j \cdot \mu_j(y_j)e$ where $y_j = \varphi_j(t_j)$.

$\triangledown$

LEMMA 5.10. *Consider the map $\theta : \mathbb{H}^m \longrightarrow \mathbb{R}$ defined by*

$$\theta(t_1, \ldots, t_m) = \frac{1}{2}d^2(\sum_{j=1}^{m}\varphi_j(t_j) + w, \ \mathbb{R}_+^H)$$

Under assumptions B2 and B4, the map θ is differentiable, its derivative is lipschitzian and $\theta(t) \geq \epsilon^2/2 \Longrightarrow D\theta(t) \neq 0$ for every $\epsilon > 0$.

Proof: The map θ is the composition of the maps

$$f : \ \mathbb{R}^H \longrightarrow \mathbb{R}$$

$$y \longrightarrow \frac{1}{2}d^2(y, \ \mathbb{R}_+^H)$$

and $\varphi : \mathbb{H}^m \longrightarrow \mathbb{R}^H$

$$t \longrightarrow \sum_{j=1}^{m}\varphi_j(t_j) + w$$

Using the results of Lemma 5.9 and Theorem 5.7, we get

$$D\theta(t) \cdot h = q \cdot \left(\sum_{j=1}^{m}h_j - h_j \cdot \mu_j(y_j)e\right), \ \forall h \in \mathbb{H}^m$$

where

$$y_j = \varphi_j(t_j); \ \mu_j(y_j) = \frac{Dg_j(y_j)}{e \cdot Dg_j(y_j)}$$

$$q = \sum_{j=1}^{m}\varphi_j(t_j) + w - \text{proj}_{\mathbb{R}_+^H}(\sum_{j=1}^{m}\varphi_j(t_j) + w)$$

$$= \sum_{j=1}^{m}y_j + w - \text{proj}_{\mathbb{R}_+^H}(\sum_{j=1}^{m}y_j + w)$$

Therefore,

$$D\theta(t) \cdot h = \sum_{j=1}^{m}(q - q \cdot e\mu_j(y_j)) \cdot h_j$$

which implies that the gradient of θ is the vector

$$(q - q \cdot e\mu_1(y_1), \ldots, q - q \cdot e\mu_m(y_m))$$

Let us show that this gradient is always non-zero if $\theta(t) \geq \epsilon^2/2$:

$$\theta(t) \geq \epsilon^2/2 \iff \frac{1}{2}\parallel q \parallel^2 \geq \epsilon^2/2 \implies q \neq 0.$$

Therefore, if the gradient is zero, it must be that

$$q = q \cdot e\mu_j(y_j), \quad \forall j = 1, \ldots, m.$$

By Theorem 5.8, $q \cdot x \leq 0$, $\forall x \in \mathbb{R}_+^H$ and in particular $q \cdot e \leq 0$. Therefore, if the gradient of θ is zero,

$$-q \in \bigcap_j N_{Y_j}(y_j)$$

which implies that

$$-q \cdot (\sum_j y_j + w) > 0 \quad \text{by B4}$$

Since $-q \cdot \text{proj}_{\mathbb{R}_+^H}(\sum_j y_j + w) = 0$, by Theorem 5.8, it must be that $- \parallel q \parallel^2 > 0$, which is obviously impossible.

$$\triangledown$$

With Lemma 5.10, we can use Lemma 5.4 to show that the projection on $\mathbb{H}^m$ of the set ϵ is the retraction of a ball of $\mathbb{H}^m$. This is the approximate version of Lemma 5.2 that we use for the case of several firms.

LEMMA 5.11. *Let* $E_\epsilon = \{(y_j) \in \prod_j \partial Y_j \mid d(\sum_{j=1}^m y_j + w, \mathbb{R}_+^H) \leq \epsilon\}$ *denote the set of individually efficient ϵ-feasible productions and let* M_ϵ *be the projection of* E_ϵ *on* $\mathbb{H}^m$

$$M_\epsilon = \{t \in \mathbb{H}^m \mid d(\sum_{j=1}^m \varphi_j(t_j) + w, \mathbb{R}_+^H) \leq \epsilon\}$$
$$= \{t \in \mathbb{H}^m \mid \theta(t) \leq \epsilon^2/2\}$$

then there exists a ball B of $\mathbb{H}^m$ such that M_ϵ is in the interior of B and a mapping $\alpha : B \longrightarrow M_\epsilon$ such that:

$$\alpha(x) = x \text{ if } x \in M_\epsilon$$

$$\alpha(x) \in \partial M_\epsilon \text{ if } x \in B \backslash M_\epsilon$$

Proof: E_ϵ is a closed set, contained in the set

$$\left\{ (y_j) \in \prod_j Y_j \mid \sum_{j=1}^m y_j + w \geq -\epsilon e \right\}$$

which is compact by assumption B3. Therefore, E_ϵ is compact and so is its projection M_ϵ on $\mathbb{H}^m$. Thus, M_ϵ is contained in a ball B which can be made large enough to include M_ϵ in its interior.

Let $\eta = \max\{\frac{1}{2}d^2(\sum_{j=1}^m \varphi_j(t_j) + w, \mathbb{R}_+^H) \mid t \in B\}$ and $M_\eta = \{t \in \mathbb{H}^m \mid \theta(t) \leq \eta^2/2\}$.

The function θ satisfies the conditions of Lemma 5.4 for $a = \epsilon^2/2$ and $b = \eta^2/2$ (M_η is compact like M_ϵ so that $\{t \in \mathbb{H}^m \mid a \leq \theta(t) \leq b\}$ is compact and by Lemma 5.10, $D\theta(t)$ is non-zero). Therefore, it is possible to retract M_η on M_ϵ and the restriction of this retraction leads to a mapping α which has the properties asserted in Lemma 5.11.

$$\nabla$$

5.5 Proof of the Existence Theorem

Proof of Theorem 5.2: Let $\mathcal{E}((u_i, w_i))_{i=1,\dots,n}, (Y_j)_{j=1,\dots,m})$ be an economy satisfying assumptions B1 to B4.

By B3, the set $\{(y_j) \in \prod_j Y_j \mid \sum_{j=1}^m y_j + w \geq 0\}$ is compact which implies that the set

$$\left\{ (x_i) \in \mathbb{R}_+^{Hn} \mid \sum_{i=1}^n x_i \leq \sum_{j=1}^m y_j + w, \quad (y_j) \in \prod_j Y_j \right\}$$

is compact. Let X_i be the ith projection of this compact set on $\mathbb{R}_+^H$ and K_i be a compact convex set of $\mathbb{R}_+^H$ which contains X_i in its interior.

The existence of an equilibrium of $\mathcal{E}$ will follow from the existence of a fixed point of the correspondence

$$\psi = (\psi_1, \psi_2, \psi_3) : B \times K \times \Delta_{H-1} \longrightarrow B \times K \times \Delta_{H-1}$$

where

- B is the ball of $\mathbb{H}^m$ defined in Lemma 5.11,
- K is a convex compact set containing $\sum_i K_i$ which is to be defined,
- Δ_{H-1} is the simplex of prices of the H goods.

Definition of ψ_1

ψ_1 is the component of the correspondence ψ which ensures that at a fixed point the normal to each production set is colinear to p.

To an element (t, x, p) of $B \times K \times \Delta_{H-1}$ we associate the retraction $\alpha(t)$ of t on M_ϵ and its preimage (y_j) in E_ϵ. $\left(y_j = \varphi_j(\alpha_j(t)) \right)$. The vector

$$\mu_j(y_j) = \frac{Dg_j(y_j)}{e \cdot Dg_j(y_j)}$$

belongs to the simplex so that $p - \mu_j(y_j)$ belongs to the hyperplane $\mathbb{H}$. Since M_ϵ is in the interior of B, it is possible to find δ sufficiently small so that $(\alpha_j(t) + \delta(p - \mu_j(y_j)))_{j=1,\ldots,m}$ is in B for any $t \in B$.

Define

$$\psi_1(t, x, p) = \alpha\big(\alpha_1(t) + \delta(p - \mu_1(y_1)), \ldots, \alpha_m(t) + \delta(p - \mu_m(y_m))\big)$$

Note that the equality $\psi_1(t, x, p) = t$ is possible in only two cases:

- if $t \in \text{Int}(M_\epsilon)$ and $p - \mu_j(t) = 0$, $\forall j = 1, \ldots, m$
- or if $t \in \partial M_\epsilon$ and $(p - \mu_j(t))_{j=1,\ldots,m}$ points outside M_ϵ.

Definition of ψ_2

ψ_2 is the component of the correspondence ψ which ensures that, at a fixed point, x is equal to the demand of the consumers. Since, in order to work with a "well-behaved" set, we consider productions which are only ϵ-feasible, we must define an (artificial) demand for consumers with negative revenues. The most natural is to begin with the following correspondence:

$$d_i : \Delta_{H-1} \times \prod_j Y_j \longrightarrow K_i$$

$$d_i(p, (y_j)) = \left\{ \begin{array}{ll} \arg \max\{u_i(x_i) \mid x_i \in K_i, p \cdot x_i \leq r_i(p, (y_j)) & \text{if } r_i(p, (y_j)) > 0 \\ \{x_i \in K_i, \ p \cdot x_i = 0\} & \text{if } r_i(p, (y_j)) \leq 0 \end{array} \right\}$$

For each i, this correspondence has a closed graph and compact, convex values. But with this definition of demand, Walras's law is not satisfied for $(p, (y_j))$ such that $p \cdot (\sum_j y_j + w) \leq 0$—which does not matter from an economic view point, but makes difficult the application of a fixed point theorem.

To get around this difficulty, note that

$$(y_j) \in E_\epsilon \iff \sum_{j=1}^{m} y_j + w \in B(0, \epsilon) + \mathbb{R}_+^H$$

where $B(0, \epsilon)$ is a ball of $\mathbb{R}^H$ of radius ϵ centered at the origin. This implies that

$$p \cdot \left(\sum_j y_j + w \right) \geq - \parallel p \parallel \epsilon, \quad \forall p \in \Delta_{H-1} \qquad (1)$$

with equality if and only if $\sum_j y_j + w = - \dfrac{\epsilon p}{\parallel p \parallel}$.

Consider the following correspondence (modified total demand): for $p \in \Delta_{H-1}$, $(y_j) \in E_\epsilon$

$$\tilde{d}(p, (y_j)) =$$
$$CO\left\{ (1 - \lambda(p, x', (y_j)))x' - \lambda(p, x', (y_j)) \frac{\epsilon p}{\parallel p \parallel} \mid x' \in \sum_{i=1}^{n} d_i(p, (y_j)) \right\}$$

where CO denotes the convex envelope and

$$\lambda(p, x', (y_j)) = \max\left\{ 0, \frac{p \cdot (x' - \sum_j y_j - w)}{p \cdot x' + \epsilon \parallel p \parallel} \right\}$$

Inequality (1) implies that $0 \leq \lambda(p, x', (y_j)) \leq 1$, which in turn implies that:

(i) for every $(p, (y_j)) \in \Delta_{H-1} \times E_\epsilon$, $\tilde{d}(p, (y_j))$ is bounded. Therefore, there exists a compact convex set K containing the image of $\tilde{d}$.

(ii) $\tilde{d}(p, (y_j)) \subset \text{Int}(B(0, \epsilon) + \mathbb{R}_+^H)$ except if there exists $x' \in \sum_{i=1}^{n} d_i(p, (y_j))$ such that $\lambda(p, x', (y_j)) = 1$. This is possible only if $\sum_{j=1}^{m} y_j + w = \dfrac{-\epsilon p}{\parallel p \parallel}$.

On the other hand, the definition of $\tilde{d}$ implies that:

(iii) if $p \cdot (\sum_{j=1}^{m} y_j + w) > 0$, then $\lambda(p, x', (y_j)) = 0$ for all $x' \in \sum_{i=1}^{n} d_i(p, (y_j))$ and $\tilde{d}(p, (y_j)) = \sum_{i=1}^{n} d_i(p, (y_j))$,

(iv) $p \cdot (x - \sum_j y_j - w) \leq 0$, $\forall x \in \tilde{d}(p, (y_j))$.

To prove (iv), it is enough to show that $(1 - \lambda)p \cdot x' - \lambda \epsilon \parallel p \parallel -p \cdot (\sum_j y_j + w) \leq 0$, $\forall x' \in \sum_i d_i(p, (y_j))$. If $p \cdot (x' - \sum_j y_j - w) \leq 0$, $\lambda = 0$ and the inequality is satisfied. If $p \cdot (x' - \sum_j y_j - w) \geq 0$, $p \cdot (x' - \sum_j y_j - w) = \lambda(p \cdot x' + \epsilon \parallel p \parallel)$ and the inequality is again satisfied.

For $(t, x, p) \in B \times K \times \Delta_{H-1}$, define $\psi_2(t, x, p) = \tilde{d}(p, (y_j))$ (recall that $y_j = \varphi_j(\alpha_j(t))$).

Definition of ψ_3

For the adjustment of prices we follow the classical procedure

$$\psi_3(t, x, p) = \arg \max \left\{ q.(x - \sum_j y_j - w) \mid q \in \Delta_{H-1} \right\}$$

A fixed point of ψ gives an equilibrium of $\mathcal{E}$

The correspondence ψ from $B \times K \times \Delta_{H-1}$ into itself satisfies the assumptions of Kakutani's theorem and has a fixed point $(\bar{t}, \bar{x}, \bar{p})$. Denote $\bar{y}_j = \varphi_j(\alpha_j(\bar{t}))$. Let us show that there exist $\bar{x}_i \in d_i(p, (\bar{y}_j)), i = 1, \ldots, n$, such that $\bar{x} = \sum_{i=1}^n \bar{x}_i$ and $((\bar{x}_i), (\bar{y}_j), \bar{p})$ is an equilibrium of $\mathcal{E}$.

$\bar{x} \in \tilde{d}(p, (\bar{y}_j))$ implies that $\bar{p} \cdot (\bar{x} - \sum_j \bar{y}_j - w) \leq 0$ (property (iv) of $\tilde{d}$). Since $\bar{p} \in \psi_3(\bar{t}, \bar{x}, \bar{p})$, $q \cdot (\bar{x} - \sum_j \bar{y}_j - w) \leq 0$ for all $q \in \Delta_{H-1}$, which is possible only if $(\bar{x} - \sum_j \bar{y}_j - w) \leq 0$.

As we have seen in the definition of ψ_1, $\bar{t} = \psi_1(\bar{t}, \bar{x}, \bar{p})$ implies $\bar{p} = \mu_j(\bar{t})$ except if $\bar{t} \in \partial M_\epsilon$ and $(\bar{p} - \mu_j(\bar{t}))_{j=1,\ldots,m}$ points outside M_ϵ.

Suppose that $\bar{t} \in \partial M_\epsilon$. This implies that $d(\sum \bar{y}_j + w, \mathbf{R}_+^H) = \epsilon$ and since $\bar{x} \leq \sum_j \bar{y}_j + w, d(\bar{x}, \mathbf{R}_+^H) \leq \epsilon$. We have seen in the definition of ψ_2 that this is possible only if $d(\bar{x}, \mathbf{R}_+^H) = \epsilon$ and $\sum \bar{y}_j + w = \dfrac{-\epsilon \bar{p}}{\parallel \bar{p} \parallel}$.

But in this case, the vector $(\bar{p} - \mu_1(\bar{y}_1), \ldots, \bar{p} - \mu_m(\bar{y}_m))$ points to the interior of M_ϵ.

More precisely, going back to the calculations of Lemma 5.9,

$$\bar{q} = \sum_j \bar{y}_j + w - \operatorname{proj}_{\mathbf{R}_+^H}(\sum_j \bar{y}_j + w) = \sum_j \bar{y}_j + w = \dfrac{-\epsilon \bar{p}}{\parallel \bar{p} \parallel}$$

and

$$D\theta(\bar{t}) = \dfrac{-\epsilon}{\parallel \bar{p} \parallel}(\bar{p} - \mu_1(\bar{y}_1), \ldots, \bar{p} - \mu_m(\bar{y}_m))$$

Since the function θ decreases in the direction $-D\theta(\bar{t})$, for δ sufficiently small, $(\bar{t}_j + \delta(\bar{p} - \mu_j(\bar{y}_j)))_{j=1,\ldots,m}$ is in the interior of M_ϵ.

Therefore, $\bar{t} \in \operatorname{Int} M_\epsilon$ and $\bar{p} = \mu_j(\bar{y}_j), \forall j = 1, \ldots, m$. This is equivalent to $\bar{p} \in \cap_j N_{Y_j}(\bar{y}_j)$, which implies, by B4, that $\bar{p} \cdot (\sum_j \bar{y}_j + w) > 0$.

Then, $\tilde{d}(\bar{p}, (\bar{y}_j)) = \sum_{i=1}^n d_i(p, (\bar{y}_j))$ (property (iii) of $\tilde{d}$) and, therefore, there exist $\bar{x}_i \in d_i(\bar{p}, (\bar{y}_j)), i = 1, \ldots, n$, such that $\bar{x} = \sum_{i=1}^n \bar{x}_i$. Since $\sum_i \bar{x}_i - \sum_j \bar{y}_j - w \leq 0$, the demands $\bar{x}_i$ belong to X_i and the constraint $x_i \in K_i$ is not binding. Therefore,

- $\bar{p} \in \cap_j N_{Y_j}(\bar{y}_j)$

- $\bar{x}_i \in \arg\max\{u_i(x_i) \mid \bar{x}_i \geq 0,\ \bar{p} \cdot x_i \leq r_i(\bar{p}, (\bar{y}_j))\}$ $\forall i = 1, \ldots, n$
- $\sum_{i=1}^{n} \bar{x}_i \leq \sum_{j=1}^{m} \bar{y}_j + w$

and $((\bar{x}_i), (\bar{y}_j), \bar{p})$ is an equilibrium of $\mathcal{E}$.

$\triangledown$

6

THE CORE

6.1 Why the Core?

Every competitive equilibrium of an economy with convex production sets has the property that agents will voluntarily participate in the production and exchange process. At the simplest level this is true because it is individually rational for each agent to participate, in the sense that all agents are better off in the equilibrium than with their own initial endowment. This property is no longer true for the concept of a marginal cost pricing equilibrium in an economy with increasing returns. For then, as we have seen, marginal cost pricing creates a deficit which must somehow be financed. A particular mode of financing the deficit (i.e., a given income map) may make some agents worse off in the equilibrium than with their own initial endowments. Even if agents are better off in an equilibrium they may object to the allocation if they feel that they are financing too large a component of the deficit of the public sector.

In this chapter we shall adopt a more abstract approach to the problem of finding acceptable ways of financing the deficit. We consider the general problem of finding allocations (i.e., production plans for firms and consumption bundles for agents) which are acceptable to all agents in the economy. We use the framework of cooperative game theory and formulate the problem via the concept of the core as follows. *Does there exist an allocation in the core of an economy in which the production sector exhibits increasing returns to scale?*

To define the concept of the core the allocations in the economy must be viewed as the result of a cooperative process in which agents accept to exchange goods and to participate in the production of goods through the provision of inputs such as labor. Exchange and production normally generate a surplus of welfare relative to the initial endowment allocation with no production. An allocation for the economy describes a feasible way of creating and distributing the surplus. If an allocation, feasible with the resources of all agents, is worse from the point of view of a particular agent than just consuming his or her initial resources then this allocation

101

is not likely to emerge since this agent will refuse to enter into the (social) production and exchange process. What is true for a single agent is also true for a subgroup of agents, if there is perfect communication between the agents. If an allocation, feasible with the resources of all agents, is such that a subgroup of agents using only their resources, can obtain better for everyone of them, then this allocation cannot be the outcome of voluntary production and exchange. The core allocations are those allocations with which all agents would accept to cooperate.

Thus, to define the core of an economy with n agents, we must first define, for all subgroups of agents S, the allocations $A(S)$ which are feasible for S using only the resources of its members. In this context a subgroup of agents is called a *coalition*; the set $N = \{1, \ldots, n\}$ of all agents is called the *grand coalition*. The feasible allocations for the whole economy are the allocations of $A(N)$. The allocations in $A(S)$ serve as a benchmark for the agents of S to accept or refuse to cooperate with the rest of the agents in the economy. If an allocation $x = (x_i)_{i=1,\ldots,n}$ is such that a coalition S can find in $A(S)$ an allocation which the agents of S unanimously prefer to x, then we say that the coalition S "blocks" x. A feasible allocation of the economy which is not blocked by any coalition is said to be in the core of the economy. If every feasible allocation is blocked by at least one coalition then the core of the economy is empty.

For an exchange economy, it is natural to define $A(S)$ as those allocations which can be obtained by the agents of S when they redistribute the total of their initial resources among themselves. Under the standard assumption of convexity of preferences, the core is non-empty and contains in particular the competitive equilibria.

When agents have the opportunity not only to exchange but also to produce goods with an increasing returns technology, if this technology is known and available to each agent in the economy then the set $A(S)$ can be extended to include both the possibility of exchange and production. Intuition suggests that the presence of increasing returns should reinforce the advantage of the grand coalition and that, therefore, the core of the economy should be non-empty. The results that are presented in the sections that follow show that this intuition needs to be refined. As soon as production involves two or more inputs and (or) two or more outputs the possibility of a choice in the composition of inputs and (or) outputs may prevent the existence of an allocation that no subset of agents can improve on. We shall show that for multigood economies core allocations exist only if the characteristics of the consumption and production sectors are compatible in an appropriate sense. To establish these results we shall need some basic concepts of cooperative game theory which are introduced in the following section.

6.2 Cooperative Game Theory

DEFINITION. *Let $N = \{1, \ldots, n\}$ be a finite set and let $\mathcal{P}(N)$ denote the set of all subsets of N. A cooperative game with side payments is a pair (N, v) where N is the set of players and*

$$v : \mathcal{P}(N) \longrightarrow \mathbb{R}$$

is a function satisfying $v(\emptyset) = 0$.

A subset S of N $(S \in \mathcal{P}(N))$ is called a *coalition*. v is called the *characteristic function*. $v(S)$ is the maximum payoff that the members of the coalition S can achieve. It is a global payoff for the group S and can be divided in any possible way between the members of S (side payments). The concept of a cooperative game is abstract and does not require a precise description of a game in terms of possible strategies for the players and resulting payoffs. It can be applied to any situation where one can identify a total payoff that the members of a group can obtain if they cooperate independently of the actions of the agents outside this group.

DEFINITION. *An imputation $(\alpha_1, \ldots, \alpha_n)$ of the game (N, v) is a vector of $\mathbb{R}^n$.*

An imputation describes the gain received by each player at the end of the game.

DEFINITION. *An imputation $\alpha = (\alpha_1, \ldots, \alpha_n)$ of the game (N, v) is blocked by the coalition S if $\sum_{i \in S} \alpha_i < v(S)$.*

DEFINITION. *An imputation $\alpha^* = (\alpha_1^*, \ldots, \alpha_n^*)$ is in the core of the game (N, v) if and only if*

- *it is feasible by the coalition of all players: $\sum_{i=1}^n \alpha_i^* \le v(N)$*
- *it is not blocked by any coalition of $\mathcal{P}(N)$.*

To understand the concept of a core allocation, imagine a mediator proposing to each player i to cooperate with the others at the beginning of the game and to receive in exchange a portion α_i^* of the total gain. This proposal is credible since $\sum_{i=1}^n \alpha_i^* \le v(N)$ and it is acceptable by every player since it is not blocked by any coalition. If, on the contrary, α^* was blocked by a coalition S, the players of S would refuse to cooperate with the players of $N \backslash S$ on the basis of the division α^*, since they could, by themselves, obtain more than α_i^* for each player $i \in S$.

For the core to be non-empty, the characteristic function must be such that the grand coalition has an advantage over smaller coalitions of players.

For example, the following condition must be satisfied: if B is a partition of N, it must be that

$$v(N) \geq \sum_{S \in B} v(S)$$

This property is satisfied if the game is *superadditive*, that is, if

$$S \in \mathcal{P}(N), T \in \mathcal{P}(N), S \cap T = \emptyset \implies v(S \cup T) \geq v(S) + v(T)$$

Superadditivity implies that two disjoint coalitions can do better when they combine their resources than when they use their resources separately. One might conjecture that superadditivity is a sufficient condition for the existence of a core. The following counterexample shows that this conjecture is false:

Suppose (N, v) is defined as follows:

$$N = \{1, 2, 3\}$$

$$v(1) = v(2) = v(3) = 0$$

$$v(1,2) = v(2,3) = v(1,3) = 5$$

$$v(1,2,3) = 7$$

This game is superadditive but the conditions

$$\alpha_1 \geq 0, \ \alpha_2 \geq 0, \ \alpha_3 \geq 0 \tag{1}$$

$$\alpha_1 + \alpha_2 \geq 5$$

$$\alpha_1 + \alpha_3 \geq 5 \tag{2}$$

$$\alpha_2 + \alpha_3 \geq 5$$

$$\alpha_2 + \alpha_2 + \alpha_3 = 7 \tag{3}$$

which must be satisfied for an imputation to belong to the core are incompatible since the inequalities (2) imply $\alpha_1 + \alpha_2 + \alpha_3 \geq 7.5$. In this game, the coalition N does not have a sufficient advantage over the two-player coalitions to make the core non-empty.

In order to state the conditions under which a game has a non-empty core, we need the following definitions.

DEFINITION. *If B is a family of subsets of N, let B_i denote all coalitions in B to which agent i belongs, $B_i = \{S \in B | i \in S\}$. A family B of non-empty subsets of N is balanced if there exist strictly positive coefficients $(\delta_S)_{S \in B}$ such that*

$$\sum_{S \in B_i} \delta_S = 1, \quad \forall i = 1, \ldots, n$$

The concept of a balanced family generalizes the concept of a partition. A partition is a particular balanced family where all the coefficients δ_S are equal to 1; however, there are balanced families which are not partitions. For example, if $N = (1, 2, 3)$, the family $\{(1, 2), (1, 3), (2, 3)\}$ associated with the coefficients $(1/2, 1/2, 1/2)$ is balanced.

DEFINITION. *A game (N, v) is balanced if, for every balanced family B with coefficients $(\delta_S)_{S \in B}$, the following inequality is satisfied:*

$$v(N) \geq \sum_{S \in B} \delta_S v(S)$$

It is difficult to give an intuitive interpretation of the property of balancedness. While intuition suggests that superadditivity is a necessary condition for non-emptiness of the core, as we have seen, it is not a strong enough property. Balancedness, which implies superadditivity, is precisely the stronger property which is both necessary and sufficient to ensure the existence of a core imputation. This is proved in the following theorem which is used extensively in the rest of this chapter.

THEOREM 6.1. *A game (N, v) with side payments has a non-empty core if and only if it is balanced.*

Proof:

a) Suppose $\alpha = (\alpha_1, \ldots, \alpha_n)$ belongs to the core of (N, v). Let B be a balanced family with coefficients $(\delta_S)_{S \in B}$. Since α is in the core:

$$\sum_{i \in S} \alpha_i \geq v(S), \quad \forall S \in B$$

$$\sum_{i=1}^{n} \alpha_i = v(N)$$

The last equality can be rewritten as

$$v(N) = \sum_{i=1}^{n} \left(\sum_{S \in B_i} \delta_S \right) \alpha_i$$

$$= \sum_{S \in B} \delta_S \left(\sum_{i \in S} \alpha_i \right) \geq \sum_{S \in B} \delta_S v(S)$$

b) To show the converse, consider the following problem:

$$V = \min \left\{ \sum_{i=1}^{n} \alpha_i \,\middle|\, \sum_{i \in S} \alpha_i \geq v(S), \quad \forall S \in \mathcal{P}(N) \right\}$$

It is clear that $v(N) \le V < +\infty$. If $V = v(N)$, there exists a imputation (α_i), feasible for the coalition N satisfying the constraints which is
therefore, not blocked by any coalition. Thus, the core is non-empty.

Since the minimization problem is linear by the duality theorem:

$$V = \max\left\{ \sum_{S \in \mathcal{P}(N)} \delta_S v(S) | \delta_S \ge 0, \sum_{\substack{S \in \mathcal{P}(N) \\ i \in S}} \delta_S = 1, \ \forall i = 1, \dots, n \right\}$$

Let $(\bar{\delta}_S)_{S \in \mathcal{P}(N)}$ be a solution of the dual problem and let $B = \{S \in \mathcal{P}(N),$
$S \ne \emptyset, \bar{\delta}_S > 0\}$. Since $(\bar{\delta}_S)$ satisfy the constraints of the dual problem, B
is a balanced family. Therefore, if the game is balanced,

$$V = \sum_{S \in B} \bar{\delta}_S v(S) \le v(N)$$

Thus, $V = v(N)$ and the core is non-empty.

$$\nabla$$

6.3   Scarf's Negative Result

We first present the negative result obtained by Scarf (1963, published
1986), which for a while discouraged further research on existence and
properties of core allocations for economies with increasing returns.
To formalize the ideas introduced in Section 6.1, consider an economy
$\mathcal{E}(N, (u_i, w_i)_{i \in N}, Y)$ where

- $N = \{1, \dots, n\}$ is the finite set of agents. Since we want to be able to
  consider economies with a variable number of agents, it is convenient
  to specify the set of agents in the description of the economy;
- $u_i : \mathbb{R}_+^H \to \mathbb{R}$ describes the preferences of the agent $i \in N$;
- $w_i \in \mathbb{R}_+^H$, denotes the initial resources of agent $i \in N$;
- $Y \subset \mathbb{R}^H$ is the production set describing a technology which is available to every agent or coalition of agents.

The concept of the core of an economy is similar in spirit to the concept
of the core of a cooperative game. It describes consumption allocations
which are feasible for the economy and which are acceptable to all agents,
given the opportunities that they have if they withdraw from the economy.

DEFINITION. *The feasible consumption allocations for a coalition S are
defined by*

$$A(S) = \{(x_i)_{i \in S} \in \mathbb{R}_+^{H|S|} | \sum_{i \in S}(x_i - w_i) \in Y\}$$

where $|S|$ denotes the number of elements of S.

The allocations in $A(S)$ are feasible for the coalition S which has access to the technology Y if the agents in S exchange between themselves. No cooperation from agents outside S is necessary to achieve the allocations in $A(S)$.

In this chapter we shall often commit the abuse of using the term allocation instead of consumption allocation. By the definition given in section 2.1, an allocation of the economy should describe both the consumption of the agents and the production of the firms. In most of this chapter (until section 6.6B) we consider only one production set Y. To a consumption allocation $(x_i)_{i \in S}$ is implicitly associated the production plan $\sum_{i \in S}(x_i - w_i)$. The consumption allocation $(x_i)_{i \in S}$ is feasible for the coalition S if the production plan $\sum_{i \in S}(x_i - w_i)$ belongs to Y.

DEFINITION. *A consumption allocation $x = (x_1, \ldots, x_n) \in \mathbb{R}_+^{Hn}$ is blocked by the coalition S if there exists an allocation $(x_i')_{i \in S} \in A(S)$ such that $u_i(x_i') \geq u_i(x_i), \forall i \in S$ with at least one strict inequality.*

DEFINITION. *A consumption allocation $x = (x_1, \ldots, x_n) \in \mathbb{R}_+^{Hn}$ is in the core of the economy $\mathcal{E}$ if:*

- *it is feasible: $x \in A(N)$*

- *it is not blocked by any coalition.*

Note that if $Y = \mathbb{R}_-^H$, the core of the economy $\mathcal{E}$ is just the core of the exchange economy $\mathcal{E}(N, (u_i, w_i)_{i \in N})$.

The result obtained by Scarf (1963) is the following.

THEOREM 6.2. *Let $Y \subset \mathbb{R}^H$ be a production set with the following properties:*

P.1 Y is closed

P.2 $0 \in Y$

P.3 $y \in Y \implies y - \mathbb{R}_+^H \subset Y$

P.4 $w + Y \cap \mathbb{R}_+^H$ is compact, $\forall w \in \mathbb{R}_+^H$.

Consider the set of economies $\mathcal{E}(N, (u_i, w_i)_{i \in N}, Y)$ such that $N = \{1, \ldots, n\}$ *for some positive integer n, u_i is continuous and quasi-concave on $\mathbb{R}_+^H$ and $w_i \in \mathbb{R}_{++}^H$ for all $i \in N$. The core of every such economy is non-empty if and only if Y is a convex cone.*

Proof: If Y is a convex cone, the economies $\mathcal{E}(N, (u_i, w_i)_{i \in N}, Y)$ have a competitive equilibrium: it is immediate that this equilibrium is in the core.

Let us prove the converse: if all the economies satisfying the stated conditions have a non-empty core, then Y must be a convex cone. Since the proof of this property is long, we break it into the following four lemmas.

LEMMA 6.3. *Let $\mathcal{E}(N, (u_i, w_i)_{i \in N}, Y)$ be an economy in which all agents have the same utility function $u : \mathbf{R}_+^H \longrightarrow \mathbf{R}$ $(u_i = u, \forall i \in N)$, which is continuous, concave, weakly monotonic and homogeneous of degree 1. The core of this economy is non-empty if and only if the game (N, v) where v is defined by*

$$v(S) = \max\{u(x) | x \geq 0, \ x - \sum_{i \in S} w_i \in Y\}$$

has a non-empty core.

LEMMA 6.4. *Let $f : \mathbf{R}_+^H \longrightarrow \mathbf{R}$ be a continuous function. Consider the set of games V_f such that: $(N, v) \in V_f \Longleftrightarrow \exists w = (w_i)_{i \in N} \in \mathbf{R}_+^{Hn}$, $v(S) = f(\sum_{i \in S} w_i)$. All the games of V_f have a non-empty core if and only if the function f has the following property:*

(D) $\forall w \in \mathbf{R}_+^H, \exists \pi \in \mathbf{R}_+^H$ *such that*

$$\pi \cdot w = f(w)$$
$$\pi \cdot w' \leq f(w'), \ \forall w', \ 0 \leq w' \leq w$$

LEMMA 6.5. *A function $f \colon \mathbf{R}_+^H \longrightarrow \mathbf{R}$ satisfies property (D) if and only if it satisfies property (D'):*

(D') *For all finite sequences $(w_i)_{i=1,\ldots,n} \in \mathbf{R}_+^{Hn}$ and $(\alpha_i)_{i=1,\ldots,n} \in \mathbf{R}_+^n$*

$$\sum_{i=1}^n \alpha_i w_i \geq w_j, \ \forall j = 1, \ldots, n \Longrightarrow f(\sum_{i=1}^n \alpha_i w_i) \geq \sum_{i=1}^n \alpha_i f(w_i)$$

LEMMA 6.6. *Let Y be a production set having properties P.1 to P.4 in Theorem 6.2. To every utility function $u : \mathbf{R}_+^H \longrightarrow \mathbf{R}$ associate the function $f_u : \mathbf{R}_+^H \longrightarrow \mathbf{R}$ defined by*

$$f_u(w) = \max\{u(x) | x \geq 0, \ x - w \in Y\}$$

f_u satisfies the properties (D) and (D') for all $u : \mathbf{R}_+^H \longrightarrow \mathbf{R}$ continuous, concave, weakly monotonic and homogeneous of degree 1 if and only if Y is a convex cone.

Lemmas 6.3 to 6.6 prove Theorem 6.2. If all the economies associated with Y have a non-empty core, it must be true in particular for economies in which all agents have the same preferences represented by a continuous, concave, weakly monotonic and linear homogeneous function u. By the Lemmas 6.3 and 6.4, the function f_u must satisfy the equivalent properties (D) and (D') which, by Lemma 6.6, is possible if and only if Y is a convex cone.

$\triangledown$

It remains to prove the lemmas.

Proof of Lemma 6.3:

a) Let $\mathcal{E}(N, (u_i, w_i)_{i \in N}, Y)$ be an economy such that $u_i = u$, $\forall i \in N$, where u is continuous, concave, weakly monotonic and homogeneous of degree 1. Suppose that there exists an allocation $x = (x_i)_{i \in N}$ in the core of economy $\mathcal{E}$. Let $\alpha_i = u(x_i)$.
  We show that $(\alpha_i)_{i \in N}$ is an imputation of the core of v, that is,

$$\sum_{i \in S} \alpha_i \geq v(S) \quad \forall S \subset N$$

$$\sum_{i=1}^{n} \alpha_i = v(N)$$

Suppose there exists a coalition S such that $\sum_{i \in S} \alpha_i < v(S)$. This implies that there exists $\bar{x} \in \mathbb{R}_+^{H-1}$ such that

$$\bar{x} - \sum_{i \in S} w_i \in Y \text{ and } u(\bar{x}) > \sum_{i \in S} \alpha_i$$

In particular, each α_i is inferior to $u(\bar{x})$ and, therefore,

$$\exists \lambda_i, \ 0 \leq \lambda_i \leq 1 \text{ such that}$$

$$\alpha_i = u(\lambda_i \bar{x}), \quad \forall i \in S$$

$$\sum_{i \in S} \alpha_i = \sum_{i \in S} u(\lambda_i \bar{x}) = \sum_{i \in S} \lambda_i u(\bar{x}) < u(\bar{x})$$

Therefore, $\sum_{i \in S} \lambda_i < 1$. For ϵ sufficiently small, the allocation $x'_i = (\lambda_i + \epsilon)\bar{x}$ is feasible for the coalition S and

$$u(x'_i) = u\big((\lambda_i + \epsilon)\bar{x}\big) > u(\lambda_i \bar{x}) = \alpha_i = u(x_i)$$

Thus, S blocks the allocation x, which contradicts the initial assumption.

Therefore, we have

$$\sum_{i \in S} \alpha_i \geq v(S) \quad \forall S \subset N$$

This inequality is true in particular for $S = N$. But since x is feasible,

$$\sum_{i=1}^{n} x_i - \sum_{i=1}^{n} w_i \in Y$$

and, thus, $v(N) \geq u(\sum_{i=1}^{n} x_i)$.

The properties of u lead to the inequality

$$u(\sum_{i=1}^{n} x_i) \geq \sum_{i=1}^{n} u(x_i) = \sum_{i=1}^{n} \alpha_i$$

Therefore, $\sum_{i=1}^{n} \alpha_i = v(N)$.

b) Conversely, suppose that v has a non-empty core. There exist α_i such that

$$\sum_{i=1}^{n} \alpha_i = v(N),$$

$$\sum_{i \in S} \alpha_i \geq v(S), \quad \forall S \subset N$$

Let $\bar{x}$ be a consumption allocation such that $\bar{x} - \sum_{i=1}^{n} w_i \in Y$ and $v(N) = u(\bar{x})$. Let $\lambda_i \geq 0$ such that $u(\lambda_i \bar{x}) = \alpha_i$, $\forall i \in N$. Define $x_i = \lambda_i \bar{x}$. Let us show that $(x_i)_{i \in N}$ is in the core of $\mathcal{E}$. This allocation is feasible since $\sum_{i=1}^{n} \lambda_i = 1$. In fact,

$$\sum_{i=1}^{n} \alpha_i = v(N) = u(\bar{x}) \iff \sum_{i=1}^{n} u(\lambda_i \bar{x}) = u(\bar{x}) \iff \sum_{i=1}^{n} \lambda_i u(\bar{x}) = u(\bar{x})$$

If x was blocked by a coalition S there would exist $(x'_i)_{i \in S}$ such that $\sum_{i \in S} x'_i - \sum_{i \in S} w_i \in Y$ and $u(x'_i) \geq u(x_i)$, $\forall i \in N$, with at least one strict inequality. Therefore, it would be true that

$$v(S) \geq u(\sum_{i \in S} x'_i) \geq \sum_{i \in S} u(x'_i) > \sum_{i \in S} u(x_i) = \sum_{i \in S} \alpha_i$$

which contradicts the inequality $v(S) \leq \sum_{i \in S} \alpha_i$.

$$\triangledown$$

Proof of Lemma 6.4:

a) Let us show that if f satisfies property D, every game of V_f has a non-empty core. Consider any positive integer n. Let $N = [1, \ldots, n]$ and let $(w_i)_{i \in N}$ be a vector in $\mathbb{R}_+^{Hn}$ with $w = \sum_{i=1}^n w_i$. Let π be a vector in $\mathbb{R}_+^H$ such that

$$\pi \cdot \sum_{i=1}^n w_i = f(\sum_{i=1}^n w_i)$$
$$\pi \cdot w' \geq f(w'), \quad \forall w', \quad 0 \leq w' \leq w$$

Define $\alpha_i = \pi \cdot w_i$. Clearly, the vector $(\alpha_i)_{i \in N}$ is in the core of the game (N, v) defined by

$$v(S) = f(\sum_{i \in S} w_i)$$

b) Conversely, suppose that the core of all the games of V_f is non-empty. Let w be a vector in $\mathbb{R}_+^H$ and $(a_i)_{i=1,\ldots,n}$ a family of vectors such that

$$\sum_{i=1}^n a_i = w.$$

For every integer $r > 0$, consider a game with $2^r \times n$ players who are of n different types with 2^r players of each type. Define N_r as the set of these players. The players of N_r are identified by the double index (i, j) where i refers to the type $(i \in [1, \ldots, n])$ and j refers to a particular player of this type $(j \in (1, \ldots, 2^r))$. Player (i, j) has resources $w_{ij} = a_i / 2^r$. Thus, each player of the same type has the same resources and $\sum_{i,j} w_{ij} = w$. Since the game (N_r, v_r) defined by

$$v_r(S) = f(\sum_{(i,j) \in S} w_{ij}), \quad \forall S \subset N_r$$

has a non-empty core, there exist (α_{ij}) such that

$$\sum_{\substack{j=1,\ldots,2^r \\ i=1,\ldots,n}} \alpha_{ij} = f(w)$$

$$\sum_{(i,j) \in S} \alpha_{ij} \geq f(\sum_{(i,j) \in S} w_{ij})$$

Without loss of generality, we can assume that the agents are numbered so that

$$\alpha_{i1} \leq \alpha_{i2} \leq \ldots \leq \alpha_{i2^r}, \quad \forall i = 1, \ldots, n$$

Define $\delta_i = \sum_{j=1}^{2^r} \alpha_{ij}$ and for all n-tuples of integers $(k_1, \ldots, k_n)$ such that $0 \leq k_i \leq 2^r$, consider the coalition S formed by the first k_i agents of type i. We have

$$\sum_{i=1}^{n} k_i \frac{\delta_i}{2^r} \geq \sum_{(i,j) \in S} \alpha_{ij} \geq f(\sum_{i=1}^{n} \frac{k_i a_i}{2^r})$$

Therefore, for every integer r, the set A_r of vectors $\delta = (\delta_1, \ldots, \delta_n)$ satisfying

$$\begin{cases} \sum_{i=1}^{n} \delta_i = f(w) \\ \sum_{i=1}^{n} \frac{k_i \delta_i}{2^r} \geq f(\sum_{i=1}^{n} \frac{k_i a_i}{2^r}) \qquad \forall (k_i)_{i=1,\ldots,n} \quad 0 \leq k_i \leq 2^r \end{cases}$$

is non-empty.

The sets A_r are closed and it can easily be shown that A_r contains A_{r+1}. Therefore, we have a nested family of closed sets in $\mathbb{R}_+^H$ which have a non-empty intersection.

Let $\delta \in \bigcap_{r \in \mathbb{N}} A_r$. Then δ satisfies

$$\begin{cases} \sum_{i=1}^{n} \delta_i = f(w) \\ \sum_{i=1}^{n} \frac{k_i \delta_i}{2^r} \geq f(\sum_{i=1}^{n} \frac{k_i a_i}{2^r}) \qquad \forall r, \quad \forall (k_i)_{i=1,\ldots,n} \quad 0 \leq k_i \leq 2^r \end{cases}$$

The diadic numbers being dense in $[0,1]$ and f being continuous, in the limit, we have

$$\sum_{i=1}^{n} \theta_i \delta_i \geq f(\sum_{i=1}^{n} \theta_i a_i), \quad \forall (\theta_i)_{i=1,\ldots,n}, \quad 0 \leq \theta_i \leq 1$$

To see that the existence of δ implies property (D) for f, take $n = H$, $a_1 = (w_1, 0, \ldots, 0) \in \mathbb{R}_+^H, \ldots, a_H = (0, \ldots, 0, w_H)$. It is easy to see from the construction of δ that if a coordinate w_i is zero for some $i \in [1, \ldots, H]$, then $\delta_i = 0$. Let $\pi \in \mathbb{R}_+^H$ be defined by

$$\pi_i = \begin{cases} \dfrac{\delta^i}{w_i} & \text{if } w_i > 0 \quad i = 1, \ldots, H \\ 0 & \text{if } w_i = 0 \end{cases}$$

Then π satisfies

$$\pi \cdot w = f(w)$$

$$\pi \cdot w' \geq f(w'), \quad \forall w' \in \mathbb{R}_+^H, \quad 0 \leq w' \leq w$$

▽

Proof of Lemma 6.5:

a) Let us show that if a function f satisfies property (D), then it satisfies property (D'). Let $(w_i)_{i=1,\dots,n}$ be a finite set of vectors in $\mathbb{R}_+^H$ and $(\alpha_i)_{i=1,\dots,n}$ a finite set of positive coefficients such that $w = \sum_{i=1}^n \alpha_i w_i$ satisfies $w \geq w_i, \ \forall i = 1,\dots,n$. Since f satisfies (D), there exists a vector $\pi \in \mathbb{R}_+^H$ such that

$$\pi \cdot w = f(w) \quad \text{and} \quad \pi \cdot w_i \geq f(w_i), \quad \forall i = 1,\dots,n$$

Therefore,

$$f(w) = f(\sum_{i=1}^n \alpha_i w_i) = \pi \cdot (\sum_{i=1}^n \alpha_i w_i) \geq \sum_{i=1}^n \alpha_i f(w_i)$$

b) Conversely, let f be a function satisfying (D'). Let $w \in \mathbb{R}_+^H$. If some components of w are zero define the function $\tilde{f}$ from $\mathbb{R}^{H'}$ to $\mathbb{R}$ as follows: $w' \longrightarrow \tilde{f}(w') = f(w',0)$ where $w' \in \mathbb{R}^{H'}$ and $H' = \{i \mid w_i > 0\}$. It is sufficient to show that the function $\tilde{f}$ which satisfies property (D') also satisfies (D). Therefore, without loss of generality, we restrict ourself to the case $w \in \mathbb{R}_{++}^H$.

Consider the convex cone T in $\mathbb{R}^{H+1}$ defined by

$$T = \left\{ (\sum_{i=1}^n \alpha_i w_i, \sum_{i=1}^n \alpha_i y_i) \ \middle| \ \begin{array}{ll} n \in \mathbb{N} & \alpha_i \in \mathbb{R}_+ \\[2mm] w_i \in \mathbb{R}_+^H & 0 \leq w_i \leq w \quad i = 1,\dots,n \\[2mm] y_i \in \mathbb{R} & y_i \leq f(w_i) \end{array} \right\}$$

Let us show that if f satisfies (D') and $y > f(w), (w,y)$ does not belong to T. If (w,y) belongs to T, then there exist vectors w_i satisfying $0 \leq w_i \leq w$ and coefficients $\alpha_i \geq 0$ and $y_i \leq f(w_i)$ such that $w = \sum_{i=1}^n \alpha_i w_i, \ y = \sum_{i=1}^n \alpha_i y_i.$ $y = \sum_i \alpha_i y_i$ implies $y \leq \sum_i \alpha_i f(w_i)$. $y > f(w)$ and (D') imply $y > f(\sum_i \alpha_i w_i) \geq \sum_i \alpha_i f(w_i)$ which contradicts the previous inequality. Therefore, $(w, f(w))$ belongs to the boundary of T and there exists a supporting hyperplane to T at this point. Thus, there exists a non-zero vector $(p, \mu) \in \mathbb{R}^{H+1}$ such that

$$p \cdot w' + \mu y' \geq p \cdot w + \mu f(w), \quad \forall (w', y') \in T$$

Since T is a cone,

$$p \cdot w + \mu f(w) = 0$$

Since y' can tend toward $-\infty$, $\mu \leq 0$ and since all components of w' can tend to $+\infty$, $p \geq 0$. If μ is zero, $p \cdot w = 0 \Longrightarrow p = 0$ which is impossible. Defining $\pi = p/\mu$, we have a non-null vector $\pi \in \mathbb{R}_+^H$ satisfying

$$f(w) = \pi \cdot w$$

$$\pi \cdot w' \geq f(w'), \quad \forall w' \ 0 \leq w' \leq w$$

$\triangledown$

Proof of Lemma 6.6:

a) Let us show that if Y is a convex cone, for every continuous, concave, weakly monotonic and linear homogeneous function u, the function f_u satisfies property (D').

Let $(w_i)_{i=1,\ldots,n}$ be a finite set of vectors of $\mathbb{R}_+^H$ and $(\alpha_i)_{i=1,\ldots,n}$ be a set of coefficients such that

$$\sum_{i=1}^{n} \alpha_i w_i \geq w_j \quad \forall j = 1, \ldots, n$$

For every i, define the vector $\bar{x}_i$ (which exists by P.4) such that $f_u(w_i) = u(\bar{x}_i)$. Since $\bar{x}_i - w_i \in Y$ for every i and since Y is a convex cone,

$$\sum_{i=1}^{n} \alpha_i \bar{x}_i - \sum_{i=1}^{n} \alpha_i w_i \in Y$$

Therefore,

$$f_u(\sum_{i=1}^{n} \alpha_i w_i) \geq u(\sum_{i=1}^{n} \alpha_i \bar{x}_i) \geq \sum_{i=1}^{n} \alpha_i u(\bar{x}_i)$$

which proves the result.

b) Conversely, suppose f_u satisfies conditions (D) and (D') for every function u satisfying the properties mentioned earlier. We shall prove that for every $\bar{y}$ belonging to the boundary of Y, there exists a vector $\pi \in \mathbb{R}_+^H$ such that

$$\pi \cdot \bar{y} = 0 \quad \text{and} \quad \pi \cdot y \leq 0, \ \forall y \in Y$$

From this, it will be easy to deduce that Y is a convex cone.

Consider a vector $\bar{y} \in \partial Y$ and a vector $w \in \mathbb{R}_+^H$ such that $w \gg 0$ and $\bar{y} + w \gg 0$. Define a utility function u by

$$u(x) = \min\left(\frac{x_1}{y_1 + w_1}, \ldots, \frac{x_H}{y_H + w_H}\right)$$

Since f_u satisfies (D), there exists a vector $\pi \in \mathbb{R}_+^H$ such that

$$f_u(w) = \pi \cdot w$$
$$f_u(w') \leq \pi \cdot w' \quad \text{for} \quad 0 \leq w' \leq w$$

Since $\bar{x} = \bar{y} + w$ satisfies $\bar{x} - w \in Y$, we have

$$f_u(w) \geq 1$$

If $f_u(w)$ is strictly greater than 1, it is possible to find a vector x such that $y = x - w \in Y$ and $x \gg \bar{x}$. This would imply $y \gg \bar{y}$, which is impossible since $\bar{y} \in \partial Y$.

Therefore, $f_u(w) = 1$ and $\pi \cdot w = 1$. Since $w \gg 0$ and $\bar{y} + w \gg 0$, there exists $\lambda > 0$ such that $\lambda(\bar{y} + w) \leq w$. Thus,

$$\pi \cdot \lambda(\bar{y} + w) \geq f_u\big(\lambda(\bar{y} + w)\big) \geq \lambda$$

where the last inequality comes from

$$\lambda(\bar{y} + w) - \lambda(\bar{y} + w) = 0 \in Y$$

Therefore, $\lambda(\pi \cdot \bar{y}) + \lambda \geq \lambda$ and $\pi \cdot \bar{y} \geq 0$. To obtain the reverse inequality, consider the vector

$$w' = (1 - \lambda)w - \lambda \bar{y}$$

$$0 \leq w' \leq w \iff 0 \leq (1 - \lambda)w - \lambda \bar{y} \leq w \iff \begin{cases} 0 \leq w - \lambda(w + \bar{y}) \\ -\lambda(w + \bar{y}) \leq 0 \end{cases}$$

The second inequality is satisfied for every $\lambda \geq 0$ and, since $w \gg 0$, the first inequality holds for λ sufficiently small. Thus, for λ sufficiently small,

$$\pi \cdot [(1 - \lambda)w - \lambda \bar{y}] \geq f_u[(1 - \lambda)w - \lambda \bar{y}] \geq 1 - \lambda$$

where the second inequality follows from

$$(1 - \lambda)(w + \bar{y}) - [(1 - \lambda)w - \lambda \bar{y}] = \bar{y} \in Y$$

Thus $(1 - \lambda)(\pi \cdot w) - \lambda \pi \cdot \bar{y} \geq 1 - \lambda$ which implies $\pi \cdot \bar{y} \leq 0$ (since $\pi \cdot w = 1$), so that $\pi \cdot \bar{y} = 0$.

Let $y \in Y$. If this vector satisfies

$$\frac{1}{2}(\bar{y} - w) \leq y \leq \frac{1}{2}(\bar{y} + w)$$

then $0 \leq 1/2(\bar{y} + w) - y \leq w$ and

$$\pi \cdot \left(\frac{1}{2}(\bar{y} + w) - y\right) \geq f[\frac{1}{2}(\bar{y} + w) - y] \geq \frac{1}{2}$$

which implies $\pi \cdot y \leq 0$.

Therefore, for every vector $w \gg 0$ satisfying $\bar{y} + w \gg 0$ there exists a vector π of $\mathbb{R}_+^H$ satisfying

$$\pi \cdot \bar{y} = 0 \quad \text{and}$$
$$\pi \cdot y \leq 0 \quad \text{for every } y \in Y \text{ satisfying } \frac{\bar{y} - w}{2} \leq y \leq \frac{\bar{y} + w}{2}$$

Consider a sequence of vectors (w^ν) such that $(w_h^\nu) \longrightarrow +\infty$, $\forall h = 1, \ldots, H$. To every vector w^ν of the sequence associate the non-empty set π_ν consisting of vectors π which satisfy the previous property for w^ν. Clearly, $\pi_{\nu+1} \subset \pi_\nu$. Thus, we have a nested family of closed sets of $\mathbb{R}_+^H$ whose intersection is non-empty. Therefore, there exists a vector $\pi \in \mathbb{R}_+^H$ such that

$$\pi \cdot \bar{y} = 0 \quad \text{and} \quad \pi \cdot y \leq 0 \quad \forall y \in Y$$

We can now show that Y is a convex cone. Let $(y_i)_{i=1,\ldots,n}$ be a finite set of vectors of Y, $(\alpha_i)_{i=1,\ldots,n}$ a finite set of positive coefficients and let $y = \sum_{i=1}^n \alpha_i y_i$. Since Y is closed and satisfies the assumption of free disposal, if y does not belong to Y then there exists $a > 0$ such that

$$y - ae \in \partial Y$$

where $e = (1, \ldots, 1)$ is the unit vector in $\mathbb{R}^H$. By earlier results, there exists a vector $\pi \in \mathbb{R}_+^H$ such that

$$\pi \cdot y_i \leq 0, \quad \forall i = 1, \ldots, n$$
$$\pi \cdot (y - ae) = 0$$

The last equality implies that $\pi \cdot y > 0$, while $\pi \cdot y_i \leq 0$, $\forall i = 1, \ldots, n$ imply that $\pi \cdot y \leq 0$. Thus, y belongs to Y so that Y is a convex cone.

$$\triangledown$$

6.4 One Input, One Output

The previous theorem can be expressed as follows: If Y is a production set with increasing returns which is not a convex cone, it is possible to find an economy, (i.e., a set of agents, preferences, and initial resources for the agents) whose core is empty. This theorem excludes all results of the type: if the returns to scale are "sufficiently" large, the core of every economy associated with Y is non-empty. A combination of assumptions on the production possibilities, the preferences of the agents, and the initial resources is required to obtain the existence of a core allocation.

The following example shows why it is impossible to obtain an existence result valid for any set of utility functions and any distribution of initial resources.

Example 6.1: Consider the following economy:

- there is one factor of production (denoted by x or z) and one output (denoted by y),

- the technology is described by the production function $y = f(z) = z^2$,

- there are three agents who consume positive amounts of the two goods. They have identical preferences represented by the utility function $u(x, y) = \min(x, y)$. The initial resources are: $w_1 = w_2 = (6, 0)$ for agents 1 and 2, $w_3 = (0, 6)$ for agent 3.

To show that the core of this economy is empty, it is enough to show by Lemma 6.3, that the game (N, v) has an empty core where

$$N = \{1, 2, 3\}$$

$$v(S) = \max\{\, \min(x, y) \mid y \le f(\textstyle\sum_{i \in S} w_i - x)\}, \quad \forall S \subset N$$

By Theorem 6.1, it is sufficient to show that this game is not balanced. Consider the balanced family $\{(1, 2), (1, 3), (2, 3)\}$ associated with the coefficients $(1/2, 1/2, 1/2)$. The coalition $(1,2)$ has initial resources $(12, 0)$. The maximum value of v is obtained by using 3 units of the input to equalize the quantities of the two goods. Thus

$$v(1, 2) = 9$$

Coalitions $(1,3)$ and $(2,3)$ own 6 units of each good. Therefore the maximum of v is achieved without production and

$$v(1, 3) = v(2, 3) = 6$$

Consider the coalition $\{1, 2, 3\}$. Its vector of resources is $(12, 6)$. In order to equalize the disposable quantity of each good, it needs to use x units of the input where x satisfies

$$12 - x = 6 + x^2$$

The solution to this equation is $x = 2$ and

$$v(1,2,3) = 10 < \frac{1}{2}(6+6+9) = 10.5$$

Therefore, $v(1,2,3) < 1/2\big(v(1,2) + v(1,3) + v(2,3)\big)$. The game is not balanced and, hence, the core is empty.

The basic idea behind this example is simple. The initial resources are such that the only coalition with two players which uses production is the coalition $(1, 2)$. This coalition, however, takes more advantage of the economies of scale than the grand coalition $(1,2,3)$. Thus, the emptiness of the core is caused by the presence in the initial resources of the good which can be produced with increasing returns to scale. The distribution of endowments is such that the coalition of all agents has no clear advantage over smaller coalitions. To translate the intuition that increasing returns in production gives an advantage to large coalitions, we must assume that the only initial resources are the factors of production. Scarf (1973) has shown that in a one-input one-output economy this assumption is sufficient to imply the existence of a core allocation.

THEOREM 6.7. *Let $\mathcal{E}(N, (u_i, w_i)_{i \in N}, Y)$ be an economy such that:*

- *$u_i : \mathbb{R}_+^2 \mapsto \mathbb{R}$ is a continuous function which is increasing in all its arguments $\forall i = 1, \ldots, N$*
- *$w_i = (a_i, 0)$, $a_i \geq 0$, $\forall i = 1, \ldots, N$*
- *$Y = \{(-z,y) \in \mathbb{R}^2 \mid z \geq 0, y \leq f(z)\}$ where f is a continuous function satisfying $f(0) = 0$ and $f(\lambda z) \geq \lambda f(z), \forall z \geq 0, \forall \lambda \geq 1$*

then the core of $\mathcal{E}$ is non-empty.

Proof: This proof is not Scarf's original proof but the proof given by Mas-Colell (1980). This latter proof is chosen because it is more intuitive and based on the geometry of the problem. The idea is to consider the properties of the following sets:

for $p \in \mathbb{R}_+$, define

$$B_i(p) = \{(x_i, y_i) \in \mathbb{R}^2 \mid 0 \leq x_i \leq a_i, y_i \geq 0, px_i + y_i \leq pa_i\}$$

$$A_i(p) = \{(x_i, y_i) \in \mathbb{R}_+^2 \mid u_i(x_i, y_i) \geq u_i(x_i', y_i'), \forall (x_i', y_i') \in B_i(p)\}$$

$$V_i(p) = A_i(p) - (a_i, 0)$$

These sets are shown in Figure 6.1. $V_i(p)$ is the set of net exchanges that give agent i a higher level of utility than any consumption satisfying

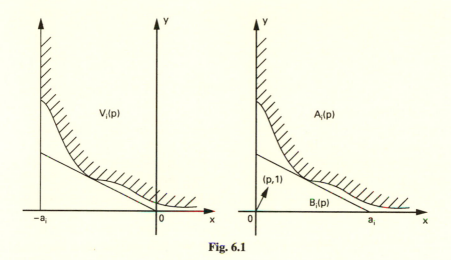

Fig. 6.1

his budget constraint at prices $(p, 1)$. Since u_i is monotonic and $B_i(p)$ is compact, $V_i(p)$ is never empty.

Let us show that every vector (z_i, y_i) of $V_i(p)$ satisfies the inequality

$$pz_i + y_i \geq 0$$

If $pz_i + y_i < 0$ with $z_i = x_i - a_i, x_i \geq 0, (x_i, y_i)$ would belong to the interior of $B_i(p)$ and it would be possible to find a consumption (x_i', y_i') in $B_i(p)$, such that $u_i(x_i', y_i') > u_i(x_i, y_i)$ which contradicts the definition of $V_i(p)$.

Define $V_S(p) = \sum_{i \in S} V_i(p)$ for $S \subset N$. Let us show that if there exists a price $p \geq 0$ such that $Y \cap V_N(p) \neq \emptyset$, and Int $Y \cap V_S(p) = \emptyset, \forall S \neq N$, then there exists an allocation in the core of the economy.

Suppose these conditions hold. Let $(z, y) \in Y \cap V_N(p)$. There exist $(x_i, y_i)_{i=1,\ldots,N} \in \mathbb{R}_+^{2n}$ such that

$$z = \sum_{i \in N} x_i - \sum_{i \in N} a_i \text{ and}$$

$$u_i(x_i, y_i) \geq u(x_i', y_i'), \; \forall(x_i', y_i') \in B_i(p), i = 1, \ldots, N$$

If $(x_i, y_i)_{i=1,\ldots,N}$ was not in the core of $\mathcal{E}$, there would exist a coalition S and consumptions $(\tilde{x}_i, \tilde{y}_i)_{i \in S}$ such that

$$\left(\sum_{i \in S} \tilde{x}_i - \sum_{i \in S} a_i, \sum_{i \in S} \tilde{y}_i \right) \in Y$$

and $u_i(\tilde{x}_i, \tilde{y}_i) \geq u_i(x_i, y_i), \forall i \in S$, with at least one strict inequality for an agent i_0. It would be possible to obtain a vector in Int $Y \cap V_S(p)$ by slightly reducing the components of $(\tilde{x}_{i_0}, \tilde{y}_{i_0})$. This contradicts the assumption that $\text{Int } Y \cap V_S(p) = \emptyset$.

Next, we show that for every $p \geq 0$,

$$V_S(p) \subset \bigcup_{0 \leq \lambda \leq 1} \lambda V_N(p), \quad \forall S \subset N$$

Define $V(p) = \bigcup_{0 \leq \lambda \leq 1} \lambda V_N(p)$. $V(p)$ is represented by the shaded region of Figure 6.2. Let (z, y) be in $V_S(p)$. Since $pz + y \geq 0$, for every $i \notin S$, there exists $\mu_i \geq 0$ such that $(\mu_i z, \mu_i y) \in V_i(p)$ (Figure 6.3). Therefore, $(1 + \sum_{i \notin S} \mu_i)(z, y) \in V_N(S)$ and $(z, y) \in \lambda V_N(S)$ with $\lambda = 1/(1 + \sum_{i \notin S} \mu_i)$.

Thus, the existence of an allocation in the core of the economy is implied by the existence of a price $p \geq 0$ such that

$$Y \bigcap V_N(p) \neq \emptyset \quad \text{and} \quad \text{Int } Y \bigcap V(p) = \emptyset$$

The assumption of increasing returns implies that if $\text{Int } Y \bigcap V_N(p) = \emptyset$ then $\text{Int } Y \bigcap V(p) = \emptyset$. Therefore, if there exists a price $p \geq 0$ such that $Y \bigcap V_N(p) \neq \emptyset$ and $\text{Int } Y \bigcap V_N(p) = \emptyset$, there exists an allocation in the core of the economy (Figure 6.4).

If $p = 0$, $Y \bigcap V_N(0) \neq \emptyset$ since $(0,0) \in V_N(0)$. If $p \mapsto \infty$, $Y \bigcap V_N(p) = \emptyset$ as soon as $p > f(\sum_{i=1}^n a_i)/\sum_{i=1}^n a_i$. Since $V_i(p)$ depends continuously on p (in the sense of the topology of closed convergence), by the intermediate value theorem, there exists $p \geq 0$ such that $Y \bigcap V_N(p) \neq \emptyset$ and $\text{Int } Y \bigcap V_N(p) = \emptyset$.

$$\triangledown$$

Theorem 6.7 gives conditions under which the intuition is correct that the grand coalition has an advantage over smaller coalitions because of the presence of increasing returns: it is true for a one-input one-output economy in which agents have initial resources of the input only. It is remarkable that no assumption of convexity of the preferences is needed to obtain the result of existence of the core.

We will see that as soon as there are two or more inputs or two or more outputs, the difficulty in obtaining an agreement among many agents on a common production plan can offset the gains due to economies of scale. Additional assumptions linking agents' preferences and production possibilities are necessary to obtain the existence of a core allocation.

6.5 Many Inputs, One Output

Let $\mathcal{E}(N, (u_i, w_i)_{i=1,\ldots,N}, Y)$ be an economy with n agents and $H = L + 1$ goods. The first L goods ($L > 1$) are inputs for the production of good

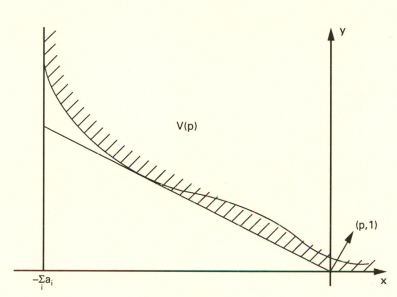

Fig. 6.2

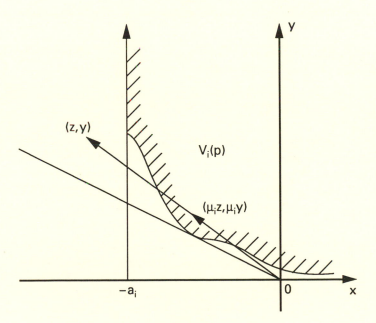

Fig. 6.3

121

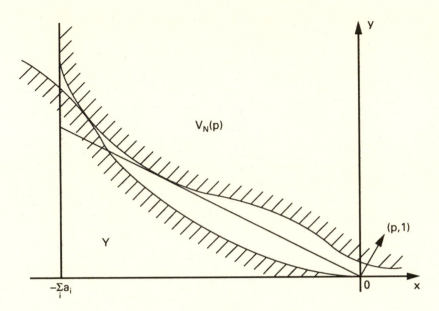

Fig. 6.4

$L + 1$. The production set Y lies in $\mathbb{R}^L_- \times \mathbb{R}$ and can be described by a production function $f : \mathbb{R}^L_+ \mapsto \mathbb{R}$:

$$Y = \{(-z, y) \in \mathbb{R}^L_- \times \mathbb{R} \mid y \leq f(z)\}$$

We first show that even if Y exhibits increasing returns and if the initial resources of the agents consist only of the inputs, the core of the economy may be empty. The conditions which are sufficient for the existence of a core allocation in the one input case are no longer sufficient in the many input case.

Example 6.2: The economy has three goods, three agents with identical utility functions $u(x_1, x_2, y) = \min(x_1, x_2, y)$ and initial resources

$$w_1 = (0, 3, 0) \text{ for agent 1}$$
$$w_2 = (3, 0, 0) \text{ for agent 2}$$
$$w_3 = (9, 9, 0) \text{ for agent 3}$$

These agents have access to the technology described by the production function

$$y = z_1^2 + z_2^2$$

By Lemma 6.3, the economy has a non-empty core if the game (N, v) with $N = \{1, 2, 3\}$ and

$$v(S) = \max \left\{ u(x_1, x_2, y) \;\middle|\; \begin{array}{l} y \le f(w_{S1} - x_1, w_{S2} - x_2) \\[4pt] 0 \le x_1 \le w_{S1} \\[4pt] 0 \le x_2 \le w_{S2} \end{array} \right\}$$

has a non-empty core (where $w_{Sl} = \sum_{i \in S} w_{il}$, $l = 1, 2$). The initial resources of the coalition (1,2) are (3,3,0). Therefore,

$$v(1, 2) = \max_{z_1, z_2} [\min(3 - z_1, 3 - z_2, z_1^2 + z_2^2)]$$

The maximum is attained at $z_1 = z_2$ and $3 - z_1 = 2z_1^2$, which implies $z_1 = 1$ and $v(1, 2) = 2$. The coalition $(1, 3)$ has initial resources $(9, 12, 0)$ and it can be easily verified that $v(1, 3) = 9$. Similarly, $v(2, 3) = 9$.

$$v(1, 2, 3) = \max(12 - z, 12 - z, 2z^2) = \frac{49 - \sqrt{97}}{4}$$

$$\sqrt{97} > 9 \Rightarrow v(1, 2, 3) < 10 = \frac{1}{2}[v(1, 2) + v(2, 3) + v(1, 3)]$$

Therefore, (N, v) is not balanced and has an empty core.

In this example, the distribution of inputs between agents is such that the coalitions (2,3) and (1,3) are the most efficient, given the common utility function of agents. The goods used as inputs by these coalitions would not bring them any utility otherwise. On the contrary, the factors used by the grand coalition for production are not "free." This situation could not occur if the inputs were not desired for consumption.

Inputs not consumed

It might seem that if agents initially own inputs which cannot be consumed directly but are used to produce a consumption good, the assumption of increasing returns should lead to the existence of an allocation in the core. The following example shows that even in this case, additional assumptions on the production function are necessary to imply non-emptiness of the core.

Example 6.3: Consider an economy with

- two inputs, goods 1 and 2.

- three possible ways of producing a third good (the output).

The first technique requires a fixed investment of one unit of each factor. Then the output can be produced with constant returns to scale, 5/14 units of each factor being necessary to produce one unit of output. The production function associated with this technology is

$$f_1(x_1, x_2) = \min\left(\frac{x_1 - 1}{5/14}, \frac{x_2 - 1}{5/14}\right) \text{ if } x_1 \geq 1, \ x_2 \geq 1$$

$$= 0 \text{ otherwise.}$$

The second technique requires a fixed investment of 3 units of the first factor. Then it takes 1/4 unit of each input to produce 1 unit of output. The associated production function is

$$f_2(x_1, x_2) = \min\left(\frac{x_1 - 3}{1/4}, \frac{x_2}{1/4}\right) \text{ if } x_1 \geq 3, \ x_2 \geq 0$$

$$= 0 \text{ otherwise.}$$

The third technique is similar to the second with the roles of the factors reversed. The associated production function is

$$f_3(x_1, x_2) = \min\left(\frac{x_1}{1/4}, \frac{x_2 - 3}{1/4}\right) \text{ if } x_1 \geq 0, \ x_2 \geq 3$$

$$= 0 \text{ otherwise.}$$

Any one of the three techniques may be used (it is of course inefficient to use two at a time). The production set Y of the economy is given by the production function

$$f(x_1, x_2) = \max\{f_1(x_1, x_2), f_2(x_1, x_2), f_3(x_1, x_2)\}$$

The consumption sector consists of three agents who own the factors and consume the output produced. The initial resources are given by: $w_1 = (3, 0, 0)$ for agent 1, $w_2 = (0, 3, 0)$ for agent 2, $w_3 = (3, 3, 0)$ for agent 3.

The coalition $\{1, 2\}$ has initial resources $(3,3,0)$. Therefore it uses the first technique and

$$v(1, 2) = 28/5$$

The coalition $\{1, 3\}$ has initial resources $(6,3)$. It can produce $2 \times 14/5$ units of the ouput using technique 1 and $4 \times 3 = 12$ units of ouput using technique 2. Therefore,

$$v(1, 3) = 12$$

By symmetry, $v(2, 3) = 12$.

The grand coalition has initial resources (6,6,0). Using technique 1, it obtains $5 \times 14/5 = 14$ units of output. Using technique 2 or 3, it obtains $3 \times 4 = 12$ units.

Thus,

$$v(1,2,3) = 14 < 1/2(v(1,2) + v(2,3) + v(1,3)) = 12 + 14/5$$

so that the core is empty.

The additional assumption on f needed to obtain the existence of a core allocation is the property (D) in Lemma 6.4. Since agents only consume the single output, they have the same utility function $u : \mathbf{R}_+^{L+1} \mapsto \mathbf{R}_+$, $u(x,y) = y$, $\forall x \in \mathbf{R}_+^L$, $\forall y \in \mathbf{R}^+$. Thus, Lemma 6.3 can be applied and we obtain the following result.

THEOREM 6.8. *Let $f : \mathbf{R}_+^L \mapsto \mathbf{R}_+$ be a continuous, monotonic production function. Let $\mathcal{E}_f$ be the set of economies with $L+1$ goods in which the agents consume only the good produced. Every economy of $\mathcal{E}_f$ has non-empty core if and only if the function f satisfies property (D):*

(D) *For all $z \in \mathbf{R}_+^L$, there exists $\pi \in \mathbf{R}_+^L$ such that $\pi \cdot z = f(z)$, $\pi \cdot z' \geq f(z')$, $\forall z' \in \mathbf{R}_+^L$, $0 \leq z' \leq z$.*

Proof: By Lemma 6.3, we know that all the economies of $\mathcal{E}_f$ have a non-empty core if all games (N, v) with $v(S) = \max\{u(x) \mid x \geq 0, \ x - \sum_{i \in S} w_i \in Y\}$ have a non-empty core. If we denote $w_i = (a_i, \bar{y}_i)$, $a_i \in \mathbf{R}_+^L, \bar{y}_i \in \mathbf{R}_+$, then

$$v(S) = \sum_{i \in S} \bar{y}_i + f\left(\sum_{i \in S} a_i\right)$$

It is easy to see that (N, v) has a non-empty core if and only if $(N, \tilde{v})$ with $\tilde{v}(S) = f(\sum_{i \in S} a_i)$ has a non-empty core. Lemma 6.2 then gives the result.

$\triangledown$

Remark: In this case, the existence of initial resources in output does not matter. It is easy to understand why: whatever the initial resources in the consumption good, each coalition is going to use all its inputs to produce since these goods have no other use. The emptiness or non-emptiness of the core depends only on the respective productivity of the grand coalition compared to the subcoalitions.

Example 6.3 shows one reason for which the core may be empty. In this example the technique of production fits better the composition of inputs

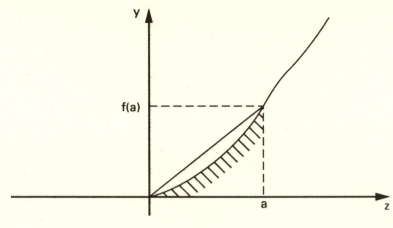

Fig. 6.5

of some coalitions than the composition of inputs of the total economy. If a production function satisfies property (D), the positive effect of an increase in the scale of production always offsets the (potentially) negative effect of a change in the composition of the inputs.

Following the terminology introduced by Scarf (1963, published 1986) we refer to a production function satisfying property (D) as a distributive function. Then Lemma 6.5 can be expressed as follows

THEOREM AND DEFINITION 6.9. *A continuous and weakly monotonic function* $f : \mathbb{R}_+^L \longrightarrow \mathbb{R}_+$ *is distributive if it satisfies one of the two equivalent properties:*

(D) *For all* $z \in \mathbb{R}_+^L$, *there exists* $\pi \in \mathbb{R}_+^L$, $\pi \neq 0$, *such that*
$$\pi \cdot z = f(z), \pi \cdot z' \geq f(z'), \forall z' \in \mathbb{R}_+^L, 0 \leq z' \leq z.$$

(D′) *For all* $(z_i \alpha_i)_{i=1,\ldots,r}$, $z_i \in \mathbb{R}_+^L$, $\alpha_i \in \mathbb{R}_+$
$$\sum_{i=1}^r \alpha_i z^i \geq z_j, j = 1, \ldots, r \Rightarrow f(\sum_{i=1}^r \alpha_i z_i) \geq \sum_{i=1}^r \alpha_i f(z_i).$$

The property (D) can be given a geometric interpretation: if f is a distributive function and $z \in \mathbb{R}_+^L$ is a vector of available factors, there exists a hyperplane passing through the origin and the point $(z, f(z))$ such that every production plan using fewer resources than z lies below this hyperplane. If f is distributive, Figure 6.5 can be generalized to the $L + 1$ dimensional space.

The property (D′) shows that a distributive production function becomes more efficient when larger quantities of inputs are used. If a combination $z = \sum_{i=1}^r \alpha_i z_i$ of r vectors of inputs $(z_1, \ldots, z_r)$ is such that z uses more of each input than any of the vectors $(z_1, \ldots, z_r)$, then it is more efficient to produce with z than to produce with the smaller input vectors (z_i) in the sense that

$$f(z) \geq \sum_{i=1}^{r} \alpha_i f(z_i)$$

In particular, property (D′) implies that a distributive function exhibits increasing returns to scale $(f(\alpha z) \geq \alpha f(z), \forall z \in \mathbb{R}_+^L, \forall \alpha \geq 1)$ and is superadditive $(f(z_1 + z_2) \geq f(z_1) + f(z_2), \forall z_1 \in \mathbb{R}_+^L, \forall z_2 \in \mathbb{R}_+^L)$.

The following theorem shows that the production functions commonly used in economic models with increasing returns are distributive.

THEOREM 6.10.

(i) *A continuous, quasi-concave, linear homogeneous function is distributive*

(ii) *A sum, product or minimum of distributive functions is a distributive function*

(iii) *If f is a distributive function and $\alpha \geq 1$, f^α is a distributive function.*

Proof: To prove (i), we can without loss of generality consider vectors $z_i \in \mathbb{R}_+^L$, $i = 1, \ldots, r$, such that $f(z_i) \neq 0$. It is then enough to note that

$$\frac{f(\sum_{i=1}^{r} \alpha_i z_i)}{\sum_{i=1}^{r} \alpha_i f(z_i)} = f\left(\sum_{j=1}^{r} \frac{\alpha_j f(z_j)}{\sum_{i=1}^{r} \alpha_i f(z_i)} \frac{z_j}{f(z_j)}\right) \geq \min_j f\left(\frac{z_j}{f(z_j)}\right) = 1$$

so that the property

$$f\left(\sum_{i=1}^{r} \alpha_i z_i\right) \geq \sum_{i=1}^{r} \alpha_i f(z_i)$$

holds for all $r \geq 0$, $z_i \in \mathbb{R}_+^L$, $\alpha_i \in \mathbb{R}$, $i = 1, \ldots, r$.

The proof of (ii) and (iii) is straightforward and left to the reader. $\triangledown$

The definition of a distributive function f ensures that for any vector of inputs z, there exist prices π for these inputs such that a firm whose technology in described by f breaks even at prices $(\pi, 1)$ with the production plan $(-z, f(z))$ and makes losses with any production using less input than z. It is thus possible to decentralize a core allocation by giving the firm an objective of profit maximization at the condition that the firm perceives a constraint on the total amount of available inputs. This is precisely described by the following theorem.

THEOREM 6.11. *Let $f : \mathbf{R}_+^L \mapsto \mathbf{R}$ be a distributive production function and let $(w_i)_{i=1,\ldots,n} \in \mathbf{R}^{L+1}$ be the initial resources of n agents who consume only the output. Denote $w_i = (a_i, \bar{y}_i)$ with $a_i \in \mathbf{R}_+^L$, $\bar{y}_i \in \mathbf{R}_+$. Let π be the price vector associated with f at the point $\sum_{i=1}^{n} a_i$. If $((y_i^*)_{i=1,\ldots,n}, y^*)$ is such that*

- $(0, y_i^*)$ *maximizes agent i's utility subject to budget constraint at prices $(\pi, 1)$,*

- $(\sum_{i=1}^{n} a_i, y^*)$ *maximizes, at prices $(\pi, 1)$, the profits of a firm producing the consumption good with the production function f over the set of productions which use at most $\sum_{i=1}^{n} a_i$ of inputs,*

then $\sum_{i=1}^{n} y_i^* = y^* + \sum_{i=1}^{n} \bar{y}_i$ and the consumption allocation $(0, y_i^*)_{i=1,\ldots,n}$ is in the core of the economy.

Proof: Let $\pi \in \mathbf{R}_+^L$ be a price vector for inputs such that $\pi \cdot \sum_{i=1}^{n} a_i = f(\sum_{i=1}^{n} a_i)$, $\pi \cdot a' \geq f(a')$, $\forall a' : 0 \leq a' \leq \sum_{i=1}^{n} a_i$. It is immediate that a firm maximizing profit under the constraint that the inputs do not exceed $\sum_{i=1}^{n} a_i$ will choose the production level $y^* = f(\sum_{i=1}^{n} a_i)$ at the prices $(\pi, 1)$. On the other hand, the revenue of an agent i at the prices $(\pi, 1)$ is $\pi a_i + \bar{y}_i$ so that agent i's demand for the consumption good is $y_i^* = \pi a_i + \bar{y}_i$. The allocation $\{(0, y_i^*)_{i=1,\ldots,n}, (-\sum_{i=1}^{n} a_i, y^*)\}$ is feasible since

$$\sum_{i=1}^{n} y_i^* = \pi. \sum_{i=1}^{n} a_i + \sum_{i=1}^{n} \bar{y}_i = y^* + \sum_{i=1}^{n} \bar{y}_i$$

The consumption allocation $(0, y_i^*)_{i=1,\ldots,n}$ is in the core of the economy since

$$\sum_{i \in S} y_i^* = \pi. \sum_{i \in S} a_i + \sum_{i \in S} \bar{y}_i \geq f(\sum_{i \in S} a_i) + \sum_{i \in S} \bar{y}_i$$

so that no coalition S can improve on the allocation.

$$\triangledown$$

Thus, in an economy with only one consumption good produced from privately owned factors with a distributive production function, it is possible to obtain an allocation in the core of the economy in a decentralized manner: a single firm produces the output and private agents sell their factors to this firm at price π. The firm maximizes its profit given the maximum amount of factors available in the economy. With a well-chosen price π for the inputs it is optimal for the firm to use all the disposable factors and its production corresponds exactly to the demands of the agents.[1]

Inputs consumed

The assumption that inputs have no use for consumption is very restrictive, especially for the important class of inputs composed of the labor inputs provided by agents in the economy. Assuming that these inputs have no use in consumption is equivalent to assuming no disutility for work, which is not especially realistic. So we are going to study the more complex case where the same goods can be used for consumption and as factors of production, still keeping the simplifying assumption that there is only one output. From the one-input one-output case we know that a necessary condition for the non-emptiness of the core is that agents have no initial resources in the output. Example 6.2 has shown that this condition is not sufficient. This example is constructed with the production function $y = z_1^2 + z_2^2$. This function, although it is distributive (as a sum of distributive functions), has a "bad" property: its input requirement sets are not convex since the sets $S_Y(y) = \{(z_1, z_2) \in \mathbb{R}_+^2 \mid z_1^2 + z_2^2 \geq y\}$ are non-convex for all $y > 0$.

We have seen in chapter 2 that the economies associated with such production sets have unintuitive properties when the inputs enter the preferences of the agents (for example, efficiency does not always require minimization of costs). One might think that the counterexample 6.2 to the existence of a core allocation is due to the unfortunate choice of the production function and that Theorem 6.3 on non-emptiness of the core for the one-input one-output economies extends to the multi-input case with the following assumptions:

- convexity and monotonicity of preferences,

- increasing returns to scale and convex input requirement sets for the technology,

- no initial resources of the output.

The only existence theorem which exists for this case (Quinzii 1982) is made under the assumptions of Theorem 4.2., which are stronger that the conditions just stated. But since we have seen in section 4.4 that these assumptions hold for nearly all Cobb-Douglas-CES economies, it is difficult to construct a counterexample of an economy with nice preferences and production sets for which the core is empty. We conjecture, however, that an assumption ensuring the compatibility of the consumption sector with the production sector is needed to ensure the existence of a core allocation.

Recall that an economy $\mathcal{E}(N, (u_i, w_i)_{i \in N}, Y)$ satisfies the assumptions of Theorem 4.2 if

- $Y = \{(-z, y)) \in \mathbb{R}_-^L \times \mathbb{R} \mid y \leq f(z)\}$ where f is continuous, monotonic on $\mathbb{R}_+^{L+1}$, satisfies $f(0) = 0$ and is such that the sections

$$S_Y(y) = \{z \in \mathbb{R}_+^L \mid y \leq f(z)\}$$

are strictly convex for $y > 0$. f is C^∞ on $\bigcup_{y>0} S_Y(y)$ with a non-zero gaussian curvature. (There may be a fixed cost.)

The cost function

$$c(p, y) = \inf\{p \cdot z \mid z \in S_Y(y)\}$$

is then continuous on $\Delta_{L-1} \times \mathbb{R}_{++}$ and C^∞ for $p \gg 0$ and $y > 0$. The input combination which minimizes the cost of producing $y > 0$, $z(p, y)$, is the unique solution to the first order conditions of the problem of cost minimization.

- $N = \{1, \ldots, n\}$
- For all $i = 1, \ldots, n$, $u_i : \mathbb{R}_+^{L+1} \mapsto \mathbb{R}$ is continuous, strictly quasi-concave monotonic on $\mathbb{R}_+^{L+1}$. It is zero on the boundary of $\mathbb{R}_+^{L+1}$ and C^∞ on $\mathbb{R}_{++}^{L+1}$. This implies that for a utility level of $v_i > 0$, the compensated demand $(\tilde{x}_i(p, \theta, v_i), \tilde{y}_i(p, \theta, v_i))$ is differentiable with respect to (p, θ) for $(p, \theta) \gg 0$.
- For all $i = 1, \ldots, n$ $w_i \in \mathbb{R}_+^L \times \{0\}$ (no initial resources in output).
- $(w + Y) \cap \mathbb{R}_+^{L+1}$ is compact with a non-empty interior.
- In addition to these assumptions of regularity, one of the two conditions hold: for all $p \gg 0$, $\theta > 0$, $v \in \rho(A)$.

(i) $c''(p, y) \mid_{y = \tilde{y}(p, \theta, v)} \times \dfrac{\partial \tilde{y}}{\partial \theta}(p, \theta, v) < 1$

(ii) $e(p, y) \mid_{y = \tilde{y}(p, \theta, v)} \times \epsilon(p, \theta, v) < 1$

where $\rho(A)$ denotes the set of Pareto optimal utility vectors, e the elasticity of the marginal cost of production with respect to the level of output y and ϵ the elasticity of the total compensated demand for output $\tilde{y}(p, \theta, v)$ with respect to the output price θ. If we add the assumption that the production set Y exhibits increasing returns, then we can prove that the core of the economy $\mathcal{E}$ is non-empty.

THEOREM 6.12. *The core of an economy* $\mathcal{E}\big(N, (u_i, w_i)_{i \in N}, Y\big)$ *satisfying the assumptions of Theorem 4.2 and such that* Y *exhibits increasing returns to scale is non-empty.*

Proof: For clarity of exposition the proof is presented under the form of a series of lemmas. The proof of the lemmas are given later. The notation is the same as in section 4.4.

The proof uses a dual approach. Instead of working with the set $A(S)$ of assumption allocations which are feasible for a coalition given its initial resources and the associated utility levels, we consider the cost that a coalition S must incur to guarantee a given vector of utilities to its members.

For $p \in \Delta_{L-1}$, $v \in \mathbb{R}^n_+$, define the cost of the imputation v for a coalition S by

$$\varphi(p, v, S) = \inf\{p \cdot \sum_{i \in S} x_i + c(p, \sum_{i \in S} y_i) \mid u_i(x_i, y_i) \geq v_i, \ \forall i \in S\}$$

The proof of Theorem 6.12 is based on the following two lemmas.

LEMMA 6.13. *Let $v_i = u_i(x_i, y_i)$ for $i = 1, \ldots, n$. If $(x_i, y_i)_{i \in N}$ is a consumption allocation blocked by a coalition S,*

$$\varphi(p, v, S) < p \cdot \sum_{i \in S} w_i, \ \forall p \in \Delta_{L-1}$$

LEMMA 6.14. *For every $p \in \Delta_{L-1}$, $v \in \mathbb{R}^n_+$, the game (N, V) defined by*

$$V(S) = -\varphi(p, v, S)$$

is balanced.

Lemma 6.13 is fairly obvious but it has the following consequence: if there exist consumptions $(x_i, y_i)_{i \in N}$ associated with a vector of utilities $v = (v_i)_{i \in N}$ such that:

- the consumption allocation is feasible in the economy,
- $\exists p \in \Delta_{L-1}$, $\varphi(p, v, S) \geq p \sum_{i \in S} w_i$, $\forall S \subset N$,

then this allocation is in the core of the economy.

By Lemma 6.14, for all $p \in \Delta_{L-1}, v \in \mathbb{R}^n_+$, there exist $(\beta_i(p, v))_{i \in N}$ such that:

- $\sum_{i \in S} \beta_i(p, v) \leq \varphi(p, v, S)$, $\forall S \subset N$
- $\sum_{i \in S} \beta_i(p, v) = \varphi(p, v, N)$.

Therefore, if there exists an allocation $(x_i, y_i)_{i \in N}$ associated with the utility levels $(v_i)_{i \in N}$ and a price $p \gg 0$ such that:

- $(x_i, y_i)_{i \in N}$ is feasible,
- $\beta_i(p, v) = p \cdot w_i$, $\forall i = 1, \ldots, n$,

then this allocation is in the core of the economy.

The last equality just means that the numbers $(-p \cdot w_i)_{i \in N}$ are in the core of the game $-\varphi(p, v, \cdot)$. (The negative sign comes from the fact that

φ is a cost and not a gain to the coalition S.) The proof is completed by the following lemma.

LEMMA 6.15. *There exists a Pareto optimal consumption allocation* $(x_i^*, y_i^*)_{i \in N}$ *corresponding to the utility levels* $(v_i^*)_{i \in N}$ *such that if* (p^*, θ^*) *is the price of support of this allocation,* $(-p^* \cdot w_i)_{i \in N}$ *is in the core of the game* $-\varphi(p^*, v^*, \cdot)$.

$$\triangledown$$

It remains to prove the lemmas.

Proof of Lemma 6.13: Suppose that an allocation $(x_i, y_i)_{i \in N}$ is blocked by a coalition S. There exists an allocation $(x_i', y_i')_{i \in S}$ feasible for S such that $u_i(x_i', y_i') \geq u_i(x_i, y_i)$, $\forall i \in S$, with strict inequality for some $i_0 \in S$. Let $v_i = u_i(x_i, y_i)$. Let $(x_i', y_i')_{i \in S}$ is feasible for S

$$\left(\sum_{i \in S} x_i' - \sum_{i \in S} w_i, \sum_{i \in S} y_i' \right) \in Y$$

and therefore,

$$c\left(p, \sum_{i \in S} y_i'\right) \leq p \cdot \left(\sum_{i \in S} w_i - \sum_{i \in S} x_i' \right), \ \forall p \in \Delta_{L-1}$$

Since $u_{i_0}(x_{i_0}', y_{i_0}') > v_{i_0} \geq 0$, $x_{i_0} \gg 0$. By continuity of u_{i_0}, it is possible to reduce each component of x_{i_0}' and still have a consumption strictly preferred to (x_{i_0}, y_{i_0}). Therefore, for ϵ sufficiently small the allocation

$$(x_i'', y_i'') = (x_i', y_i') \ i \in S, \ i \neq i_0, \ (x_{i_0}'', y_{i_0}'') = (x_{i_0}' - \epsilon e, y_{i_0}')$$

(where e is the unit vector of $\mathbb{R}^L$) gives a utility level of at least $(v_i)_{i \in S}$ and

$$p \cdot \sum_{i \in S} x_i'' + c\left(p, \sum_{i \in S} y_i''\right) < p \cdot \sum_{i \in S} x_i' + c\left(p, \sum_{i \in S} y_i'\right) \leq p \cdot \sum_{i \in S} w_i$$

Therefore,

$$\varphi(p, v, S) < p \cdot \sum_{i \in S} w_i$$

$$\triangledown$$

Proof of Lemma 6.14: (This proof is adapted from Scarf 1973.) Let $\mathcal{B} = (S_r)_{\mathbb{R}}$ be a balanced family of subsets of $N = \{1, \dots, n\}$ associated with weights $(\delta_r)_{\mathbb{R}}$. Let $p \in \Delta_{L-1}$ and $v \in \mathbb{R}_+^n$. We want to show that

$$\sum_{r=1}^{R} \delta_r \varphi(p, v, S_r) \geq \varphi(p, v, N)$$

Let us assume without loss of generality that $v_i > 0, \forall i \in \{1, \ldots, n\}$. If there exists a set of players I_0 with $v_i = 0$, $i \in I_0$, I_0 can be eliminated from the set of players without altering anything.

Define

$$U(S_r) = \{(x_i, y_i)_{i \in S_r} \mid u_i(x_i, y_i) \geq v_i, \quad \forall i \in S_r\}$$

If one of these sets is empty, $\varphi(p, v, S_r) = +\infty$, $\varphi(p, v, N) = +\infty$ and both sides of the inequality are equal to $+\infty$. If none of these sets is empty, choose for $\epsilon > 0$ and $r = 1, \ldots, R$ an allocation $(x_i^r, y_i^r)_{i \in S_r}$ of $U(S_r)$ such that

$$p \cdot \sum_{i \in S_r} x_i + c(p \cdot \sum_{i \in S_r} y_i^r) \leq \varphi(p, v, S_r) + \epsilon$$

and define

$$a(S_r) = \frac{c(p, \sum\limits_{i \in S_r} y_i^r)}{\sum\limits_{i \in S_r} y_i^r}$$

The numbering of the sets $(S_r)_\mathbf{R}$ can be assumed to be such that

$$a(S_1) \leq a(S_2) \leq \ldots \leq a(S_R)$$

Let us show that we can also assume that there exists an index r_0 such that

$$\delta_1 + \delta_2 + \ldots + \delta_{r_0} = 1$$

Since the family $\mathcal{B}$ is balanced, $\delta_1 \leq 1$ and $\delta_1 + \ldots + \delta_R \geq 1$. If $\delta_1 < 1$, there exists an index $r_0 > 1$ such that

$$\delta_1 + \ldots + \delta_{r_0 - 1} < 1$$
$$\delta_1 + \ldots + \delta_{r_0} \geq 1$$

If the second inequality is strict, we can replace $\mathcal{B}$ by the balanced family derived from $\mathcal{B}$ by counting the set S_{r_0} twice, first associated with the weight δ'_{r_0} such that $\delta_1 + \ldots + \delta_{r_0 - 1} + \delta'_{r_0} = 1$ and then associated with δ''_{r_0} such that $\delta'_{r_0} + \delta''_{r_0} = \delta_{r_0}$.

Define

$$\mathcal{S} = \{S_r \in \mathcal{B} \mid 1 \leq r \leq r_0\}, \quad \mathcal{T} = \{S_r \in \mathcal{B} \mid r > r_0\}$$

Consider the random allocation constructed as follows: first select a set S_r of $\mathcal{S}$ with probability δ_r. Allocate (x_i^r, y_i^r) to the agents of S_r. Draw independently for every agent i who does not belong to S_r a set S_s from the sets of $\mathcal{T}$ containing i with conditional probability

$$\frac{\delta_s}{\sum\limits_{S_{s'} \in \mathcal{T}, i \in S_{s'}} \delta_{s'}}$$

and allocate (x_i^s, y_i^s) to agent i. Since for every realization $(x_i, y_i)_{i=1,\dots,n}$ of the random allocation each agent i, $i = 1, \dots, n$, has at least a level of utility v_i,

$$\varphi(p, v, N) \le p \cdot \sum_{i=1}^{n} x_i + c(p, \sum_{i=1}^{n} y_i)$$

Therefore, $\varphi(p, v, N)$ is less than the expected cost of the random allocation

$$\varphi(p, v, N) \le \sum_{S_r \in \mathcal{S}} \delta_r E(p \cdot \sum_{i=1}^{n} x_i + c(p, \sum_{i=1}^{n} y_i)/S_r)$$

When S_r is drawn, $\sum_{i=1}^{n} y_i \ge \sum_{i \in S_r} y_i^r$ for every realization of the random allocation and because of the increasing returns in production:

$$\frac{c\left(p, \sum\limits_{i=1}^{n} y_i\right)}{\sum\limits_{i=1}^{n} y_i} \le \frac{c\left(p, \sum\limits_{i \in S_r} y_i^r\right)}{\sum\limits_{i \in S_r} y_i^r} = a(S_r)$$

Hence,

$$\varphi(p, v, N) \le \sum_{S_r \in \mathcal{S}} \delta_r E(p \cdot \sum_{i=1}^{n} x_i + a(S_r) \cdot \sum_{i=1}^{n} y_i/S_r)$$

Calculation of the conditional expectation gives

$$\varphi(p, v, N) \le$$

$$\sum_{S_r \in \mathcal{S}} \delta_r \left[\sum_{i \in S_r} (p \cdot x_i^r + a(S_r) \cdot y_i^r) + \sum_{i \notin S_r} \sum_{\substack{S_s \in \mathcal{T}, \\ i \in S_s}} \frac{\delta_s(p \cdot x_i^s + a(S_r)y_i^s)}{\sum\limits_{S_{s'} \in \mathcal{T}, i \in S_{s'}} \delta_{s'}} \right]$$

By changing the order of summation, this inequality can be written as:

$$\varphi(p, v, N) \le \sum_{S_r \in \mathcal{S}} \delta_r (p \cdot \sum_{i \in S_r} x_i^r + c(p, \sum_{i \in S_r} y_i^r))$$

$$+ \sum_{S_s \in \mathcal{T}} \delta_s \sum_{i \in S_s} \frac{\sum\limits_{S_r \in \mathcal{S}, i \notin S_r} \delta_r(p \cdot x_i^s + a(S_r)y_i^s)}{\sum\limits_{S_{s'} \in \mathcal{T}, i \in S_{s'}} \delta_{s'}}$$

But for every $S_r \in \mathcal{S}$ and $S_s \in \mathcal{T}$,

$$a(S_r) \leq a(S_s)$$

Also,

$$\sum_{S_r \in \mathcal{S}, i \in S_r} \delta_r + \sum_{S_s \in \mathcal{T}, i \in S_s} \delta_s = 1$$

since $\mathcal{B}$ is a balanced family and

$$\sum_{S_r \in \mathcal{S}, i \in S_r} \delta_r + \sum_{S_r \in \mathcal{S}, i \notin S_r} \delta_r = 1$$

by the definition of $\mathcal{S}$. This leads us finally to the inequality

$$\varphi(p, v, N) \leq \sum_{S_r \in \mathcal{S}} \delta_r (\varphi(p, v, S_r) + \epsilon)$$

$$+ \sum_{S_s \in \mathcal{T}} \delta_s \sum_{i \in S_s} (p \cdot x_i^s + a(S_s)y_i^s) \frac{\displaystyle\sum_{S_r \in \mathcal{S}, i \notin S_r} \delta_r}{\displaystyle\sum_{S_r \in \mathcal{S}, i \notin S_r} \delta_r}$$

that is,

$$\varphi(p, v, N) \leq \sum_{r=1}^{R} \delta_r [\varphi(p, v, S_r) + \epsilon]$$

Since this is true for every $\epsilon > 0$, the result follows.

$\triangledown$

Proof of Lemma 6.15: Recall the notation of chapter 4, Theorems 4.1 to 4.4. Let A be the set of optimal allocations of the economy $\mathcal{E}$ and ρ be the utility map which gives the associated utilities

$$\rho: A \longmapsto \mathbb{R}_+^n$$

$$(x_i, y_i)_{i=1,\ldots,n} \longmapsto (u_i(x_i, y_i))_{i=1,\ldots,n}$$

Note that we commit the abuse of neglecting the production part in the description of an allocation of A. The complete description is

$$\left((x_i, y_i)_{i=1,\ldots,n}, \left(\sum_{i=1}^{n} (x_i - w_i), \sum_{i=1}^{n} y_i \right) \right)$$

We know that under the assumptions of Theorem 6.12, ρ is a one-to-one map of A on $\rho(A)$ and that $\rho(A)$ is homeomorphic to the simplex Δ_{n-1} of $\mathbb{R}^n$ (Theorem 4.1). Let h denote this homeomorphism:

$$h: \quad \rho(A) \longmapsto \Delta_{n-1}$$

$$v \longmapsto \frac{v}{\sum\limits_{i=1}^{n} v_i}$$

Consider the mapping $\psi = (\psi_1, \psi_2)$ from

$$\Delta_{n-1} \times \Delta_{L-1} \longmapsto \Delta_{n-1} \times \Delta_{L-1}$$

$$(\alpha, p) \longmapsto \big(\psi_1(\alpha, p), \psi_2(\alpha, p)\big)$$

defined as follows: let $v = h^{-1}(\alpha)$ be the vector of Pareto optimal utilities corresponding to $\alpha \in \Delta_{n-1}$. Let $\varphi(p, v, \cdot)$ denote the game describing the cost of a utility level v at input prices p for every coalition. The mapping $(p, v) \longmapsto \varphi(p, v, S)$ is continuous on $\Delta_{L-1} \times \rho(A)$. By Lemma 6.14, the game $-\varphi(p, v, \cdot)$ has a non-empty core. It is possible to find an imputation in the core which depends continuously on (p, v) (for example, the nucleolus has this property). Suppose that $\big(-\beta_i(p, v)\big)_{i=1,\dots,n}$ is a continuous selection in the core of the game $-\varphi(p, v, \cdot)$. Define

$$\psi_1(\alpha, p) = \{\alpha' \in \Delta_{n-1} \mid \alpha'_i = 0 \text{ if } \beta_i(p, v) > p \cdot w_i\}$$

The interpretation of this correspondence is straightforward. $\beta_i(p, v)$ represents the cost of the imputation v attributed to player i. If this cost exceeds the value of the resources, player i is penalized and given 0 utility.

Since ρ is a one-to-one mapping of A onto $\rho(A)$, the correspondence ψ_2 can be defined as follows: To the utility level $v = h^{-1}(\alpha)$, associate the unique Pareto optimal allocation $(x_i, y_i)_{i=1,\dots,n}$ which gives utilities $(v_i)_{i=1,\dots,n}$. Consider the price (p', θ'), $p' \in \Delta_{L-1}$, which supports this allocation (the utilities are assumed to be differentiable so that, given the normalization $p' \in \Delta_{L-1}$, this price is unique). Define $\psi_2(\alpha, p) = p'$. The map ψ_2 is continuous on $\Delta_{n-1} \times \Delta_{L-1}$.

Kakutani's fixed point theorem applied to the correspondence ψ implies that there exists a vector of utilities $v^* = h^{-1}(\alpha^*)$ associated with a Pareto optimal allocation $(x_i^*, y_i^*)_{i=1,\dots,n}$ supported by a price (p^*, θ^*), $p^* \in \Delta_{L-1}$ such that

$$\alpha^* \in \psi_1(\alpha^*, p^*)$$

The assumptions on the preferences imply $p^* \gg 0$. From the proof of Theorem 4.2, we can deduce that if condition (i) or (ii) holds,

$$\varphi(p^*, v^*, N) = p^* \cdot \sum_{i=1}^{n} w_i.$$

Therefore, if $-\beta_i(p^*, v^*)$ is the chosen selection in the core of $-\varphi(p^*, v^*, \cdot)$, we have

$$\sum_{i=1}^{n} \beta_i(p^*, v^*) = p^* \cdot \sum_{i=1}^{n} w_i$$

Suppose that for some agent i

$$\beta_i(p^*, v^*) > p^* \cdot w_i \geq 0$$

Then, $\alpha_i^* = 0$ and $v_i^* = 0$. But it must also be true that

$$0 < \beta_i(p^*, v^*) \leq \varphi(p^*, v^*, \{i\}) = 0$$

which is impossible (v_i^* costs nothing for any coalition and therefore, no cost can be imputed to agent i). Therefore,

$$\beta_i(p^*, v^*) \leq p^* \cdot w_i, \ \forall i = 1, \ldots, n$$

Since $\sum_{i=1}^{n} \beta_i(p^*, v^*) = \sum_{i=1}^{n} p^* \cdot w_i$, these inequalities are actually equalities.

$\triangledown$

6.6 Many Inputs, Many Outputs

This section generalizes the results of the preceding sections to the case where the production set Y includes several outputs:

- If some inputs are not used for consumption, the concept of a distributive production function can be extended to the notion of a distributive production set.

- If every good can be consumed, the assumption of Theorem 4.5 together with the assumption of increasing returns imply the existence of a core allocation.

Some inputs not consumed

Consider an economy with of $H = L + K$ goods in which the first L goods are not consumed but are only used as inputs. The production possibilities are represented by a production set $Y \subset \mathbb{R}_-^L \times \mathbb{R}^K$. The last K goods can contain other factors besides the goods produced. A feasible production plan in Y will be denoted by $t = (-z, y)$ where $z \in \mathbb{R}_+^L$, $y \in \mathbb{R}^K$.

THEOREM AND DEFINITION 6.16. *A production set $Y \subset \mathbb{R}_-^L \times \mathbb{R}^K$ is distributive with respect to the first L goods if it satisfies one of the following equivalent conditions:*

(D) $\forall t = (-z, y) \in \partial Y$, $\exists \pi \in \mathbb{R}_+^{L+K}$, $\pi \neq 0$, such that
$\pi \cdot t = 0$, $\pi \cdot t' \leq 0$, $\forall t' = (-z', y') \in Y$, $0 \leq z' \leq z$.

(D′) $\forall (t_i, \alpha_i)_{i=1,\ldots,r}$, $t_i = (-z_i, y_i) \in Y$, $\alpha_i \in \mathbb{R}_+$, $\sum_{i=1}^r \alpha_i z_i \geq z_j$, $j = 1, \ldots, r$ $\Rightarrow$ $\sum_{i=1}^r \alpha_i t_i \in Y$.

The notion of a distributive production set clearly generalizes the notion of a distributive production function. A function f is distributive if and only if the associated production set $Y = \{(-z, y) \mid y \leq f(z)\}$ is distributive with respect to the factors. The proof of the equivalence of properties (D) and (D′) in the general case is exactly similar to the proof of Lemma 6.3 and is not repeated here.

The following theorem due to Scarf (1963) generalizes Theorems 6.9 and 6.11.

THEOREM 6.17. *Let Y be a production set in $\mathbb{R}_-^L \times \mathbb{R}^K$ satisfying assumptions P1 to P4 of Theorem 6.2.*

Let E_Y denote the set of economies with $L + K$ goods composed of agents who do not consume the first L goods, have convex, locally non-satiated preferences over the other K goods and in which the aggregate production possibilities are described by Y.

If all the economies in E_Y have a non-empty core, then Y must be distributive with respect to the first L factors.

Conversely, if Y is distributive with respect to the first L factors, if $\mathcal{E}(N, (u_i, w_i)_{i \in N}, Y)$ is an economy of E_Y with $w_i = (a_i, \bar{y}_i)$ $w_i \gg 0$, $\forall i \in N$, there exists an allocation $(0, y_i^*)_{i=1,\ldots,n}$ and a price $\pi \neq 0 \in \mathbb{R}_+^{L+H}$ such that:

- $(0, y_i^*)$ *maximizes agent i's utility under i's budget constraint evaluated at price π,*

- $t^* = (-\sum_{i=1}^n a_i, \sum_{i=1}^n y_i^* - \sum_{i=1}^n \bar{y}_i)$ *maximizes the profit of a firm with production set Y, over the set of production plans using at most the available quantity $\sum_{i=1}^n a_i$ of the first L factors.*

Moreover, the consumption allocation $(0, y_i^*)_{i=1,\ldots,n}$ is in the core of the economy $\mathcal{E}$.

Proof:

a) Let us show that if all the economies of E_Y have a non-empty core, Y is distributive. The proof is similar to that of Theorem 6.1, so we just outline the principal steps.

If all the economies of E_Y have a non-empty core, it is in particular true for the economies in which all agents have the same utility function u concave, weakly monotonic and homogeneous of degree 1 on $\mathbb{R}_+^K$. By Lemmas 6.3 and 6.4, the function f_u defined over $\mathbb{R}_+^{L+K}$ by

$$f_u(w) = \max\{u(x) \mid (0, x) - w \in Y\}$$

must be distributive.

Let $\bar{t} = (-a, \bar{y})$ be a vector on the boundary of Y. Let us show that it is possible to associate a price π with $\bar{t}$ such that

$$\pi \cdot \bar{t} = 0$$

$$\pi \cdot t \leq 0 \quad \forall t = (-a', y) \in Y, \quad 0 \leq a' \leq a.$$

For this, consider a vector $w = (a, \tilde{w})$ such that $\tilde{w} \gg 0$, $\bar{y} + \tilde{w} \gg 0$ and a utility function u defined on $\mathbb{R}_+$ by

$$u(x) = \min\left(\frac{x_1}{\tilde{w}_1 + \bar{y}_1}, \ldots, \frac{x_k}{\tilde{w}_k + \bar{y}_k}\right)$$

This gives $f_u(w) = 1$. Therefore, there exists $\pi \neq 0 \in \mathbb{R}_+^{L+K}$ such that

$$\pi \cdot w = f_u(w) = 1$$

$$\pi \cdot w' \geq f_u(w') \quad \forall w' \in \mathbb{R}_+^{L+K}, \quad 0 \leq w' \leq w$$

(if any component of w_k is zero, $\pi_k = 0$). In particular, since $\tilde{w} + \bar{y} \gg 0$, for α sufficiently small,

$$w' \stackrel{\text{def}}{=} \alpha(\bar{t} + w) = \alpha(0, \tilde{w} + \bar{y})$$

satisfies the inequality $0 \leq w' \leq w$. From the inequality $\pi \cdot w' \geq f_u(w') \geq \alpha$, we get $\pi \cdot \bar{t} \geq 0$.

Since $\tilde{w} \gg 0$, for α sufficiently small,

$$w'' \stackrel{\text{def}}{=} (1 - \alpha)w - \alpha \bar{y} = (a, (1 - \alpha)\tilde{w} - \alpha \bar{y})$$

satisfies $w'' \geq 0$. Since $\tilde{w} \gg -y$, we have $w'' \leq w$. Therefore, $\pi \cdot w'' \geq f_u(w'') \geq 1 - \alpha$, which leads to the inequality $\pi \cdot \bar{t} \leq 0$. Thus, $\pi \cdot \bar{t} = 0$.

Let $t \in Y$ be such that $t = (-a', y)$ with

$$0 \leq a' \leq a$$

$$\frac{\bar{y} - \tilde{w}}{2} \leq y \leq \frac{\bar{y} + \tilde{w}}{2}$$

The vector $w''' \overset{\text{def}}{=} \frac{1}{2}(w + \bar{t}) - t = (a', \frac{1}{2}(\tilde{w} + \bar{y}) - y)$ satisfies $0 \leq w''' \leq w$ and, therefore, $\pi \cdot w''' \geq f(w''') \geq \frac{1}{2}$ which gives $\pi \cdot t \leq 0$.

Consider a sequence $\tilde{w}^\nu$ which tends to $+\infty$ and associate with every element of this sequence the non-empty set of prices π^ν which satisfy

$$\pi^\nu \cdot \bar{t} = 0 \text{ and } \pi^\nu \cdot t \leq 0 \text{ for all } t = (-a', y) \in Y$$

such that $0 \leq a' \leq a$ and $(\bar{y} - \tilde{w}^\nu)/2 \leq y \leq (\bar{y} + \tilde{w}^\nu)/2$.

This gives a sequence of nested closed sets whose intersection contains at least a price π such that

$$\pi \cdot \bar{y} = 0$$

$$\pi \cdot y \leq 0 \text{ for every } y = (-a', y) \in Y, \quad 0 \leq a' \leq a$$

Therefore, Y satisfies the property (D) and is distributive with respect to the first L goods.

b) Conversely, let $Y \in \mathbb{R}^L_- \times \mathbb{R}^K$ be a distributive production set with respect to the first L factors and $\mathcal{E}(N, (u_i, w_i)_{i \in N}, Y)$ be an economy of E_Y with $w_i = (a_i, \bar{y}_i)$, $i = 1, \ldots, n$.

Consider the economy $\tilde{\mathcal{E}}(N, (u_i, w_i)_{i \in N}, T)$, where T is smallest closed convex cone containing the set

$$\hat{Y} = \{t = (-a', y) \in Y \mid 0 \leq a' \leq \sum_{i=1}^{n} a_i\}$$

To prove that the convex economy $\tilde{\mathcal{E}}$ has a competitive equilibrium, it is enough to show that T satisfies the usual properties P1 to P4 of production sets.

T is closed, contains 0 since $0 \in Y$ and inherits the property of free disposal from Y. It only remains to show that $w + T \cap \mathbb{R}^{L+K}_+$ is compact. Let us show that $T \cap \mathbb{R}^{L+K}_+ = \{0\}$. If $\bar{t} \in T \cap \mathbb{R}^{L+K}_+$, $\bar{t}$ must be of the form $\bar{t} = (0, \bar{y})$ since the first L elements of all the vectors of Y and hence of T are either zero or negative. The vector

$$\tilde{t} = \left(-\sum_{i=1}^{n} a_i, \bar{y}\right) = \left(-\sum_{i=1}^{n} a_i, 0\right) + (0, \bar{y})$$

then belongs to T. Let us show that this vector actually belongs to Y. If not, there would exist an $\epsilon > 0$ such that $\left(-\sum_{i=1}^{n} a_i, \bar{y} - \epsilon e\right) \in \partial Y$ (where $e = (1, \ldots, 1) \in \mathbb{R}^K$) and therefore, a price π satisfying

$$\pi \cdot \tilde{t} > 0$$
$$\pi \cdot t \leq 0 \qquad \text{if } t \in Y \text{ and utilizes less than } \sum_{i=1}^{n} a_i \text{ of inputs}$$

But this would imply that $\pi \cdot t \leq 0, \quad \forall t \in T$ which contradicts the inequality $\pi \cdot \tilde{t} > 0$.

This argument holds for every vector $(0, \lambda \bar{y})$. If $\bar{y}$ were different from zero, the set of vectors $(-\sum_{i=1}^{n} a_i, \lambda \bar{y})$ would not be bounded and would belong to Y which is impossible since Y satisfies assumption P4. Therefore, the economy $\tilde{\mathcal{E}}$ has a competitive equilibrium

$$\left((0, y_i^*)_{i=1,\ldots,n}, \quad t^* = (-z^*, y^*), \quad \pi^*\right)$$

Since t^* maximizes the profit of a firm with production set T, in particular it maximizes profit over $\hat{Y}$. Let us prove that $t^* \in Y$.

The conditions for equilibrium are

$$z^* \leq \sum_{i=1}^{n} a_i$$
$$\sum_{i=1}^{n} y_i^* \leq y^* + \sum_{i=1}^{n} \bar{y}_i$$

If any component z_h^* is strictly smaller than $\sum_{i=1}^{n} a_h^i$, the associated price π_h^* is zero. Since T satisfies the assumption of free disposal, $(\sum_{i=1}^{n} a_i, y^*) \in T$ and gives the same profit as y^*. Therefore, the equilibrium of $\tilde{\mathcal{E}}$ can be written in the form

$$\left((0, y_i^*)_{i=1,\ldots,n}, \quad t^* = (-\sum_{i=1}^{n} a_i, y^*), \quad \pi^*\right)$$

If $t^* = (-\sum_{i=1}^{n} a_i, y^*)$ does not belong to Y, the same reasoning as above shows that there would exist a price $\pi' \neq 0$ such that

$$\pi' \cdot t^* > 0 \text{ and } \pi' \cdot t \leq 0, \qquad \forall t \in T$$

which is impossible.

Finally, let us show that $(0, y_i^*)_{i=1,\ldots,n}$ is in the core of the original economy $\mathcal{E}$. If a coalition S could block this allocation with an allocation $(0, y_i')_{i \in S}$, this allocation would be such that

$$\pi^* \cdot (0, y_i') \geq \pi^* \cdot (a_i, \bar{y}_i), \qquad \forall\, i \in S$$

with at least a strict inequality. This would imply

$$\pi^* \cdot \left(-\sum_{i \in S} a_i, \sum_{i \in S} y_i' - \sum_{i \in S} \bar{y}_i\right) > 0$$

The allocation $\left(-\sum_{i \in S} a_i, \sum_{i \in S} y_i' - \sum_{i \in S} \bar{y}_i^i\right)$ would belong to Y, use less inputs than $\sum_{i=1}^{n} a_i$ and give a positive profit. This is impossible since the allocation $\left(-\sum_{i=1}^{n} a_i, \sum_{i=1}^{n} y_i^* - \sum_{i=1}^{n} \bar{y}_i\right)$ which maximizes profit over $\hat{Y}$ yields zero profit.

$$\triangledown$$

It is not difficult to deduce from the characteristic property (D') that a distributive production set Y has the following property: the set of productions which are feasible with a given vector $z \in \mathbb{R}_-^L$ of the first L factors is convex. This explains why, in the case where these factors are not desired for consumption, a core allocation can almost be decentralized by a price system π. Theorem 6.17 shows that the consumers' decisions can be completely decentralized by the price system π while the firm which operates the increasing returns technology needs more information than just the price vector π. The firm needs to know the total amount of the L factors available in the economy and maximizes profit within this constraint. The price vector π can be set such that the output which maximizes profit exactly matches the demand of the consumers. This concept of equilibrium was introduced by Scarf (1963, published 1986) under the name of a "social equilibrium."

Note that a social equilibrium is different from a marginal cost pricing equilibrium. To simplify the discussion, suppose that the K goods which are not the factors with respect to which the production set is distributive are all outputs. If we denote by $\pi^* = (\pi_L^*, \pi_K^*)$ the price vector which decentralize a social equilibrium, typically π^* does not belong to $N_Y(t^*)$ $\left(t^* = (-\sum_{i=1}^{n} a_i, y^*)\right)$ as shown in Figure 6.6

Since y^* maximizes profit when the quantities of the L factors are fixed at $-\sum_{i=1}^{n} a_i$, there exists $\pi_L' \in \mathbb{R}_+^L$ such that $\pi' = (\pi_L', \pi_K^*) \in N_Y(t^*)$. At a marginal cost pricing equilibrium, the firm would be instructed to minimize the cost of producing y^* at price π'. Since distributive sets do not necessarily have convex input requirement sets, the result may be different from $\sum_{i=1}^{n} a_i$. Even if $\sum_{i=1}^{n} a_i$ were chosen as the optimal combination of

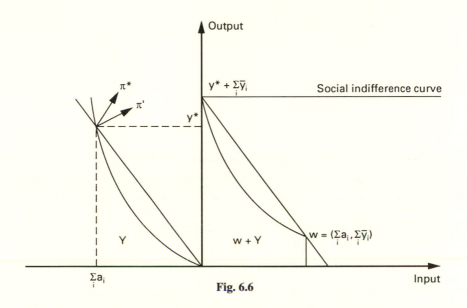

Fig. 6.6

inputs, selling y^* at marginal cost would create a deficit to be covered through taxation.

Since the consumers do not have any use for the inputs there is, however, no reason to impose marginal conditions on the input prices. The only requirement for efficiency is that the firm be induced to use all of the available factors $\sum_{i=1}^{n} a_i$. The assumption of distributivity ensures that there exists a way of pricing the factors, π_L^*, which leads to this result when the firm is restricted to a limited quantity of inputs. The pricing of outputs, π_K^*, is proportional to the marginal costs since efficiency requires that the marginal rates of substitution of consumers for outputs equal their technical rate of substitution at the given vector of inputs $\sum_{i=1}^{n} a_i$.

Thus, the assumptions of Theorem 6.17 describe the circumstances under which efficiency requires only that the prices of outputs be *proportional* to their marginal cost so that marginal conditions can be satisfied without a deficit for the firm. Theorem 6.17 shows that there is a way of pricing the factors at average product such that the resulting distribution of outputs is acceptable to all agents.

Note finally that at a social equilibrium the firm operating the technology Y does not need to be protected from entry of potential competitors.[2] If potential entrants take the prevailing price π^* as a guide to evaluate their profit after entry and are realistic about the available quantity of factors, no entry will take place as long as the existing firm minimizes cost. If one accepts the idea that potential competition is as effective as actual competition on markets with several firms, the threat of entry can in this case be the force that incites the existing firm to minimize costs.

Every good consumed

Once again we consider a production set $Y \subset \mathbb{R}_-^L \times \mathbb{R}^K$ with increasing returns but now assume that

- every good can be consumed,
- initial resources are in the first L goods,
- the last K goods can be produced from these factors.

Instead of assuming that the convex sector of the economy consists only of consumers, we now allow for the existence of competitive firms as in section 4.5. The definition of the core of an economy must therefore, be generalized to describe the possibilities of a coalition of agents which have both initial resources in goods and shares in convex firms.

Let $\mathcal{E}\left(N, (u_i, w_i)_{i=1,\ldots,n}, (Y_j)_{j=1,\ldots,m}, (\theta_{ij})_{\substack{i=1,\ldots,n \\ j=1,\ldots,m}}, Y\right)$ be an economy as introduced in section 4.5 where the ownership of the convex firms is distributed among agents according to the shares $(\theta_{ij})_{\substack{i=1,\ldots,n \\ j=1,\ldots,m}} \in \mathbb{R}_+^{nm}$, $\sum_{i=1}^n \theta_{ij} = 1, \forall j = 1, \ldots, m$. We adopt the following definition of the feasible allocations for a coalition $S \subset N = \{1, \ldots, n\}$.

DEFINITION. *The feasible consumption allocations for a coalition are defined by*

$$A(S) = \left\{ (\xi_i)_{i \in S} \in \mathbb{R}_+^{(L+K)|S|} \ \Big| \ \sum_{i \in S} \xi_i - \sum_{i \in S} w_i \in Y + \sum_{j=1}^m \sum_{i \in S} \theta_{ij} Y_j \right\}$$

This definition, which comes from the literature on "coalition production economies" and was developed in the 1970s (Hildenbrand 1968, 1970, 1974; Böhm 1973a, 1973b, 1974a, 1974b; Sondermann 1974; Oddou 1976) is less natural than the definition given in section 6.3 in the case where there are no private firms. To assume that a coalition S of agents has access to the production sets $(\sum_{i \in S} \theta_{ij} Y_j)_{j=1,\ldots,m}$ is pushing the notion of ownership of a firm much beyond the competitive assumption that a share θ_{ij} of firm j entitles i to receive the corresponding share of the profit. It first implies that when a production plan y_j is chosen by firm j, the coalition S physically provides a share $\sum_{i \in S} \theta_{ij}$ of the factors of production and receives the same share of the outputs. Secondly, it implies that the agents of the coalition S can impose on the firms in which there are shareholders the production plans which are the most beneficial to the coalition S, which is not realistic for small coalitions.

But we have to remember that the allocations in $A(S)$ are only used as a benchmark to decide whether or nor a coalition S blocks a proposed allocation. If we assume that the coalitions have access to a large set of allocations—some perhaps outside the range of the allocations that a coalition could realistically achieve with its own means—then the existence of a core allocation is a powerful result and the core allocations have an important property of stability.

Once the definition of $A(S)$ is given for each $S \subset N$, the definition of the core of the economy follows: it is the set of feasible allocations of the economy which are not blocked by any coalition, a coalition S being limited to the allocations of $A(S)$ to block a proposed allocation.

Note that with this definition for $A(S)$, the core on the economy is always non-empty if the production set Y is reduced to 0 since it contains the competitive equilibrium allocations of the convex economy. We are going to show that under the assumptions of Theorem 4.5, core allocations still exist if all agents in the economy have access to a production technology Y with increasing returns.

THEOREM 6.18. *The core of an economy*

$$\mathcal{E}\left((u_i, w_i)_{i=1,\ldots,n}, (Y_j)_{j=1,\ldots,m}, (\theta_{ij})_{\substack{i=1,\ldots,n \\ j=1,\ldots,m}}, Y\right)$$

satisfying the assumptions of Theorem 4.5 and where Y exhibits increasing returns to scale is non-empty.

Proof: (The notation is the same as in section 4.5.) The proof of this theorem combines the ideas of the proofs of Theorems 4.5 and 6.8.

For a vector $(p, \theta q)$ of prices of the $L+K$ goods with $p \in \Delta_{L-1}, q \in \Delta_{K-1}, \theta \geq 0$, we define the cost $\varphi(p, q, v, S)$ of a utility vector $v \in \mathbb{R}^n_+$ for a coalition S as the value of the program

$$\inf\left(p \cdot \sum_{i \in S}(x_i - \sum_{j=1}^{m}\theta_{ij}x_j) + c(p, q, \eta)\right)$$

subject to
$$\begin{cases} u_i(x_i, y_i) \geq v_i \ \forall i \in S. \\ (x_j, y_j) \in Y_j, \ j = 1, \ldots, m \\ q \cdot \sum_{i \in S}(y_i - \sum_{j=1}^{m}\theta_{ij}y_j) = \eta \end{cases}$$

The proof is based on the following lemmas which generalize lemmas 6.13 to 6.15.

LEMMA 6.19. *If an allocation $(x_i, y_i)_{i \in N}$ is blocked by a coalition S and if v is the corresponding vector of utilities $(v_i = u_i(x_i, y_i), \ i = 1, \ldots, n)$, then*

$$\varphi(p, q, v, S) < p \cdot \sum_{i \in S} w_i, \qquad \forall p \in \Delta_{L-1}, \qquad \forall q \in \Delta_{K-1}$$

LEMMA 6.20. *For all* $p \in \Delta_{L-1}$, $q \in \Delta_{K-1}$, $v \in \mathbb{R}^n_+$, *the game* $(N, -\varphi(p,q,v,\cdot))$ *is balanced.*

Lemma 6.19 implies that if there exists a feasible allocation $(x_i, y_i)_{i=1,\dots,n}$, prices p and q such that

$$\varphi(p,q,v,S) \geq p \cdot \sum_{i \in S} w_i \qquad \forall\ S \subset N$$

where v is the vector of utilities $(u_i(x_i,y_i)_{i=1,\dots,n})$, then this allocation is in the core of the economy.

If $-\beta_i(p,q,v)_{i=1,\dots,n}$ is a continuous selection from the core of the game $-\varphi(p,q,v,\cdot)$ which is non-empty by Lemma 6.20, it is sufficient to show that there exists a feasible allocation $(x_i,y_i)_{i=1,\dots,n}$ and a pair (p,q) such that

$$\beta_i(p,q,v) = p \cdot w_i \quad \forall i = 1,\dots,n$$

The next lemma shows that this is possible.

LEMMA 6.21. *There exists a Pareto optimal consumption allocation* $(x_i^*, y_i^*)_{i=1,\dots,n}$ *such that if* $v_i^* = u_i(x_i^*, y_i^*)$ *and* $(p^*, \theta^* q^*)$ *is the price vector which supports this allocation, then* $(-p^* \cdot w_i)$ *is in the core of the game* $(N, -\varphi(p^*, q^*, v^*, \cdot))$.

$$\nabla$$

Proof of Lemma 6.19: The proof is similar to the proof of Lemma 6.5 and is not repeated.

$$\nabla$$

Proof of Lemma 6.20: The proof is an adaptation of the proof of Lemma 6.6. We sketch the idea.

Let $\mathcal{B} = \{(S_r)_{r=1,\dots,R}\}$ be a balanced family of subsets of $N = \{1,\dots,n\}$, with coefficients $(\delta_r)_{r=1,\dots,R}$. For every subset S_r, let

$$\{(x_i^r, y_i^r)_{i \in S_r}, \quad (x_j^r, y_j^r) \in Y_j, \quad j = 1,\dots,m\}$$

be an allocation such that

$$p \cdot \sum_{i \in S}(x_i^r - \sum_{j=1}^m \theta_{ij} x_j^r) + c(p,q,\eta^r) \leq \varphi(p,q,v,S_r) + \epsilon$$

$$u_i(x_i^r, y_i^r) \geq v_i, \ \forall i \in S_r$$

where $\eta^r = q \cdot \sum_{i \in S}(y_i^r - \sum_{j=1}^m \theta_{ij} y_j^r)$. Let $a(S_r) = c(p,q,\eta^r)/\eta^r$ and suppose that the ordering of coalitions is such that

$$a(S_1) \leq a(S_2) \leq \dots \leq a(S_R)$$

and the family is such that for an index r_0

$$\delta_1 + \ldots + \delta_{r_0} = 1$$

Define $\forall = \{S_r \in \mathcal{B} \mid r \leq r_0\}$, $\mathcal{T} = \{S_r \in \mathcal{B} \mid r > r_0\}$, and consider a random allocation defined as follows:

- a coalition S_r from the family $\forall$ is drawn with probability δ_r, ($r = 1, \ldots, r_0$).
- the agents of S_r receive the allocation (x_i^r, y_i^r). Independently for each $i \notin S_r$, a coalition S_s is drawn from the coalitions of $\mathcal{T}$ which contain i with probability

$$\frac{\delta_s}{\displaystyle\sum_{S_{s'} \in \mathcal{T}, i \in S_{s'}} \delta_{s'}}$$

  Agent i receives (x_i^s, y_i^s).

- if S_r has been drawn first and for $i \notin S_r$, S_{s_i} has been chosen, the convex firm j produces

$$\Big(\sum_{i \in S_r} \theta_{ij}\Big)(x_j^r, y_j^r) + \sum_{i \notin S_r} \theta_{ij}(x_j^{s_i}, y_j^{s_i})$$

This production belongs to Y_j since Y_j is convex and $\sum_{i \in N} \theta_{ij} = 1$. The total cost of the realization of the random allocation is

$$p \cdot \sum_{i \in S_r}(x_i^r - \sum_j \theta_{ij} x_j^r) + p \cdot \sum_{i \notin S_r}(x_i^{s_i} - \sum_j \theta_{ij} x_j^{s_i})$$

$$+c\Big(p, q, \sum_{i \in S_r} q \cdot (y_i^r - \sum_j \theta_{ij} y_j^r) + \sum_{i \notin S_r} q \cdot (y_i^{s_i} - \sum_j \theta_{ij} y_j^{s_i})\Big)$$

By assumption C_2'' of Theorem 4.5, $y_j^{s_i} \leq 0$ and, therefore,

$$q \cdot \Big(\sum_{i \in S_r}(y_i^r - \sum_j \theta_{ij} y_j^r) + \sum_{i \notin S_r}(y_i^{s_i} - \sum_j \theta_{ij} y_j^{s_i})\Big)$$

$$\geq q \cdot \sum_{i \in S_r}(y_i^r - \sum_j \theta_{ij} y_j^r) = \eta_r.$$

Since Y exhibits increasing returns, the function $\eta \to c(p, q, \eta)/\eta$ is decreasing. Since the allocation considered gives each agent i at least the utility level v_i, we get the following inequality:

$$\varphi(p, q, v, N) \leq p \cdot \sum_{i \in S_r}(x_i^r - \sum_j \theta_{ij} x_j^r) + p \cdot \sum_{i \notin S_r}(x_i^{s_i} - \sum_j \theta_{ij} x_j^{s_i})$$

$$+a(S_r)\left(\eta_r + q\cdot\sum_{i\notin S_r}(y_i^{s_i}-\sum_j\theta_{ij}y_j^{s_i})\right)$$

Following the same steps as in Lemma 6.14, taking the expectation of the second term leads to the inequality

$$\varphi(p,q,v,N)\le\sum_{r=1}^R\delta_r\varphi(p,q,v,S_r)$$

$\triangledown$

Proof of Lemma 6.21: The proof is a generalization of the proof of Lemma 6.15. We indicate the main steps of the proof. Consider the correspondence

$$\psi:\ \Delta_{L-1}\times\Delta_{K-1}\times\Delta_{n-1}\to\Delta_{L-1}\times\Delta_{K-1},\Delta_{n-1}$$

$$(p,q,\alpha)\to(\psi_1(p,q,\alpha),\psi_2(p,q,\alpha),\psi_3(p,q,\alpha),)$$

defined as follows.

To an element α of the simplex Δ_{n-1}, associate the vector of utilities v on the boundary of the feasible inputations. By Theorem 4.5, there is only one feasible allocation that gives a level of utility v to the agents. If $(p',\theta'q')$ is the price that supports this allocation, let $\psi_1(p,q,\alpha)=p'$ and $\psi_2(p,q,\alpha)=q'$.

Let $(-\beta_i(p,q,v))_{i=1,\ldots,n}$ be a continuous function in the core of the game $-\varphi(p,q,v,\cdot)$, and define ψ_3 by

$$\psi_3(p,q,\alpha)=\{\alpha'\in S_{n-1}\mid\alpha_i'=0\ \ \text{if}\ \ \beta_i(p,q,v)>p\cdot w_i\}$$

ψ has a fixed point (p^*,q^*,α^*). Using the property $\varphi(p^*,q^*,v^*,N)=p^*\cdot\sum_{i=1}^n w_i$ proved in Theorem 4.5, it is easy to show that $\beta_i(p^*,q^*,v^*)=p^*\cdot w_i$ which completes the proof.

$\triangledown$

Theorems 4.7 and 6.18 identify a class of economies which have the following properties even though they contain a production sector with increasing returns: there is a unique way of realizing a Pareto optimal imputation; a marginal cost pricing equilibrium exists for every income map; all these equilibria are Pareto optimal; the core of the economy is non-empty.

However, these economies differ from convex economies in an important respect. Unlike the competitive equilibria of convex economies, not all the marginal cost pricing equilibria are in the core of the economy. A structure of revenues implicitly defines a rule for sharing the losses of the public sector among the agents. Some of these rules may be so unfavorable to some agents that they generate equilibrium allocations which are not even individually rational. This explains in particular why it has been difficult to prove non-emptiness of the core of an economy with increasing returns. In a convex economy the result is much more easily obtained since there is only to check that the competitive equilibrium allocations are in the core of the economy.

Once we have conditions which imply existence of core allocations for an economy with increasing returns, one would like to characterize the rules for sharing the losses of the public sector which lead to equilibrium allocations in the core. Such rules would not be subject to the criticism that they induce income redistribution among agents since no agent would contribute more than he or she benefits from the consumption of the publicly produced goods. Unfortunately, no such rule has yet been found and it is unlikely that a simple one can be defined since the core of an economy depends on all the characteristics of the agents, their preferences as well as their initial resources.

A notion of equilibrium which decentralizes allocations in the core of the economy has been proposed by Ichiishi and Quinzii (1983) in the article "Decentralization for the Core of a Production Economy with Increasing Returns." Consider an economy $\mathcal{E}(N, (u_i, w_i)_{i=1,\dots,n}, Y)$ without a private production sector, satisfying the assumptions of Theorem 6.18. (The absence of a convex production sector simplifies the exposition but is not crucial.) Let $p \in \Delta_{L-1}$ be a vector of relative prices for the first L goods (which are both consumption goods and factors of production), $q \in \Delta_{K-1}$ a vector of relative prices for the outputs. Agent $i, i = 1, \dots, n$, receives an income ξ_i to spend on the first L goods and an income η_i to spend on the outputs but cannot transfer income from one category of goods to the other. Agent i then faces two budget constraints and solves the program

$$\max\{u_i(x_i, y_i) \mid x_i \in \mathbb{R}_+^L, \quad y_i \in \mathbb{R}_+^K, \quad p \cdot x_i \leq \xi_i, \quad q \cdot y_i \leq \eta_i\}$$

The value of the program gives the indirect utility $v_i(p, q, \xi_i, \eta_i)$. The demand of the agent is

$$\left(\tilde{x}_i(p, q, \xi_i, \eta_i), \quad \tilde{y}_i(p, q, \xi_i, \eta_i)\right)$$

The production is undertaken by a firm with the production set Y, which buys inputs at prices p and sells output at prices q. Its objective is to realize a production of value $\eta = \sum_{i=1}^{n} \eta_i$ at least cost. It solves the program

$$\inf\{-p \cdot z \mid (z, y) \in Y, \quad q \cdot y = \eta\}$$

whose value is $c(p, q, \eta)$. The production plan of the firm is

$$\left(\tilde{z}(p, q, \eta), \quad \tilde{y}(p, q, \eta)\right)$$

An equilibrium is characterized by incomes $(\bar{\xi}_i, \bar{\eta}_i)$ and prices $(\bar{p}, \bar{q})$ such that:

1. $(\bar{\xi}_i, \bar{\eta}_i)$ are in the core of the simplified two-good economy $\mathcal{E}_{\bar{p}, \bar{q}}$ where the preferences of agent i on vectors $(\xi_i, \eta_i) \in \mathbb{R}_+^2$ is given by $v_i(\bar{p}, \bar{q}, \cdot, \cdot)$, its initial resources are $(\bar{p} \cdot w_i, 0)$ and the possibilities of production are represented by the cost function $\eta \to c(\bar{p}, \bar{q}, \eta)$. The core of such an economy is the determined by the feasible sets

$$A_{\bar{p}, \bar{q}}(S) = \left\{ (\xi_i, \eta_i)_{i \in S} \mid \sum_{i \in S} \xi_i + c(\bar{p}, \bar{q}, \sum_{i \in S} \eta_i) \leq \bar{p} \cdot \sum_{i \in S} w_i \right\}$$

2. The prices $(\bar{p}, \bar{q})$ are such that the plans of the agents and of the firm are compatible:

$$\sum_{i=1}^{n} \tilde{x}_i(p, q, \eta_i) = \sum_{i=1}^{n} w_i + \tilde{z}(p, q, \sum_{i=1}^{n} \eta_i)$$

$$\sum_{i=1}^{n} \tilde{y}_i(p, q, \eta_i) = \tilde{y}(p, q, \sum_{i=1}^{n} \eta_i)$$

Ichiishi and Quinzii prove that under assumptions slightly stronger than those of Theorem 6.18 (boundary conditions have to be added) such an equilibrium exists and is in the core of the economy. The proof is based on a fixed point theorem developed by T. Ichiishi (1981). The proof is not given here since the non-emptiness of the core has been proved by a simpler method.

An institutional framework where such an equilibrium could emerge can be described as follows: The first L goods are ordinary private goods for which there exists a market at prices $\bar{p}$. Agents can exchange their initial resources on this market and bargain with the firm which produces the K other goods. The firm sets the relative prices of its outputs equal to $\bar{q}$ and proposes contracts to the agents of the following form: in exchange for a quantity of inputs of value $\bar{p} \cdot w_i - \bar{\xi}_i$, agent i receives a coupon for a value $\bar{\eta}_i$ of the firm's production. To decide whether or not to accept the contracts proposed by the firm, the agents evaluate if they can do better by undertaking themselves the production of the outputs, alone or in coalitions. Their calculations are not completely detailed but they are based on the cost function $c(\bar{p}, \bar{q}, \cdot)$. Agents accept the contracts proposed by the firm if no coalition $S \subset N$ can find a vector $(\xi_i, \eta_i)_{i \in S}$ in $A_{\bar{p}, \bar{q}}(S)$ preferred by the agents of S. Then the economy functions in a decentralized manner. Given the prices $(\bar{p}, \bar{q})$ and their constraints (ξ_i, η_i) agents optimize their transactions on the market and their demand to the firms. The firm produces at minimum cost an output of value $\bar{\eta} = \sum_{i=1}^{n} \bar{\eta}_i$ with the factors provided by the agents or bought on the market.

Note that there is no need to prevent the existence of a market for the coupons given by the firm. Since the equilibrium that we consider is in the core of the economy, it is in particular Pareto optimal and there exists a rate of substitution $\bar{\theta}$ between dollars spent on the first L good and dollars spent on the outputs which is common to all agents. With a price $\bar{\theta}$ the market for coupons would be in equilibrium and the agents, instead of facing two budget constraints, would have the usual budget constraint

$$\left\{ (x_i, y_i) \in \mathbb{R}_+^{L+K} \mid \bar{p} \cdot x_i + \bar{\theta}\bar{q} \cdot y_i \le \xi_i + \bar{\theta}\bar{\eta}_i \right\}$$

This would not change their demands. It is easy to check that $\bar{\theta}\bar{q}$ is the vector of marginal costs of the firm when the input prices are $\bar{p}$. The equilibrium described is thus, a marginal cost pricing equilibrium where the contributions of the agents to the financing of the public firm are

$$\bar{t}_i = \bar{p} \cdot w_i - \bar{\xi}_i - \bar{\theta}\bar{\eta}_i, \qquad i = 1, \dots, n$$

The fact that $(\bar{\xi}_i, \bar{\eta}_i)_{i=1,\dots,n}$ are in the core of the simplified two-good economy $\mathcal{E}_{\bar{p}, \bar{q}}$ ensures that these contributions—which can be considered either as taxes or as fixed fees of a two-part tariff—are acceptable by all agents.

The advantage of letting the firm finance its production by signing contracts with the agents instead of subsidizing its deficit is that it makes possible to expose the firm to potential entry of competitors, thus creating the necessary incentives to minimize cost.

Let us show that a potential entrant which can use the technology Y does not perceive the possibility of making a positive profit by entering the market of the K outputs produced by the existing monopoly, under the simplifying assumption that agents have to buy all their goods from only one firm. Whatever is proposed by the new firm to consumers will result, for the consumers who join the new firm, in vectors $(\xi_i', \eta_i')_{i \in I}$, where I is the set of consumers captured by the new firm, $\eta_i' = \bar{q} \cdot y_i'$ is the value of the outputs bought by agent i and $\bar{p} \cdot w_i - \bar{\xi}_i'$ is the total price paid by consumer i. (The entrant may decide to sell at linear prices $q' \in \mathbb{R}^K$ in which case $\bar{p} \cdot w_i - \xi_i' = q' \cdot y_i'$ or may decide to propose personalized contracts.)

The budget of the new firm is balanced if

$$g(\bar{p}, \sum_{i\in I} y_i') \leq \sum_{i\in I}(\bar{p}\cdot w_i - \xi_i')$$

which implies

$$c(\bar{p}, \bar{q}, \sum_{i\in I} \eta_i') \leq \sum_{i\in I}(\bar{p}\cdot w_i - \xi_i')$$

But there does not exist a coalition I and vectors $(\eta_i', \xi_i')_{i\in I}$ preferred by agents of the coalition I such that the above inequality is verified.

Notes

1. Note that the prices π correspond to the average product of the inputs and not to their marginal product; however, since there is no other use for the inputs than the production of a single good in a single firm, no marginal condition is necessary to ensure that these goods are used efficiently. The only question is how to allocate the output of the consumption good between agents in the economy.
2. The link between the core of an economy and the notion of "sustainable price" for a monopoly under the assumptions of Theorem 6.17 has been noticed by W. Sharkey (1979).

7

CONCLUSION

The general equilibrium analysis that has been presented shows that there are even more problems in using marginal cost pricing with increasing returns technologies than has been discussed at the time of the "marginal cost pricing controversy," but also that, in some circumstances, the problems can be solved.

The earlier literature raised objections to the income redistribution induced by financing the deficit of public firms through income taxes and questioned the incentives that a subsidized public firm would have to minimize costs. The additional difficulties which appear when studying the equilibria of a closed economy functioning with marginal cost pricing are two-fold. First, some income distributions may be inefficient not because of considerations of equity but because they yield equilibria which are all inefficient (section 4.1). When several firms produce the same good, one of them with a non-convex technology, marginal cost pricing is not sufficient to ensure a good coordination of the production plans and the resulting equilibria may be productively inefficient (section 5.2).

This last difficulty arises from the inability of the price mechanism to coordinate production decisions in presence of non-convexities and is not really a critique of marginal cost pricing. Once a good can be produced with increasing returns, its total production should be supervised by a central agency to avoid inefficient use of different units of production. The example of Beato and Mas-Colell described in section 5.2 shows that such an agency cannot rely on equalization of marginal costs to ensure productive efficiency. In cases where the economies of scale in the production of a good are large enough to justify its production by a public (or regulated) sector, it seems unlikely that there exist alternative techniques available to the private sector to produce small quantities at the same marginal cost. A solution to the problem shown in section 5.2 lies more in refining the planning procedures used in the public sector than in abandoning the rule of pricing at marginal cost to sell the goods to the private sector.

Consider economies in which the non–convex sector is aggregated and produces goods which are different from those held or produced by the private sector (to avoid the issue of productive efficiency just discussed). Then there are (at least) two classes of economies which have efficient equilibria,

153

in which the public sector can be financed without abusive income redistribution and which can be exposed to entry of potential competitors to keep the pressure on cost minimization without the danger of wasteful entry. The first class consists of economies satisfying the assumptions of Theorem 6.17, in which the inputs used by the sector with increasing returns have no alternative use. In this case, efficiency only requires that the prices of output be proportional to their marginal cost so that the deficit of the public sector can be avoided. The second class consists of economies satisfying the assumptions of Theorem 6.18, in which the inputs of the convex sector have alternative uses. In these economies a combination of marginal cost pricing and discriminatory contracts can yield a satisfactory solution to the problem of resource allocation.

These results can be interpreted negatively if emphasis is placed on the restrictiveness of the assumptions of Theorems 6.17 to 6.18 and on the difficulty of obtaining the information on agents' characteristics needed to design acceptable contracts. Or they can be interpreted positively if emphasis is placed on the fact that a first best allocation of resources is not always out of reach of a market economy in which the sectors of production with increasing returns are managed with some ingenuity, following the precepts of marginal cost pricing. The preferences of the author, impressed by the French tradition of producing great economists from the engineers in charge of the public sector, clearly lean in the second direction.

REFERENCES

Arrow, K., and Hahn, F. (1971). *General Competitive Analysis*. San Francisco: Holden Day.

————, Hurwicz, L. (1960). "Decentralization and Computation in Resource Allocation" in *Essays in Economics and Econometrics*, pp. 34–104. Chapel Hill: University of North Carolina Press.

Aumann, R. (1964). "Markets with a Continuum of Players." *Econometrica* 32: 39–54.

Babbage, C. (1832). *On the Economy of Machinery and Manufacture*. London: C. Knight.

Balasko, Y. (1988). *Foundations of the Theory of General Equilibrium*. Boston: Academic Press.

Baron, D., and Myerson R. (1982). "Regulating a Monopoly with Unknown Costs." *Econometrica*, 50: 911–30.

Baumol, W.; Panzar, J.; and Willig, E. (1982). *Contestable Markets and the Theory of Industry Structure*. New York: Harcourt Brace Jovanovitch.

Beato P. (1976). "Marginal Cost Pricing Equilibria with Increasing Returns." Ph.D. dissertation, University of Minnesota.

————. (1982). "The Existence of Marginal Cost Pricing Equilibria with Increasing Returns." *Quarterly Journal of Economics* 97: 669–689.

————, Mas-Colell, A. (1983). "Gestion au Coût Marginal et Efficacité de la Production Agrégée: un Exemple." *Annales de l'INSEE* 51: 39–45.

————. (1985). "On Marginal Cost Pricing with Given Tax Subsidy Rules." *Journal of Economic Theory* 37: 356–365.

Böhm, V. (1973). "Firms and Market Equilibria in a Private Ownership Economy." *Zeitschrift für Nationalökonomie* 33: 81–102.

————. (1973). "On Cores and Equilibria of Productive Economies with a Measure Space of Consumers: An Example." *Journal of Economic Theory* 6: 409–12.

————. (1974). "The Core of an Economy with Production." *Review of Economic Studies* XLI: 423–36.

————. (1974). "The Limit of the Core of an Economy with Production." *International Economic Review* 15: 143–48.

Boiteux, M. (1956). "Sur la Gestion des Monopoles Publics Astreints à l'Equilibre Budgétaire," *Econometrica* 24: 22–40.

Bonnisseau, J. M., and Cornet, B. (1988a). "Existence of Equilibria when Firms Follow Bounded Losses Pricing Rules." *Journal of Mathematical Economics* 17: 119–148.

————. (1988b). "Valuation Equilibrium and Pareto Optimum in Non-Convex Economies." *Journal of Mathematical Economics* 17: 293–315.

————. (1990a). "Existence of Marginal Cost Pricing Equilibria in an Economy with Several Non Convex Firms." *Econometrica* 58: 661–820.

————. (1990b). "Existence of Marginal Cost Pricing Equilibrium: The Non-Smooth Case." *International Economic Review* 31: 685–708.

Brown, D., and Heal, G. (1979). "Equity, Efficiency and Increasing Returns." *Review of Economic Studies* 46: 571–85.

————. (1980). "Two Part Tariffs, Marginal Cost Pricing and Increasing Returns in a General Equilibrium Model." *Journal of Public Economics* 13: 25–50.

————. (1982). "Existence, Local Uniqueness and Optimality of a Marginal Cost Pricing Equilibrium in an Economy with Increasing Returns". Social Science Working Paper, No. 415, California Institute of Technology.

————; Kahn, M.; and Vohra, R. (1986). "On a General Existence Theorem for Marginal Cost Pricing Equilibria." *Journal of Economic Theory* 38: 371–79.

Brown, D.; Heller, W. P.; and Starr, R. M. (1990). "Two-Part Marginal Cost Pricing Equilibria: Existence and Efficiency." Stanford Discussion Paper.

Caillaud, B.; Guesnerie, R.; Rey, P.; and Tirole, J. (1988). "Government Intervention in Production and Incentive Theory: a Review of Recent Contributions." *Rand Journal of Economics* 19: 1–26.

Chamberlin, E. (1933). *The Theory of Monopolistic Competition.* Cambridge, Mass.: Harvard University Press.

Clarke, F. H. (1983). *Optimization and Nonsmooth Analysis.* New York: Wiley Interscience Publication.

Cornet, B. (1988). "Tarification au Coût Marginal et Pareto Optimalité" in *Melanges Economiques: Essais en l'Honneur de Edmond Malinvaud,* edited by EHESS. Paris: Economica.

————. (1990). "Existence of Equilibria in Economies with Increasing Returns" in *Contributions in Operations Research and Econometrics: the XXth Anniversary of Core,* Edited by B. Cornet and H. Tulkens. Cambridge, Mass.: MIT Press. Discussion Paper (1982).

Cremer, J. (1977). "A Quantity-Quantity Algorithm for Planning Under Increasing Returns to Scale." *Econometrica* 45: 1339–348.

Debreu, G. (1959). *Theorie of Value.* New York: Wiley.

Dierker, E. (1986). "When Does Marginal Cost Pricing Lead to Pareto Efficiency?" *Zeitschrift für Nationalökonomie* Supplement no. 5, pp. 41–66.

———; Guesnerie, R.; and Neuefeind, W. (1985). "General Equilibrium when Some Firms Follow Special Pricing Rules." *Econometrica* 53: 1369–394.

Dreze, J. H. (1964). "Some Postwar Contributions of French Economists to Theory and Public Policy." *American Economic Review* 54: 1–64.

Gramain, A. (1971). *Topologie des Surfaces.* Paris: Presses Universitaires de France.

Guesnerie, R. (1975). "Pareto Optimality in Non Convex Economies." *Econometrica* 43: 1–30.

———. (1980). *Modèles de l'Economie Publique.* Monographie du Séminaire d'Econométrie. Paris: Editions du Centre National de la Recherche Scientifique.

———. (1984). "First Best Allocations of Resources with Non-Convexities in Production." Stanford Discussion Paper.

Heal, G. (1973). *A Theory of Economic Planning.* Amsterdam: North Holland.

Henry, C., Zylberberg, A. (1978). "Planning Algorithms to Deal with Increasing Returns," *Review of Economic Studies* 15: 67–68.

Hildenbrand, W. (1968). "The Core of an Economy with a Measure Space of Economics Agents." *Review of Economic Studies* 35: 443–52.

———. (1970). "Existence of Equilibria with Production and a Measure Space of Consumers." *Econometrica* 38: 608–23.

———. (1974). *Core and Equilibria in a Large Economy.* Princeton N.J.: Princeton University Press.

Hotelling, H. (1938). "The General Welfare in Relation to Problems of Taxation and of Railway Utility Rates." *Econometrica* 6: 142–69.

Ichiishi, T. (1981). "A Social Coalitional Equilibrium Existence Lemma." *Econometrica* 49: 369–77.

———, and Quinzii, M. (1983). "Decentralization for the Core of a Production Economy with Increasing Returns." *International Economic Review* 24: 397–412.

Kamiya, K. (1988a). "Existence and Uniqueness of Equilibria with Increasing Returns." *Journal of Mathematical Economics* 17: 149–78.

———. (1988b). "On the Survival Assumption in Marginal (Cost) Pricing." *Journal of Mathematical Economics* 17: 261–74.

Khan, A., and Vohra, R. (1987). "An Extension of the Second Welfare Theorem to Economies with Non Convexities and Public Goods." *Quarterly Journal of Economics* 102: 223–41.

———. (1988). "Pareto Optimal Allocations of Non-Convex Economies in Locally Convex Spaces." *Nonlinear Analysis* 12: 943–50.

Mantel, R. (1979). "Equilibrio con Redimentos Crescientes a Escala." *Anales de l'Association Argentina de Economia Politica* 1: 271–82.

Marshall, A. (1890). *Principles of Economics*. London: Macmillan.

Mas-Colell, A. (1980). "Remarks on the Game Theoretic Analysis of a Simple Distribution of a Surplus Problem." *International Journal of Game Theory* 9: 125–40.

——— . (1985). *The Theory of General Economic Equilibrium—A Differentiable Approach*. Cambridge: Cambridge University Press.

Mill, J. S. (1848). *Principles of Political Economy*. London: J. W. Parker.

Milnor, J. (1969). *Morse Theory*, Annals of Mathematical Studies. Princeton N.J.: Princeton University Press.

Negishi, T. (1960). "Welfare Economics and Existence of an Equilibrium for a Competive Economy." *Metroeconomica* 12: 92–97.

Oddou, C. (1976). "Théorèmes d'Exisence et d'Equivalence pour des Economies avec Production." *Econometrica* 44: 265–82.

Oi, W. (1971). "A Disneyland Dilemma: Two Part Tariffs for a Mickey Mouse Monopoly." *Quarterly Journal of Economics* 85: 77–96.

Quinzii, M. (1982). "An Existence Theorem for the Core of a Productive Economy with Increasing Returns." *Journal of Economic Theory* 28: 32–50.

——— . (1982). "Définition et Existence du Noyau dans un Modèle d'Economie où la Production Présente des Rendements Croissants." *Cahier du Séminaire d'Econométrie* 23: 105–19.

——— . (1986). *Rendements Croissants et Equilibre Général*. Thesis, University Paris II.

——— . (1988a). *Rendements Croissants et Efficacité Economique*. Monographie d'Econométrie. Paris: Editions du Centre National de la Recherche Scientifique.

——— . (1988b). "Efficiency of Marginal Cost Pricing Equilibria," forthcoming in *Equilibria and Dynamics, Essays in Honor of David Gale*. London: Macmillan.

Robinson, J. (1933). *The Economics of Imperfect Competition*. London: Macmillan.

Ruggles, N. (1949). "The Welfare Basis of the Marginal Cost Pricing Principle." *Review of Economic Studies* 17: 29–46.

——— . (1950). "Recent Developments in the Theory of Marginal Cost Pricing." *Review of Economic Studies* 17: 107–26.

Scarf, H. (1973). *The Computation of Economic Equilibria*. New Haven: Yale University Press.

——— . (1986). "Notes on the Core of a Production Economy" in *Contributions to Mathematical Economics (in Honor of Gerard Debreu)* ch. 21. Amsterdam: North Holland. Discussion Paper (1963).

Sharkey, W. (1979). "Existence of a Core When There Are Increasing Returns." *Econometrica* 47: 869–76.

——— . (1982). *The Theory of Natural Monopoly*. Cambridge: Cambridge University Press.

Smith, A. (1776). *An Inquiry into the Nature and Causes of the Wealth of Nations*. Edited by R. H. Campbell and A. S. Skinner. Oxford: Oxford University Press.

Sondermann, D. (1974). "Economies of Scale and Equilibria in Coalition Production Economies." *Journal of Economic Theory* 8: 259–91.

Spulber, D. (1989). "The Second Best Core." *International Economic Review* 30: 623–31.

Sraffa, P. (1920). "The Laws of Returns under Competitive Conditions." *The Economic Journal* 26: 535–50.

Varian, H. R. (1978). *Microeconomic Analysis*. New York: Norton.

Vohra, R. (1988). "On the Existence of Equilibria in Economies with Increasing Returns." *Journal of Mathematical Economics* 17: 179–92.

——— . (1990a). "Marginal Cost Pricing under Bounded Marginal Returns." Brown University Discussion Paper.

——— . (1990b). On the Inefficiency of Two-Part Tariffs, *Review of Economic Studies* 57: 415–38.

Walras, L. (1874). *Elements d'Economie Politique Pure*. Lausanne: L. Corbaz.

——— . (1898). *Etudes d'Economie Politique Appliquée (Théorie de la Production de la Richesse Sociale)*. Lausanne: Rouge; Paris: Pichon.

INDEX